The Psychology of Teaching and Learning

A Three Step Approach

Manuel Martinez-Pons

CONTINUUM
London and New York

Continuum
The Tower Building
11 York Road
London SE1 7NX

370 Lexington Avenue
New York
NY 10017-6550

First published 2001

British Library Cataloguing-in-Publication Data
A catalogue record for this book is available from the British Library

ISBN: 0-8264-5355-4 (paperback) 0-8264-5354-6 (hardback)

Printed and bound in Great Britain by Biddles Ltd, *www.biddles.co.uk*

Contents

vi

Preface

This book was written as an introduction to the process of instruction. The reader can use it as an orientation to the study of this process, or as reference to the more general aspects of the instructional enterprise.

The work takes a contextual approach to its topic, examining the roles played in the teaching-learning effort by a number of social and psychological processes. It also takes a systems approach to the subject, dividing the instructional process into three sequentially occurring phases: that set of activities the instructor conducts before he or she engages the student in the teaching-learning venture, that set of activities the instructor conducts as he or she engages the student in the learning experience, and that set of activities the instructor conducts following engagement. For each phase, the book considers current theory and research underlying various approaches to instruction, issues attending such theory and research, and ways of integrating positions deemed tenable into one cohesive model of the instructional process.

The book is divided into four parts spanning five chapters. Part 1, addressing the pre-engagement phase of instruction, consists of Chapter 1. It discusses the role played by educational psychology in the study of the teaching-learning effort, the three-phase model underlying the present approach to teaching and learning, and the role played by scientific research in the study of instruction. Part 2 addresses the engagement phase of instruction and consists of two chapters. Chapter 2 addresses information gathering as the instructor prepares to engage the student in the teaching-learning endeavor, and Chapter 3 covers planning of the activities to be carried out in the engagement phase. Part 3, consisting of Chapter 4, addresses the actual engagement of the student in the teaching-learning undertaking. And Part 4, consisting of Chapter 5, covers the post-engagement phase of instruction—that set of activities the instructor carries out to assess the effectiveness of the teaching-learning enterprise and to modify the structure of the effort for future use.

MMP   Brooklyn College, 2001

PART 1

OVERVIEW OF THE INSTRUCTIONAL PROCESS

The study of instruction is complex, concerned as it is with contextual and substantive matters ranging as far and wide as political, economic, social and psychological processes; administrators' and teachers' capabilities; program planning and evaluation, research design, assessment and statistical analysis of assessment data; behavioral processes; mental ability, learning principles and academic self-regulation; and academic achievement. Part 1, consisting of Chapter 1, serves as an overview of the study of the instructional process and discusses the role played by educational psychology in addressing the complex nature of the instructional enterprise.

Chapter 1

Overview

INTRODUCTION

Although some of the factors impacting on the process of instruction do so tangentially, the success of the instructional effort depends in large part on the degree to which each factor is given its due attention. Whether tangential or central to the instructional process, many different factors come into play in the teaching-learning effort, and some way is needed of thinking in a coherent manner about their impact on the outcome of instruction. Educational psychology, which places much emphasis on the numerous contextual factors that impact on the success of the teaching-learning enterprise, has evolved during the past century as the premier discipline addressing this task. Chapter 1 begins by looking at the field of educational psychology and its relevance to the study of the process of instruction.

EDUCATIONAL PSYCHOLOGY

Educational psychology has emerged during the past 100 years as the primary field concerned with the conduct of theory building and research in education. The field is broad, concerned with such matters as "theoretical conceptions about mind, the development of children, and the nature of effective educational environments" (Pressley & McCormick, 1995, p. 1). In the words of Crow and Crow (1954), educational psychology seeks

> to discover and to interpret (1) the extent to which the factors of heredity and environment contribute to learning, (2) the nature of the learning process, (3) the forces and factors that influence learning, and (4) the degree to which a scientific attitude can serve the cause of education. (p. 6)

Davis (1983) listed seven areas of education addressed by educational psychology: social dynamics in the classroom; physical, social and cognitive development; the psychology of learning; motivation; teaching theory; individual differences in such areas as personality, creativity and intelligence; and measurement, research design and statistics.

Although in addressing matters falling within its purview it often relies on theory and research found in other branches of social science, educational psychology is an established scientific discipline in its own right, responsible for some of the more important advances in educational theory and research that have been made during the past 100 years. Edward L. Thorndike is credited with founding of the field with publication of his text *Educational Psychology* in 1903. Other notable contributors to the establishment of educational psychology as a legitimate discipline were William James, G. Stanley Hall and Charles H. Judd (Crow & Crow, 1954). The discipline has grown steadily in breadth and rigor, and in present times workers in this field continue to make groundbreaking contributions in theory building and research to the educational enterprise.

Because of the broad perspective it takes in its approach to the process of instruction, educational psychology is uniquely equipped to provide the educator with ideas and procedures he or she can use for the conduct of the teaching-learning effort. This effort can be described as a well-defined process.

THE PROCESS OF INSTRUCTION

As already suggested, the process of instruction is complex; and in discussing it, it is advantageous to consider the major contexts in which it occurs and the phases in which it takes place.

The Major Contexts of Instruction

For present purposes, there can be said to be two major contexts in which instruction takes place: The curricular context and the programmatic context. The difference between the two is important because it determines the way in which instruction is planned and carried out.

The curricular context of instruction usually involves a primary or secondary school or higher educational setting; it involves instructional efforts that are part of an on-going curriculum whose activities are repeated cyclically. For example, math instruction in fourth grade is part of the regular, on-going school curriculum.

The programmatic context of instruction entails teaching-learning activities designed to meet some specific organizational goal such as bringing employees up to date on aspects of their work; or to meet some social need such as education in some aspect of public health. In contrast to curricular education, programmatic instruction usually involves a one-time instructional effort in the form of a project, with a set beginning and a set end. Although reference will be made to the programmatic context in the following chapters, this work focuses mainly on the curricular context.

Whether its context be curricular or programmatic, it is useful to think of instruction in terms of phases in which specific activities are carried out to facilitate the teaching-learning effort. The following paragraphs introduce a frame of reference for thinking about the process of instruction in terms of such phases.

The Phases of Instruction

The instructional endeavor can be thought of as a three-phase process. These phases are termed here the *pre-engagement* phase, the *engagement* phase and the *post-engagement* phase. The activities involved in each of these phases are summarized in Table 1.

Table 1. The Phases of Instruction

PRE-ENGAGEMENT	ENGAGEMENT	POST-ENGAGEMENT
Needs Assessment	**Situational Assessment & Final Adjustments**	**Summative evaluation**
	Physical environment	Targets
Diagnostics	Materials	Student performance
Environmental influences	Students	Teacher performance
Prior experience	System support	School support
Self-regulation		Methodology
Mental ability		Sources
Emotional functioning		Students
Goal orientation	**Module Implementation**	Teachers
	Execution and adjustment	Others
Instructional Objectives &	Social-cognitive processes	Assessment methods
Task Analysis	Modeling	Observations
Domains	Encouragement	Tests
Cognitive	Facilitation	Questionnaires
Knowledge,	Rewards	Consultations
comprehension,		Critical incident reports
application, analysis,	**Formative evaluation and**	
synthesis, evluation	**Corrective Activity**	**Remediation**
Affective	Targets	Student performance
Attending, responding,	Student performance	Teacher performance
valuing, performing,	Teacher performance	School support performance
integrating	System support	Methodological revisions
Psychomotor	Assessment methods	Pre-engagement
Gross, fine, goal-oriented	Observations	Engagement
Properties	Tests and quizzes	Post-engagement
Observability	Consultations	
Performance conditions	Critical incident reports	
Performance criteria	Areas	
	Curricular	
Test Development/Selection	Objectives-related	
Assessment theory	Non objectives-related	
Validity	Behavioral	
Reliability	Group discipline problems	
Types of tests	Individual discipline	
Teacher-made *vs.* published	problems	
Norm- *vs.* criterion-	Decrement in self-efficacy	
referenced		
Objectives-related test		
properties		
Domain and domain level		
Performance conditions		
Performance criteria		
Testing research design		
Pre-Testing & Grouping		
Instructional Module		
Development/Debugging		
Attention to learning processes		
Module structure		
Introduction		
Demonstration/description		
Questions and answers		
Student enactment		
Feedback and corrective		
action		
Summary		

The Pre-Engagement Phase of Instruction

The pre-engagement phase of instruction involves those tasks the educator performs to prepare before engaging the student in the teaching-learning effort. As shown in Table 1, activities such as *needs assessment, diagnostic assessment, development of instructional objectives* and *instructional module development* form integral parts of this phase of the instructional process.

The Engagement Phase of Instruction

In the engagement phase of instruction, the educator involves the student in the teaching-learning effort. As shown in Table 1, activities such as *situational assessment, module implementation* and *formative evaluation* form parts of this phase of the instructional process.

The Post-Engagement Phase of Instruction

In the post-engagement phase of instruction, the educator assesses the effectiveness of the teaching-learning effort he or she has just completed, and makes corrections as necessary to ensure the success of future attempts in the same direction. As shown in Table 1, activities such as *summative evaluation, student remediation* and *methodological revisions* form parts of this phase of the instructional process.

Thus, in the pre-engagement phase of instruction, the educator prepares to engage the student in the teaching-learning effort; in the engagement phase, the educator actually involves the student in this process; and in the post-engagement phase the educator looks back and assesses the success of the effort—and takes corrective action to improve the likelihood of success in subsequent efforts.

A number of questions can be posed for each of the phases of instruction introduced above:

1. How is each phase best conceptualized?

2. How relevant is each phase to the success of the teaching-learning effort?

3. What are areas of each phase in need of theoretical elaboration or further research?

As will become clear, educational psychology has much to say about the activities that take place in each of the major phases of instruction.

Much of the educational work cited in the following pages takes the form of ideas, theories and research findings offered by leading workers in the field. Because of its complexity and innovative nature, this work is often accompanied by issues that arise in its discussion among members of the educational community—and to be well-informed concerning the process of instruction, the modern educator must be conversant with such issues. The following paragraphs describe the manner in which issues regarding the process of instruction are addressed in this book.

Issues Regarding the Process of Instruction

An issue is the expression of a reservation concerning some set of propositions. A useful way of approaching any issue raised concerning the process of instruction is to consider the position and validity of the reservation involved.

An Issue's Position

An issue's position can fall into one of three categories, ordered in terms of the degree of reservation at hand: *Cautionary, questioning* or *dismissive*. A cautionary issue is one whose reservation takes the form of a caveat concerning the set of propositions involved; it states that the proposition can be accepted only if certain conditions not yet satisfied are met. A questioning issue is one whose reservation notes the need for clarification of the terminology used or of the rationale underlying the proposition in question. A dismissive issue is one whose reservation posits that there are enough flaws in the set of propositions to render it untenable.

The Validity of an Issue's Underlying Reservation

As treated in this text, an issue's validity can be gauged in terms of the tenability of its underlying reservation. A *valid* issue is one whose reservation can be accepted as defensible. A *debatable* issue is one whose reservation can be shown to be inconclusive, requiring elaboration for its clarification or defense. An *invalid* issue is one whose reservation can be shown to be indefensible.

Table 2 depicts a frame of reference for considering issues that arise in the discussion of the process of instruction. The cells in this table represent the intersections of the categories of the position and validity dimensions introduced above. For example, Cell *a* represents a cautionary issue considered valid, Cell *e* represents questioning issue considered debatable, and Cell *i* represents a dismissive issue judged to be invalid. This frame of reference will be used to address issues that arise as educational psychologists conduct research to explore the activities of the instructional process covered in this work.

Table 2. Frame of Reference for Considering Issues that Arise in Discussing the Process of Instruction

Reservation Level	Validity Level		
	Valid	Debatable	Invalid
Cautionary	*a*	*b*	*c*
Questioning	*d*	*e*	*f*
Dismissive	*g*	*h*	*i*

EDUCATIONAL RESEARCH

The Process of Educational Research

When he or she conducts educational research, the investigator embarks on a process beginning with the selection of a topic for study and ending with the analysis of data germane to the research interest. First, the investigator selects a topic for research and decides on the specific aspect of it that he or she wants to investigate. Second, on the basis of what is known about the subject, the researcher develops a conceptual framework, or model, to guide in his or her research effort. Third, the investigator develops a set of research questions whose answer he or she will seek through the remainder of his or her research effort. Fourth, he or she develops hypotheses as tentative answers to the research questions. Finally, he or she tests the hypotheses by generating and analyzing information pertinent to the matter at hand.

Rules exist for the conduct of each of these facets of the research process, and the credibility merited by research findings is a function of the degree to which the investigator adheres to these rules.

Martinez-Pons (1997) describes in detail the process of research in the social sciences and education and the rules governing this process.

Issues Concerning Research in Education

A number of issues have been raised concerning the function of research in the field of education. According to Miller (1999), these issues revolve around three principal reservations: first, in the view of some critics,

> scholars eschew research that shows what works in most schools in favor of studies that observe student behavior and teaching techniques in a classroom or two. They employ weak research methods, write turgid prose and issue contradictory findings. (p. 17)

This appears to be a Type *b* (cautionary, debatable) issue; it seems cautionary because it warns of the danger in employing too narrow a focus when conducting research in education and of the need to use strong research methods and to write prose that is not turgid; and it seems debatable because of the nebulousness of the phrase "what works in most schools": What works in one school (say, a small, affluent college preparatory school) may not work in another (say, a large, inner-city secondary school), making attention to "what works in most schools" a seemingly questionable goal.

At any rate, large-scale studies unrestricted to one or two classrooms are periodically conducted by scholars to address important educational matters. One such study is the *National Education Longitudinal Studies* (NELS; US Department of Education, 1996) a long-term effort addressing the educational experiences of students from three time periods in the US: The 1970s, 1980s, and 1990s. The project examines "the educational, vocational, and personal development of students at various grade levels, and the personal, familial, social, institutional, and cultural factors that may affect that development" (Ingels & Baldridge, 1995, p. 1). NELS consists of three major studies: (1) The *National Longitudinal Study of the High School Class of 1972* (NLS-72); (2) *High School and Beyond* (HS&B); and (3) the *National Education Longitudinal Study of 1988* (NELS:88). Each study examines the educational lives of large numbers of students throughout the US. For example, NELS:88, initiated in 1986 with follow-ups conducted in 1990 and 1995, includes data from 25,000 students in 1,296 schools. For each student, one or more teachers completed a questionnaire addressing his or her perceptions of the student's behavior and various aspects of the school's setting. (The data set generated by this study is used in Chapter 2 to investigate such student-related matters as the relation between socioeconomic status (SES), self-concept and academic achievement; and such teacher-related matters as principal's leadership behavior and teacher job satisfaction and commitment to teaching.) The HS&B examines 1980 seniors and sophomores in the US, and is designed to provide information on these students through early adulthood. The base year data includes information on 58,270 students from 1,015 public and private schools.

Another example of a large-scale educational study is the Tennessee Study (Pate-Bain, Boyd-Zaharias, Cain, Word and Binkley, 1997), a four-year investigation of the effect of small class size on academic achievement. The study was conducted with 6,000 students in grades K to 3; Chapter 4 discusses this study in some detail. Such large-scale efforts examining thousands of students in upward of thousands of schools would seem to render the claim that scholars eschew large-scale works in favor or research involving a classroom or two something of an overstatement.

A second issue regarding educational research involves an on-going debate concerning what constitutes good research in this field. On the one hand, one camp calls for the use of so-called *qualitative* research, in which the investigator "becomes part of the thing being studied", and in this way gains a degree of intimacy with the topic in question not otherwise possible. On the other hand, an opposing camp calls for the use of *quantitative* methods that, in the view of its adherents, afford the type of explanatory and predictive power that is possible only through the use of rigorous research design and statistical data analysis. The objections of these camps relative to each other's positions seem to be Type *i* (dismissive, invalid) issues. Martinez-Pons (1997) argued that the incompatibility between "qualitative" and "quantitative" research is more apparent than real:

> It is the position of this author that the so-called positivist [quantitative] and post-positivist [qualitative] views are not mutually exclusive. A good scientist always becomes deeply immersed in the things that interest him/her. But...it is possible, following this deep level of immersion, to abstract and symbolically manipulate those aspects of experience about which it is possible to truly provide explanations and predictions with some degree of accuracy. In the final analysis, while something may be gained by the scientist's going through a phase of "phenomenological immersion" in the thing he or she is studying, at some point he or she will have to do something to explain and predict (and possibly control) the thing of interest—and to test the accuracy of

such explanation and prediction. That dual function of explanation and prediction, after all, is the ultimate purpose of science, and as evidenced by the work carried out in the more established scientific disciplines, it is only through the generation and processing of quantitative information that this function can be fulfilled with any degree of confidence. (p. 108) [1]

Finally, disagreement exists among researchers concerning that which educational research should be about because, in the words of one university official, "We haven't agreed on the key issue of what the purpose of the school is" (Miller, 1999, p. 18). This seems to be a Type *d* (questioning, valid) issue. It seems questioning because it calls for further dialogue concerning the major goals of education, and hence, of the major goals of educational research. And it seems valid because the very definition of achievement—i.e., performance on standardized tests of basic skills—is being disputed, with many calling for an expanded account to include such matters as molding citizens, teaching critical thinking and practical skills, and overcoming obstacles raised by poverty (Miller, 1999).

Although disagreement exists concerning what educational research should be *about*, in this writer's opinion there can be little disagreement concerning its *approach* to whatever its subject matter happens to be. As proposed above, this approach is scientific in nature, following a process beginning with the selection of a topic for inquiry and ending with the testing of theoretical models through the collection and statistical analysis of data.

SUMMARY

---

[1] The present author considers this point so important that he has placed heavy emphasis throughout this text on the "dual function of explanation and prediction" of science in the study instruction. Thus, while highlighting a concept of inquiry spanning the qualitative-quantitative research continuum, he has treated variables involved in the process of instruction from a largely quantitative perspective. To this end, in making a particular point, whenever possible the author has referred to statistically-oriented research—and where he has found no statistical study for ready reference, he has tried to use existing data bases to test statistical models germane to the matter at hand (for the benefit of the reader unfamiliar with statistical methodology, the author has devoted a "frame" or "box" to a discussion of a given statistical procedure or concept when referring to it for the first time).

In summary, the process of instruction can be divided into three phases: The pre-engagement phase, in which the instructor prepares to interact with the student in the teaching-learning effort; the engagement phase, in which the instructor involves the student in the teaching-learning enterprise; and the post-engagement phase, in which the instructor assesses the success of the teaching-learning effort following its completion. Educational psychology is that field which specializes in exploring, through scientific research, the psychological, social and systemic dynamics involved in the three phases of instruction. Finally, not all of the issues that inevitably arise as educators perform research on the various phases of instruction are valid, and some frame of reference is necessary for addressing the nature and validity of such issues when they arise. Table 2 presented a frame of reference that will be used throughout this work to approach the matter.

Table 1 offered an overview of the activities involved in each phase of the instructional process. The rest of this work is devoted to an exploration of the elements appearing in Table 1. For each element, the work discusses a) the theoretical work that has been used to describe it, b) the research that has been conducted in support of theory addressing it, c) issues revolving around the area, and d) significance of the area for the success of the instructional enterprise. The following pages begin this exploration by examining the pre-engagement phase of instruction.

PART 2

THE PRE-ENGAGEMENT PHASE OF INSTRUCTION

In the pre-engagement phase instruction, the educator prepares to enable the student to acquire the information, values or skills that will constitute the objectives of the teaching-learning effort. In this phase, the instructor embarks on a wide variety of activities, each instrumental in preparation for the teaching-learning effort that lies ahead. The pre-engagement phase of instruction can be divided into two facets: investigation of the needs to be addressed in the teaching-learning effort, and investigation of student and instructor characteristics relevant to the instructional goals at hand; and preparation of the instructional modules to be implemented to reach these goals. Chapter 2 addresses the information-gathering part of the pre-engagement phase of instruction, and Chapter 3 addresses the preparation part of this phase of the instructional effort.

Chapter 2

Information Gathering

INTRODUCTION

The first set of activities the instructor undertakes in the pre-engagement phase of instruction involves the gathering of information that he or she can use in the planning of the teaching-learning effort. First, through *needs assessment*, the educator determines the general needs to be addressed through the instructional endeavor; and then, through *diagnostic activities*, he or she assesses key student and instructor attributes that may impact on the success of attempts to meet these needs.

Each of these topics will be discussed in terms of the way in which it is approached and of the role it plays in the process of instruction; in terms of the activities it entails in the instructional process; and in terms of issues that have been raised regarding the way in which the topic has been approached. The chapter begins with a discussion of needs assessment.

NEEDS ASSESSMENT

Definition of *Needs Assessment*

Needs assessment involves the identification of general educational needs to be addressed through the educational enterprise. According to King (1999), the importance of needs assessment as part of the pre-engagement phase of instruction lies in the fact that

> Well-meaning efforts by instructional developers to design instructional materials that enhance performance may fail if the performance problem is not accurately identified and instructional needs are not fully assessed. (p. 1)

Levels of Needs Assessment

Needs assessments can be conducted at different levels, ranging from the national, through the state, city and school district levels, down to the neighborhood level in which the school operates—and to the level of the school and of the classroom in which instruction takes place. At each level, interested parties or "stakeholders" (Edward & Newman, 1982) express opinions, concerns and demands regarding the general goals to be sought through education—and it is the function of needs assessment to sort out these demands, opinions and concerns.

In the end, what the educator does as he or she engages in the process of instruction is framed to no small degree by information generated through the needs assessment effort, and the variety of opinions that emerge in the process presents a special challenge to the instructor because of often conflicting positions. According to Taba (1962),

> Society's concept of the function of the public school determines to a great extent what kind of curriculum schools will have. Yet, in a complex culture with a pluralistic value system, it is difficult to establish a single central function for any agency. In a democratic society these formulations are further complicated by the fact that different layers of society participate in the process of determining what education in general and public schools specifically should be and do...Our society has by no means agreed about what the central function of the school should be. (p. 2)

Schultz (1998) identified three major conflicting views that often emerge in the process of needs assessment: the conservative view represented by Mortimer Adler (1982); the liberal-progressive view represented by John Dewey (1916); and the critical pedagogical view represented by Paolo Freire (1970). The debate between adherents of these positions can become heated, as evidenced by their writings on each other's perspectives. For example, addressing what he saw as the conservative tradition of education represented by Adler, Freire (1970) wrote:

> Education thus becomes an act of depositing, in which the students are the depositories and the teacher is the depositor. Instead of communicating, the teacher issues communiqués and makes deposits which the students patiently receive, memorize, and repeat. This is the "banking" concept of education, in which the scope of action allowed to the students extends only as far as receiving, filing, and storing the deposits. (p. 64)

On the other hand, referring to what he saw as the critical pedagogical position on education represented by Freire, Barber (1992) wrote:

> The methodologies deployed by critics of power and convention in the academy do not always find the dialectical center, however, and are subject to distortion and hyperbole...In its postmodern phase, where the merely modern is equated with something vaguely reactionary and post-modernism means a radical battering down of all certainty, this hyperskeptical pedagogy can become self-defeating. (p. 204)

Whatever the information garnered through the process of needs assessment, the educator will frequently find that he or she must come to some sort of compromise in considering the multiplicity of opinions, values and demands—including his or her own—that often surface in this facet of the instructional process.

The perception of educational needs can vary across time as well as across philosophical stance, particularly in terms of behavioral problems faced by students. About half a century ago, Thorpe (1946) reported that the ten major concerns among educators regarding student behavior at the time were 1) rationalization, 2) showing off, 3) resentment against authority and advice, 4) refusal to face reality, 5) lack of consistency in conduct or emotion, 6) selfishness, 7) avoidance of difficult tasks, 8) jealousy, 9) decided crushes on individuals of the same sex, and 10) hero worship. In 1997, the Federation of Families for Children's Mental Health reported that the ten major areas of concern among educators at that time regarding student behavior were 1) truancy, 2) stealing, 3) fighting, 4) substance abuse, 5) mugging, 6) vandalizing, 7) arson, 8) physical cruelty to people or animals, 9) sexual assault, and 10) homicide (Huff, 1999).

Ultimately, the potential benefit of a needs assessment will come to fruition with the success of the program it is intended to serve. For this reason, in discussing the topic it is important to consider conditions that influence the probability of success of any program needs assessment is designed to inform. One such condition is the level at which the assessment is conducted. For example, regarding school reform, it has been suggested that the less global the level at which needs assessment is carried out, the more fully the information generated is likely to be used; and that the more global the level, the less likely this is to happen. Using *transaction-cost economics* theory (Williamson, 1975, 1985), House (1996) proposed that the likelihood of the success of any school reform effort depends largely on the degree to which three key attributes of educational reform initiatives are attended to: *bounded rationality,* or limits in information or information-processing capability people bring to the reform task, and limits in the degree to which people can foresee problems that can arise in the reform effort; *opportunism,* or the degree to which people place their interests ahead of the interests of the organization involved in educational reform; and *asset specificity,* or the unique skills—e.g., "craftsmanship so deeply embedded in the personal experience that they cannot be known by others or can be inferred only with great difficulty" (p. 7)—people bring to the reform task. House's argument is that these three attributes can be fully addressed to the point where the reform effort can best succeed at the local, school level. According to House, at the national level, at which broad educational goals and standards are set, bounded rationality and opportunism are most difficult to address effectively.

To show the feasibility of successfully attending to bounded rationality, opportunism and asset specificity in needs assessment at the local level, House (1996) cited one case in which, attending to these factors, educators were able to succeed in efforts at reform. The institution cited by House was Central Park East School (CPE). Located in New York City, CPE was initiated as a set of "alternative" elementary and secondary schools for East Harlem families. According to Bensman (1994), because of its singular makeup (small student population, close ties with parents and active participation of students in curriculum development), CPE can boast a number of accomplishments that set it apart from other schools at the same grade level: although CPE graduates have come from backgrounds more closely associated with school failure than the New York City public school population as a whole, they have attained higher school graduation and college entrance rates and more favorable occupational outcomes than have students in the rest of the New York public school system. In House's (1996) view, the success of CPE would have been impossible had the reformers not developed a clear idea through needs assessment activities of what they wanted to accomplish and how to go about doing so (unbounded rationality), had the teachers not seen the benefits to themselves of implementing the reforms (bounded opportunism), or had the teachers and administrators lacked the progressive pedagogical skills (asset specificity) necessary to make the program work—matters difficult, if not impossible, to ensure at the national level.

One possible way of reconciling educational concerns ascertained through needs assessment at the national level with local reform efforts is to set key general guidelines at the federal level, and to then fund programs based on local needs assessment efforts. An example of such an approach is the presidential initiative during the 1990s termed *Goals 2000*. Although attended by some controversy (see Berliner and Biddle, 1995), the program did seem to provide a compromise between needs assessments conducted at the national and local levels. At the national level, this initiative called for schools to decide what they wanted the education of their students to be like by the year 2000. Schools were enabled to conduct needs assessments at their local levels and to then submit proposals for funding at the federal level to meet these needs. A needs assessment involving one such effort is described below.

Forms of Needs Assessment

Two forms of needs assessment exist: Formal and informal. In formal assessment, the educator uses accepted methods of social research to carry out the task. In informal needs assessment, the investigator relies on general impressions he or she forms in the course of everyday life about educational demands.

Formal Needs Assessment

Contributions have been made to the formalization of the needs assessment process, and several needs assessment models exist. A particularly rigorous form, developed by Norman Dalkey and Olaf

Helmer (Lang, 1998) is termed *The Delphi Procedure (DP)*. DP is conducted in four steps (Rothwell & Kazanas, 1997):

1. Selection of a panel of participants whose opinions and judgments the investigator will use as the basis of educational planning.

2. Solicitation of the opinions and judgments of the participants through structured questionnaires or interviews, or through unstructured, open-ended invitations to comment on the issues at hand.

3. Processing of the information gained in Step 2, and development of a more focused questionnaire.

4. Use of the more focused questionnaire to gather more detailed information from the panel.

Steps 2 through 4 are repeated until a cohesive interpretation of the participants' concerns emerges.

As an example of this part of the pre-engagement phase of instruction, the present author participated in the conduct of a formal needs assessment for a *Goals 2000* program in an elementary public school in a large metropolitan area. The needs assessment for this program, expanding on the Delphi Procedure, was conducted in the following steps.

1. Three panels of persons associated with the school were formed: Teachers ($N = 10$), parents ($N = 13$) and the school's principal and school assistant principal.

2. In focused group interviews, each panel was presented with an open-ended question: "If you had your choice and an unlimited budget, what would you like to see done in this school by the Year 2000?" The panel discussed ideas for one hour and a recorder wrote down the ideas generated in the course of the discussion.

3. The ideas gleaned from the interviews were grouped into categories for further processing. Analysis yielded 14 categories for responses by the parents' panel, 12 categories for the teachers' panel, and 11 categories for the administrators. Nine of the categories were cited in common by the participants in the three panels.

For each panel, each emergent category was formed into a questionnaire item, and a question with a forced-choice response format was posed for each item. For all panels, the direction for using the questionnaire was as follows: *For each area listed below, what priority, in your view, should the topic receive as a school goal for the Year 2000?* The response format for this question was as follows: *(1) I see this as a "nice to do" goal; (2) I see this as a "should do" goal; (3) I see this as a "must do" goal.*

4. The parent questionnaire (14 items) was distributed to the school's parents (they returned 277 completed questionnaires); the

teacher questionnaire (12 items) was distributed to the teachers (they returned 32 completed questionnaires); and the administrator questionnaire (11 items) was distributed to the principal and assistant principal. The data were analyzed to determine the mean priority given each area by each panel. The ranked priorities given by the parents, teachers and administrators for the goals for the year 2000 are shown in Table 3.

Table 3. Survey Ranking of Concerns of Parents, Teachers and Administrators in an Elementary School

Item	*Mean*
Parents	
1. Positive outlets for students to express and resolve negative feelings	2.92
2. Computer literacy for students and teachers	2.65
3. The state of the school's physical plant (water fountains, bathrooms, plumbing, intercoms, lighting, heating, air conditioning, etc.)	2.54
4. A curriculum that includes literacy, music and science, with labs and necessary equipment	2.51
5. Teacher training to ensure state-of-the-art pedagogy in reading, math, social studies and the arts	2.48
6. Safety and hygiene educational program	2.41
Teachers	
1. A literacy (reading, writing) program that works for all students	2.84
2. Safety	2.50
3. All students free of drugs, violence, alcohol and weapons	2.48
4. Teacher training to ensure state-of-the-art pedagogy in reading, math, social studies and the arts	2.33
5. Computer literacy for students and teachers	2.31
6. Positive outlets for students to express and resolve negative feelings	2.26
Administrators	
1. A literacy (reading, writing) program that works for all students	3.00
2. Computer literacy for students and teachers	2.50
3. Positive outlets for students to express and resolve negative feelings	2.50
4. Safety	2.50
5. Teacher training to ensure state-of-the-art pedagogy in reading, math, social studies and the arts	2.50
6. Parental involvement in the school's activities	2.50

Partly on the basis of these needs assessment outcomes, the school administrators began to plan curricular changes and other activities in order to implement a federally funded *Goals 2000* program in the school. Although this needs assessment was largely programmatic in nature, the procedures generated for the *Goals 2000* project based on the findings eventually became regular components of the school's on-going curriculum.

Informal Needs Assessment

In informal needs assessment, the investigator develops a general, typically amorphous, impression of opinions, interests and concerns expressed regarding the general goals of education. Casual conversations; reading of newspapers and other periodicals, and exposure to the general media; and reviewing of directives passed down through administrative channels are the sources of information the instructor uses when he or she performs an informal needs assessment. One advantage in using this approach is that it saves the time and effort required to assemble and formally interview the panel of participants, as well as the survey and data analysis activities involved in formal assessment. A potential disadvantage is the relative lack of validity and reliability typically found in the informal approach to seeking any sort of information.

Issues Regarding Needs Assessment

The following are three major issues that can be raised concerning this part of the pre-engagement phase of instruction: first, in the view of some, it is usually those with social mobility and the ability to articulate concerns who influence decision-making in the determination of educational needs. Those without social power or in general lacking the ability to articulate their educational concerns are usually left out of the needs assessment process, so that their educational needs are seldom addressed. This appears to be a Type *a* (cautionary, valid) issue, and it can be addressed by ensuring that all interested parties, including groups deemed to be underrepresented—or advocates of such groups—are represented in needs assessment panels.

Second, needs may change between the time an assessment is conducted and the time services based on the findings are delivered, so that the services may end by not addressing present needs. This also appears to be a Type *a* issue, and it can be addressed through formative evaluation procedures involving a continuous dialogue with interested parties regarding changing needs.

Finally, it might be argued that the basic "existential" needs of students cannot be easily determined through the types of inquiry allowed by needs assessment methodology. The reason given for this objection is that, by their nature, existential needs are impossible to define clearly. This appears to be a Type *i* (dismissive, invalid) issue. At the same time that it rejects the needs assessment concept outright, it seems invalid because it seems unreasonable to expect any educator to effectively work with concepts such as "existential needs" that cannot be clearly defined.

Even after steps are taken in response to the cautionary issues noted above, two questions remain for the instructor to address concerning this part of the pre-engagement phase of instruction:

1. What are, in the end, the general goals the educator is to seek through the instructional process?

2. Given conflicting opinions regarding the goals of education, whose opinion is the instructor to accept to guide his or her instructional endeavors?

In the final analysis, these are questions only the instructor can answer following a careful consideration of ideas and opinions proffered by him or her or others.

In summary, needs assessment involves the determination of the general goals to be pursued through education. A variety of opinions are possible concerning this direction, coming from such different sources as political and community leaders, school administrators, parents, students—and instructors. The instructor who is aware of the different conceptions of general educational needs for his or her institution is in a better position to prepare for the teaching-learning endeavor than one lacking this awareness.

Following needs assessment completion, the next step in the information-gathering facet of the pre-engagement phase of instruction involves an examination of key student and instructor attributes with potential for impacting on the success of the teaching-learning effort. This matter comes under the heading of *diagnostics.*

DIAGNOSTICS

Definition of *Diagnostics*

The term *diagnostics* refers to any set of procedures designed to generate student- and instructor-related information about factors that may impact on the success with which the general goals of education are pursued through the process of instruction.

The Role Played by Diagnostics in Instruction

The role of diagnostics in the process of instruction is pivotal since, as in the case of needs assessment, a teacher equipped with information about his or her students'—as well as his or her own—preparedness to embark on the teaching-learning effort is in a better position to plan for the enterprise than a teacher lacking such information. The major question regarding diagnostics is, "What kind of information can help the educator to best prepare to interact with his or her students, and how can he or she go about obtaining it?"

While the information sought through needs assessment involves general goals to be sought through education, that sought through diagnostic procedures is specific to the students and instructors involved in a particular teaching-learning effort. The student-related information of interest involves processes that can impact on the student's *learning readiness*, and the instructor-related information sought involves processes that can impact on the instructor's *teaching effectiveness*.

Student Learning Readiness

The importance of student learning readiness in instruction was noted by Jensen (1969):

> Attempting to force instruction on a child who is not ready can cause the child either to learn the skill by a more primitive technique (one which has little transfer value to other learning) or to "turn off" to learning altogether. (p. 1)

For this reason, the success of the instructional effort largely depends on the degree to which the student's learning readiness is taken into account in preparing for the teaching-learning effort.

Historically, the matter of readiness to learn has been approached from a biological perspective. Concepts of *maturational states* (Hurlock, 1975), *maturational stages* (Piaget, 1951) and *critical stimulation periods* (Lenneberg, 1967) have been used in attempts to explain individual differences in learning. According to Siegler and Klahr (1982), however, these attempts have suffered from circularity:

> Whether we explain failures to learn in terms of the child being unready, not yet being in the critical period, or not yet possessing the appropriate logical structure makes little difference unless we can measure the hypothesized explanatory construct. Without such independent measurement, all that we know is that the younger child

did not learn what the older one did; regardless of the label, we have not explained anything, we have merely restated the data. (p. 127)

Siegler and Klahr (1982) attempted to break the circularity of learning readiness theories by first, abandoning biological condition as an explanatory factor; and by then, using the concept of *rule formation* to render learning readiness an independently measurable construct.

Although it recognizes that some form of cognitive process or structure (e.g., Siegler and Klahr's rule formation) is involved in learning readiness, the present position takes a largely contextual, probabilistic approach to the matter: Learning readiness, in terms of this stance, can be defined as *the likelihood that a student will benefit from the instructional effort.* A student with a low level of learning readiness is less likely to gain from the instructional effort than one with a high learning readiness level. The relevance of this approach to learning readiness involves decision-making. An instructor considering whether to engage a student in the teaching-learning effort must decide whether the student is likely to benefit from the experience—and in making this decision the instructor must have some idea of the factors that determine the likelihood that the student will benefit from instruction. As will become clear, the present approach seeks to address these matters through the formulation of causal models including processes found in the instructional context: it assumes that a student is more likely to learn, or benefit from the instructional effort, if these contextual factors are favorable than if they are not.

Factors Hypothesized to Contribute to Learning Readiness

Copple (1993) proposed three key factors as influential in the likelihood of a student's benefiting from instruction: good health, a stable and supportive home environment, and an engaging and responsive school environment. It is student-related factors such as these that the instructor assesses in this part of the pre-engagement phase of instruction.

In addressing factors influencing learning readiness, it is useful to think of their impact not only in terms of their direct significance for the likelihood of student success, but also in terms of the roles played by their interrelations in this respect. For example, it is possible that parents who take pains to ensure the home environment is stable and academically supportive also take pains to ensure that their offspring attend schools with academically supportive environments—and that both of these parental processes are influenced by the parents' socioeconomic status (SES: parental educational level, occupation, and income level). These interrelations are complex, and their study can shed light on the dynamics involved in the determination of academic success. The following pages will consider such interrelations.

Figure 1 shows processes assumed to influence learning readiness. The model appearing in this figure hypothesizes that interrelations among *age; environmental influences; genetic factors; health; physiology; academic self-regulation (motivation, goal setting, strategy usage and self-evaluation); prior experience; mental acuity, or ability; emotional functioning;* and *goal orientation (task mastery vs. simple desire for social recognition)* lead to learning readiness. (An additional factor proposed to influence learning readiness not appearing in Figure 1 is *learning style.* The concept is controversial and, although it is not included in the present frame of reference, it is cited often enough as a determinant of learning readiness to merit attention; it will be discussed in this chapter's *postscript.*)

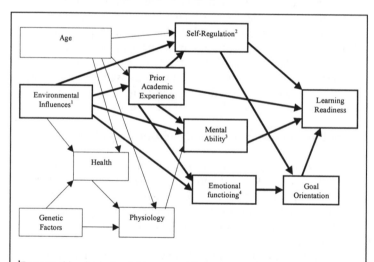

[1]Demographic, physical, and interpersonal factors
[2]Motivation, goal setting, strategy usage, self-evaluation, strategy adjustment
[3]Speed of acquisition, effectiveness of retention, and extent of utilization
[4]Being in touch with, sorting out, and regulating one's moods and emotions

Figure 1. Complex of Factors Hypothesized to Contribute to Learning Readiness

Of the processes appearing in Figure 1, those enclosed in heavy-lined boxes (i.e., *environmental influences, self-regulation, prior academic experience, mental ability, emotional functioing,* and *goal orientation*) will be addressed in detail in the following pages. The others will be discussed in passing. The major processes shown in Figure 1 will be discussed in terms of how they are defined, how they are assessed, the role they play in learning readiness, and issues involving their use in the diagnostic part of the pre-engagement phase of instruction. The processes will be addressed from left to right as they appear in Figure 1; the first discussed will be *environmental influences.*

Environmental Influences Impacting on Learning Readiness. For present purposes, environmental influences can be defined as factors in a student's surroundings that may affect his or her readiness to learn. Three aspects of the environment relevant to learning readiness are discussed in the following pages: demographic factors, physical factors and interpersonal factors.

Demographic Factors. A number of demographic factors have been found to relate to learning readiness. Relations are apparent among the locale (urban or sub-urban) in which the student functions or where the teaching-learning effort occurs, the locale's population density, the proportion of the locale's population born in the US, the proportion of the locale's population proficient in English, the proportion of the locale's adult population having graduated from high school and college, and the locale's average household income. Of particular interest in this regard is the relation of population density with key features of a student's life. In a study of school districts in five large US cities, Meyer and Levine (1977) found low SES and high population density to negatively impact on academic achievement.

Using 1990 US Census Bureau data, the present author examined these factors among seven counties in New York State: Counties considered urban (Bronx, Kings, Queens and New York counties—coded as 1 for present purposes for statistical analysis), and counties considered suburban (Suffolk, Nassau and Westchester counties—coded as 2 for present purposes for statistical analysis). He then calculated Spearman rank correlation coefficients (see Frame 1 for a description of correlational analysis) among these variables using the seven counties as the cases for study. Using data from the 1990 follow-up of the National Educational Longitudinal Study (NELS) performed by the National Center for Educational Statistics (Ingels & Baldridge, 1992), this author also calculated the Pearson correlation coefficients among the socioeconomic status, self-concept and academic achievement of 20,840 high school students residing throughout the US. The composite results of these analyses appear in Figure 2.

Frame 1. Correlational Analysis

Correlational analysis is a statistical procedure used to determine whether changes in one variable are accompanied by corresponding changes in another. For example, one may want to find out whether as a child grows older (change in age) he or she also grows taller (change in height). The most common index of correlation used today is the Pearson product moment coefficient of correlation, or Pearson correlation, signified by r and ranging between -1 through 0 and +1. A positive (+) correlation means that as one variable increases the other also increases (e.g., as children grow older, they tend to grow taller). A negative (-) correlation means that as one variable increases, the other decreases (e.g., as children grow older, they tend to become less dependent on their parents).

Disregarding the sign, an r between 0 and .20 can be considered low or weak, one between .21 and .40 can be considered moderate; one between .41 and .60 can be considered strong; and one between .61 and 1 can be considered very strong. As a general rule, r is used when a sample size is equal to or greater than 30. With smaller samples, Spearman's rank correlation coefficient, or Spearman's Rho (ρ), is calculated by first, ranking the values for the two variables and then calculating r between the two ranks.

As in all statistical procedures, the researcher may be interested in whether correlational findings for a particular sample can be generalized to the population from which the sample has been drawn. The branch of statistics addressing this question is termed *inferential statistics*. The index used in inferential statistics to address this matter is termed the p value. A p value equal to or lower than .05 is interpreted as a low probability of being wrong if one accepts the hypothesis that the sample's findings can be generalized to the population.

Thus a correlation of r = .54 with a p value of .03 shows that for the sample at hand, increase in one variable is accompanied by a corresponding increase in the other—and that the finding can be generalized to the population with some degree of confidence.

It should be noted that some controversy exists concerning the meaning of a *p* value. Martinez-Pons (1999b) discusses this controversy in detail.

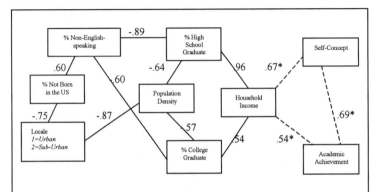

*Pearson correlation coefficient; all other coefficients shown are Spearman Rho correlations.

Figure 2. Composite Outcomes of US Census Bureau (Solid Linkages) and US Department of Education (Dashed Linkages) Data Related to Population Characteristics and Academic Achievement

As evidenced by the information appearing in Figure 2, in one geographic area key demographic factors beginning with locale (urban *vs.* sub-urban) and ending with household income came together to produce a set of relations conceptually leading to academic achievement—a student outcome post-indicative of learning readiness. In this case, it seems safe to assume that randomly selected students differing in their locale were likely to face differing environmental conditions impacting on their readiness to benefit from instruction.

Physical Factors. Physical factors are health-related and cosmetic aspects of the environment that can impact on a student's learning readiness. Of special importance regarding health-related factors are indoor health hazards found in homes and schools; concerning cosmetic factors evidence exists that aesthetic aspects of the environment have much to do with students' readiness to learn.

Environmental Health Hazards. Much work has appeared in the literature concerning environmental health hazards in the educational setting. For example, the Environmental Protection Agency has determined that indoor air pollution constitutes one of the four major environmental risks to public health; and the House of Representatives Committee on Energy and Commerce, Subcommittee on Health and Environment, has determined that the problem is especially serious in the air of American schools (Grubb, 1996). Indeed, according to Wulf (1993), the threat involves three fourths of US schools, which, in a number of cases, have become major public health concerns due to the deteriorating condition of their physical plants.

The Environmental Protection Agency (EPA) Office of Radiation and Indoor Air (1990) listed various sources of indoor health hazards. These include indoor pollutants such as smoke and chemicals; heating, ventilation, and air conditioning systems; pollutant pathways such as drinking water and unfiltered outside air; and building occupants in poor health. Grubb (1996) noted a number of school indoor health hazards in addition to those cited by the EPA: Radon gas, asbestos, and lead in paint and in the drinking water (the problem involving lead poisoning is of special concern, since as of 1993, three to four million children in the US had toxic levels of lead in their blood). According to Grubb, a particularly serious source of indoor health hazard is the *sick building syndrome*, involving a variety of nondescript illnesses assumed to be due to tightly sealed, poorly ventilated buildings.

Andrews and Neuroth (1988) noted a number of ways in which indoor environmental health hazards can negatively impact on students' learning readiness (much of the impact is assumed to occur partly through retention of toxins in the body for long periods of time): underdeveloped organs and systems, lowered immune competency, central nervous systems rendered fragile, and underdeveloped liver and kidneys.

In relation to negative effects of health hazards on cognitive functioning, Kovac, Potasova, Arochova, Biro, Halmiova and Kovac (1997) found reaction time to be negatively affected in children living in environments polluted with neurotoxins; and Raloff (1987) reported a study showing that body absorption of lead can diminish cognitive ability and learning skills in children, even when the levels are not easily detectable. In fact, as of 1993, fully 50 percent of students in special education classes were lead poisoning victims (Kimball, 1994). Finally, Marlowe (1986) reported that low metal exposure not high enough to cause actual poisoning can nevertheless cause a variety of childhood behavior disorders in addition to lowered cognitive ability.

Of special concern regarding school environmental health hazards is the relation of air pollutants with asthma which, afflicting 4.8

million children in the US, is the most common chronic childhood illness in this country. The problem is particularly serious in inner-city schools. In his review of the literature, Appea (1999) found that in one inner city school, at one time 32 percent of its students were afflicted with asthma (Newfield, 1996). Appea's review also disclosed that environmental factors associated with asthma include low socio-economic status; airborne chemical products and biological products of bacterial and fungal decay; cockroach and rodent-infested dwellings; indoor dust or tobacco smoke; and of special importance, non-existent or poor health care and lack of knowledge about asthma and its management (Field, 1996). Exacerbated by indoor air pollution, the net effect of asthma on learning readiness involves poor school attendance, behavior problems, physical activity difficulties and limitations, and academic underachievement despite normal or above normal IQ scores (American Academy of Allergy, Asthma & Clinical Immunology, 1995).

Environmental health hazards of interest to educators can come into play long before a student's birth, as evidenced by research on alcohol teratogen (*teratogen* means any factor that causes damage to the fetus). According to Streissguth, Barr, Bookstein, Sampson and Carmichael (1999), during the past 25 years,

> alcohol has been irrefutably established as a teratogen through thousands of experimental animal studies... and hundreds of studies have demonstrated the comparability of the neurobehavioral findings from human and animal research on the short-term and long-term consequences of prenatal alcohol exposure. (p. 186)

In a longitudinal study tracing 500 children from birth to the age of 14, Streissguth et al. (1999) uncovered numerous effects of prenatal alcohol exposure on mental functioning. Although a broad range of socioeconomic and ethnic groups were represented in the sample, the majority of the mothers in the study were white, married, middle class, and well educated. Twenty-four percent of the mothers reported binge drinking (5 or more drinks on any occasion) during pregnancy, and the average number of drinks per day during this time was .66; the average monthly occasion of drinking during pregnancy was 8, with the average number of drinks per occasion 2.2. Table 4 summarizes effects of fetal alcohol exposure as they were detected at various ages between birth and 14 years. The effects shown in Table 4 remained after adjustments were made for such possible confounding variables as maternal nutrition and use of drugs and medications during pregnancy, demographic factors, mother-child interactions, household stress, childhood accidents and illnesses, and child's educational experiences.

Table 4. Effects of Prenatal Alcohol Exposure on Mental Functioning After Birth. Material compiled from Streissguth et al. (1999).

Age	Observable Effect of Fetal Alcohol Exposure
Day 1	Decreased body activity, poor habituation, poor response modulation, increased tremulousness
Day 2	Lower sucking pressure
Year 4	Decreased attention and longer response latency, longer error correction latency, poorer fine motor performance, and IQ decrements
Year 7	IQ decrements, lowered reaction time, poor spatial and verbal memory and integration, lowered organization and problem-solving flexibility, heightened distractibility higher chance of being in special education classes, poor grammar and word recall, poor attention in the classroom
Year 11	Processing and reasoning problems, distractibility, impersistence and restlessness, poor academic achievement
Year 14	Problems with organization; poor attention, memory; phonological processing and arithmetic performance; poor academic progress; high impulsivity; early use of tobacco and alcohol; other substance abuse; antisocial behavior

As evidenced by an examination of the information appearing in Table 4, a mother's alcohol consumption during pregnancy can impact negatively on her child's learning readiness; the effect can be detected as early as the first day after birth with such conditions as poor response modulation and decreased body activity, and later at the age of 14 in the form of such outcomes as poor memory and poor academic progress. Alcohol teratogen cases such as these are usually referred to as *fetal alcohol effected (FAE)*. In extreme cases, the problem, known as *fetal alcohol syndrome (FAS)*, takes the form of a set of irreversible birth defects including mental retardation and facial and other physical malformations.

According to Mack (1995), the problems of FAE and FAS are widespread and growing. Eight-thousand FAS babies are born each year in the US, and many more babies go undiagnosed with FAE. The problems are particularly severe in special populations such as Native American communities. According to Asetoyer (1990), FAS affects about 1 in every 100 Native Americans born in the Northern Plains, and 1 in 50 Native American children is born with FAE.

In addition to alcohol teratogen, maternal smoking during pregnancy has been found to negatively impact on learning readiness. Ferguson (1993) found this maternal behavior to be associated with offspring disruptive conduct in childhood, and Olds (1994) found that infants whose mothers smoked ten or more cigarettes per day during pregnancy scored several points lower on standardized tests of intelligence than did infants whose mothers did not smoke during pregnancy. Other maternal practices that pose threats to the fetus—including timing, dosage, consumption patterns, and chemical properties of drugs such as marijuana, cocaine, heroin and prescription medications—were discussed by Cook (1990).

Cosmetic Factors. Aside from health hazards in students' lives, there exist cosmetic aspects of the environment with potential to impact on pupils' learning readiness. Concerning these factors' impact on readiness to learn, Earthman and Lemasters (1998) noted the following physical plant attributes of the school as significant contributors to student motivation and achievement: color, maintenance, age, climate conditions, noise and lighting. They stated,

> Studies of facilities' variables reported that student achievement scores were higher when windows, floors, heat, roofs, locker conditions, ceilings, laboratory conditions, age of the facility, lighting, interior paint, clean floors, and cosmetic conditions in general were rated above standard by school staff. Studies suggested that the facilities also affected attitudes and behaviors. (p. 1)

In a review of the research literature on lighting, Veitch and Newsham (1996) found consistent evidence that this feature of the school environment can influence visual comfort, social interaction and communication, aesthetic judgments, student behavior, and academic task performance.

   Interpersonal Factors. The third aspect of the environmental element appearing in Figure 1 hypothesized to influence learning readiness involves interpersonal factors, particularly factors involving students' interactions with parents, teachers and peers.
   Parental Influences on Student Learning Readiness. Concerning parental roles, in a ten-year longitudinal study, Bradley, Caldwell and Rock (1988) demonstrated the influence of parental behavior on academic achievement. In a separate study, Laosa (1982) showed the impact of parents' education on the manner in which they interact with their offspring, and demonstrated the effect of this relationship on student achievement in school. Finally, in a study following the Laosa investigation, Marjoribanks (1984) demonstrated the strong effect of these parental processes when such factors as occupational grouping and the clarity, timing and focus of key parental processes are taken into account.
   In another groundbreaking work, Marjoribanks (1979) showed three key parental attributes to differentiate between academically low-achieving and high-achieving students in an English-speaking country: *parental press for English*, or how much parents encourage their offspring to master the English language; *parental press for independence*, or how much autonomy parents encourage in their children; and *educational-occupational aspirations parents have for their offspring.*
   Martinez-Pons (1991) used *path analysis* (see Frame 2 for a discussion of path analysis) to test the hypothesized relations among these variables.   The researcher used data generated by Martinez-Pons and Zimmerman (1989) with 150 families of 10th and 11th grade students in a large metropolitan area. The results of the analysis appear in Figure 3. As evidenced by the results shown in this figure, *quality of the home environment* exerted an influence on *student's educational-occupational aspirations,* which in turn influenced *time spent on homework* and *academic achievement.* (The *CFI* of .99 disclosed that the linkages omitted in this figure were not required for the explanation of the data.)
   Recent work by Harris (1999) has brought a unique perspective to bear on parental influences on student behavior. While her work has concentrated most heavily on the relative effects, discussed below, of parents and peers on children's personality, an important component of her work involves the genetic influence she

believes parents exert on their children. According to Harris, whatever influence parents have on their offspring stems from genetic rather than from parent-to-child social effects. In fact, there is a complex set of interrelations involving heredity and social environmental factors in Harris' theory of socialization: "Not only do the parents provide the child's genes; they also provide the child's environment. [But] The kind of environment they provide—the kind of parents they are—is, in part, a function of their genes" (p. 31). Thus, a child's personality is partly a function of behavioral interactions that occur between him or her and the parents, and partly a function of his or her genetic makeup. In addition, the quality of the interactions between the child and the parents is a function of his or her and the parents' genetic makeup. According to Harris, the point of all this is that even when a child's behavior is found to accord with that of his or her parents, it may not be due, as believed by many socialization theorists, to the way parents treat him or her (parent-to-child social effect), but to either the genetic characteristics passed on to the child by the parents or *to the way the parents respond to the child's behavior* (child-to-parent social effect). These interrelations among genetic and parent-to-child effects in a child's development are shown in Figure 4.

Criticisms of Harris' work are discussed below, following a discussion of her treatment of peer influences on children's behavior.

Frame 2. Path Analysis

Path analysis (PA) is a statistical procedure used to test models containing intervening variables such as those appearing in Figure 3. In this figure, *quality of family environment, student's educational-occupational aspirations* and *time spent on homework* intervene between *SES* and *academic achievement*. PA enables the researcher to *decompose* the correlation between two variables into a) that which is spurious, inflated by the effects of other variables; b) that which is indirect, mediated by intervening variables, and c) that which is direct after all confounding and intervening effects have been accounted for. The procedure yields *path coefficients*, or regression weights (β), which show the direct effects involved. It also yields *multiple correlation coefficients* (R), which show the degree to which a dependent variable simultaneously correlates with two or more independent variables in the model. Finally, the procedure enables the researcher to determine the most parsimonious form the model can take—that is, it enables the researcher to identify the simplest form the model can take to address the issues at hand. It does this through *model fitting*, which

---

compares the power of the model for doing so with linkages excluded with all linkages included. One method widely used for the purpose of model fitting is termed the *comparative fit index* (*CFI;* Bentler & Bonnett, 1980). A *CFI* greater than .90 is considered indicative of the justification in omitting given linkages to tell the simplest story possible in explaining the processes involved.

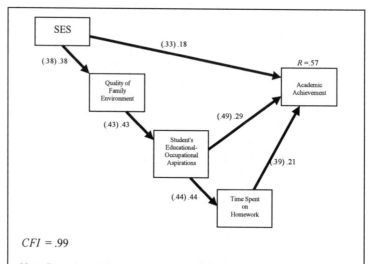

CFI = .99

Note: Pearson correlation coefficients appear enclosed in parentheses, and path coefficients, in the form of standardized regression weights (β), appear outside parentheses. All coefficients are significant beyond the .05 level.

Figure 3. Path Analysis of Quality of Family Environment and Academic Achievement

Peer Influences on Student Learning Readiness. According to Harris (1999), while in the past the assumption has been that parents exert the greatest social influence on children's behavior (with some influence also exerted by other adults such as teachers), in fact the social influence of peers can outstrip that of parents. Harris suggested that children's personality evolves largely as they watch and imitate other children. She came to this conclusion after considering the following possible influences on children's personality development: a) Parental encouragement of the typical behavior making up children's personality, b) children's imitation of parental behavior, c) children's imitation of all adults in their society, and d) children's imitation of other children. According to Harris,

> Any one, two or three of these mechanisms, or all four of them together, may be producing the observed effects on the children's behavior.... The trouble is that under ordinary conditions all the aspects of a child's environment are correlated—they all vary together— so it is impossible to tell which aspect of the environment is having the effect on the child. (p. 187)

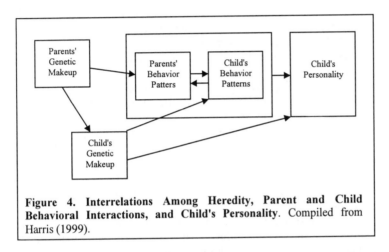

Figure 4. Interrelations Among Heredity, Parent and Child Behavioral Interactions, and Child's Personality. Compiled from Harris (1999).

To ascertain these factors' comparative influence on children's personalities, Harris reviewed the literature on immigrant families and Deaf children (the capitalized term *Deaf* denotes beliefs and values shared by hearing-impaired persons rather than hearing impairment *per se*). Concerning immigrant families, the author noted that

> When the immigrants' child joins a peer group of ordinary, non-ethnic Americans, the parents' culture is lost very quickly (the last aspects of the old culture to disappear are the things that are done only at home. Styles of cooking, for example, may survive for several generations. Children do not ordinarily learn to cook in the presence of their peers). (p. 191)

Thus, in Harris' view, despite their parents' efforts to induce them to maintain their original culture, immigrant children pick up the language and styles of their native peers (and quickly lose those of their parents) in a process pointing to the overwhelming effect of peers over that of parents in children's personality development.

Concerning the culture of the Deaf, the literature shows that groups of children with profound hearing impairment develop their own sense of "groupness", with their own world view and attitudes (Schaller, 1991). The important point in this respect concerning the development of children's personalities is that the culture of the Deaf cannot be passed down from hearing parents to deaf children; typically, hearing parents know nothing about such a culture, so they cannot pass it down to their offspring. Only peers can acculturate children into this system of perceptions and values. In fact, deaf children learn to be Deaf by interacting with other Deaf children, *in spite of the efforts of parents and teachers* to induce them to take on the values and outlook of the hearing world.

In addition to reference to immigrant families and the culture of the Deaf in support of her thesis, Harris has made reference to generational differences between parents and their offspring: "Parents and children belong to different generations; they grow up in different times. Cultural changes in the society add to the differences between parents and children" (p. 32).

Some controversy surrounds the work of Harris on socialization. For example, Williams (1999) suggested the following limitations in Harris' work:

1. Harris has failed to attend to research supporting the nurture position. For example, Williams cited work showing that infants randomly assigned to a condition of high maternal responsiveness displayed higher cognitive functioning than did children in a low maternal responsiveness condition.

2. The measures of parental influence in the studies cited by Harris have been too insensitive to detect the real parental influences that matter in children's personality development.

3. While Harris emphasizes the influence of peers on personality development, she minimizes the fact that parents influence the choice of peers.

Williams concluded her review of Harris' work by stating:

> Harris is a talented communicator, but she fails to convince us through this book that she is an empirical scientist who impartially evaluates the evidence. Her position is more that of a zealot arguing a side in a court battle than a dispassionate and independent reviewer. (p. 268)

In addition to the criticisms voiced by Williams, Plomin (1999) suggested the following limitations in Harris' work:

1. Harris' argument concerning the effects of peers involves for the most part group norms and fails to address individual differences. "In fact, however, the case for the role of peers as the answer to non-shared environments is far from proven" (p. 270).

2. Harris fails to apply to peers the same logic concerning genetic mediation that she applies to parents. But in fact, Manke, McGuire, Reiss, Hetherington and Plomin (1995) have found evidence of a genetic influence on characteristics of peer groups, "perhaps because adolescents choose peer groups and are chosen by peer groups on the basis of personality" (p. 270). These interrelations can be best represented in the diagram in Figure 5, showing a more complex set of interrelations among the factors of interest than that posed by Harris.

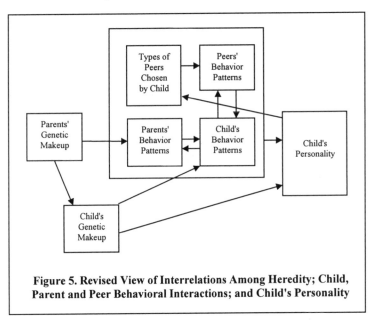

Figure 5. Revised View of Interrelations Among Heredity; Child, Parent and Peer Behavioral Interactions; and Child's Personality

Despite the criticisms leveled at Harris' work, research conducted during the past 20 years has supported parts of her thesis. For example, Reiss, Neiderheiser and Plomin (in press) have determined that

> Attempts to pin personality differences between siblings on differential treatment by parents have come to naught, because the evidence indicates that parents are responding to genetically instigated differences between siblings, rather than producing the sibling differences. (Plomin, 1999, p. 269)

What many writers seem to agree on concerning Harris' work is that she has succeeded in inducing workers to consider previously fragmented work, coming from different perspectives, for thinking about the dynamics involving *all* of the interpersonal factors that influence a child's psychological development. In doing so, she has refocused interest regarding child development from almost exclusive attention on parental influences to inclusion of the comparative influence exerted by peers. According to Williams,

> Harris does the psychological community a service by challenging the assumption that parents can craft their children out of clay. Her assault on closely held beliefs shared by many developmental psychologists forces us all to modify and clarify our thinking about why children turn out the way they do. (p. 268)

Where Harris' outlook may be relevant concerning learning readiness is in the influence that the attitudes and behavior of peers bring to bear on student's school performance. Berndt (1999) proposed a model of friends' influences on student academic achievement consisting of two major peer processes: *close friends' characteristics* and *quality and stability of friendship*. Berndt's model can be depicted as in Figure 6.

In Figure 6, the two elements of peer relations noted above are hypothesized to influence a student's motivation for schoolwork and compliance with school rules; and these variables are hypothesized to influence student academic task performance. Berndt (1999) reported research supportive of key linkages in this model.

Finally, research by Urdan (1997) and others (see Epstein, 1983; Kinderman, 1993) has demonstrated the influence of peers on academic achievement. Urdan studied 260 eight-grade students in an urban school district. Among the variables he examined were *positive school orientation of friends, negative school orientation of friends, task goals, effort avoidance goals* and *grade point average*. Students with task goals have been found to have a more positive motivational and behavioral profile than students with ability-oriented goals, and Urdan hypothesized a positive correlation of students' task goals and academic achievement with friends' school orientation. The correlation matrix among these variables, reproduced from Urdan (1997), is shown in Table 5.

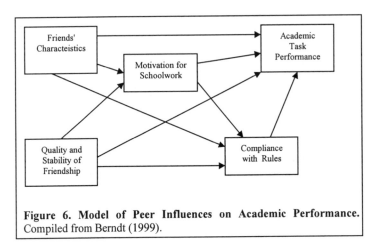

Figure 6. Model of Peer Influences on Academic Performance. Compiled from Berndt (1999).

Table 5. Correlations Among Student Academic Achivement and Peer School Orientation. From Urdan (1997).

	1	2	3	4	5
1. Positive Orientation of friends	1.00				
2. Negative orientation of friends	-.47	1.00			
3. Task goals	.53	-.42	1.00		
4. Effort avoidance goals	-.23	.45	-.47	1.00	
5. Grade point average	.35	-.41	.25	-.21	1.00

The present author tested a number of path models using this data, with positive and negative orientation of friends as the left foremost, "exogenous", predictor variables and academic achievement as the right foremost "endogenous", dependent variable. Neither task nor effort avoidance goals proved to play a role in the causal models examined. The best fitting model that emerged appears in Figure 7.

Although the Pearson correlation of friends' positive orientation with academic achievement was $r = .35$, $p < .05$, the effect proved to be indirect, through mediation of friends' negative orientation. As suggested by these outcomes, students' academic achievement is negatively affected by their friends' negative school orientation, when it occurs, and the latter is in turn negatively affected by friends' positive school orientations.

Peer influences on *academic self-regulation,* along with parental and teacher influences on academic self-regulation and *emotional functioning,* will be discussed below, after the self-regulation and emotional intelligence notions have been introduced.

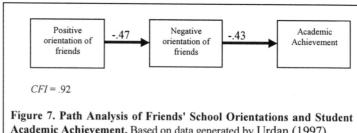

CFI = .92

Figure 7. Path Analysis of Friends' School Orientations and Student Academic Achievement. Based on data generated by Urdan (1997).

Thus, it is clear that health hazards, cosmetic factors and interpersonal factors are aspects of a student's environment that can influence the likelihood of his or her benefiting from instruction. An instructor equipped with information about the effects of such environmental factors on his or student learning readiness is in a better position to help his or her students to benefit from the teaching-learning effort than is one lacking such information.

The way in which the instructor can use information gained through environmental influences assessment is by a) rating the student's background in terms of key environmental demographic, physical and interpersonal factors; and b), in the case in which deficits in these areas are found, estimating the amount of effort it would take to remediate the condition. In the case in which the amount of effort would exceed that which the instructor feels he or she can exert, he or she can refer the matter to individuals or agencies with the resources necessary to address the problem.

Prior Academic Experience. The second major factor appearing in Figure 1 hypothesized to influence learning readiness is prior academic experience, or past events in a student's education with the potential for impacting on the likelihood of his or her benefiting from instruction. The following pages differentiate between two forms of prior experience: *prior practice* and *prior learning.*

Prior Practice. Until recently, learning theorists have believed talent to consist of native ability, something with which a person is born and which remains unchanged throughout his or her life. According to Ericsson and Charnes (1994), one previous account, termed *information-processing theory* (Newel & Simon, 1972), described in Chapter 4, has held that the basic information processing mechanism underlying given abilities remains intact during learning and that what changes in the attainment of mastery is simply the amount of acquired knowledge or skill. According to Ericsson and Charnes, another previous account, termed *multiple intelligences theory* (Gardner, 1993), has held that the neural mechanisms underlying given talents remain fixed through life and that what accounts for exceptional attainment is a close match between a specific fixed ability and situational demands. These accounts have been seemingly supported with research on high achievers, infant prodigies and savants.

The view concerning talent in relation to learning readiness has changed significantly during the past several years, with some workers challenging the traditional position on talent. For example, Ericsson and Charnes (1994) argued against the traditional view of learning readiness by noting a number of fallacies underlying it:

1. Most reports of unexplainable extraordinary performance cannot be substantiated. Actually, what is found when looking at such cases more closely is that for the individuals involved, intensive training in the skill at hand had started at an early age, usually before the age of five or six.

2. According to the traditional view, exceptional skills or talent occur irrespective of the environment: The genius "is born that way and stays that way". However, research has shown that the more pronounced the skill, the greater the need for long-term support from skilled mentors.

3. The great majority of talented adults were never child prodigies. They reached their skill level through an early start in instruction and intensive parental support.

4. While the parents of prodigies often report that their offspring's talent appeared suddenly, it turns out that what occurred suddenly was the discovery of the talent—which had been there all along due to opportunities, support and encouragement for mastery.

5. While the traditional view has it that special talent such as immediately naming the day of the week for an arbitrary date (e.g., July 3, 1800) is innate, research has shown that such a skill can be taught to college students within a month of training.

On the basis of such findings, Ericsson and Charnes (1994) concluded that

In summary, the evidence from systematic laboratory research on prodigies and savants provides no evidence for giftedness or innate talent but shows that exceptional abilities are acquired often under optimal environmental conditions. (p. 729)

The major thesis propounded by Ericsson and Charnes and others is that highly skilled, or expert, performance is a function of *deliberate practice*. For example, Ericsson, Krampe, and Tesch-Romer (1993) have determined that it takes an average of 10 years and upward of 10,000 hours of systematic practice under expert supervision to attain the mastery level characteristic of outstanding individuals in such fields as music and sports. The important thing about this point of view relative to learning readiness is that the principle of deliberate practice applies to everyday activities such as thinking, comprehension and problem solving instrumental in academic performance as well as to expert performance in art, science and sports.

Some reservations have been expressed concerning the position of Ericsson and Charnes on deliberate practice. For example, Gardner (1995) argued against the concept of deliberate practice on two points. First, referring to the work of Hernstein and Murray (1994), he contended that *g*, or intelligence, does not seem amenable to variation on the basis of deliberate practice—that in fact, only those with high psychometric ability to begin with can gain enough from deliberate practice to become experts—and that this outcome is to be expected in the case of any complex task. Second, he argued that in order to persist long enough at deliberate practice to succeed, a person must originally experience some level of success at it—and that early success at deliberate practice must be dependent on initial ability. In summary, according to Gardner,

> Ericsson and Charnes help us to understand some hitherto less-appreciated aspects of training, but in belittling the role of individual differences in interest, motivation, and above all, *relevant computational power or "intelligences,"* they undercut the power of their case. (p. 803)

In effect maintaining that the reservations expressed by Gardner underlie Type *i* (dismissive, invalid) issues, Ericsson and Charnes (1995) argued that Gardner's position represents a confusion between cause and effect:

> Experts' superior domain-specific memory performance doesn't reflect a separate ability but is an integral aspect of their skill. Their

memory improves without any specific training of memory as an indirect consequence of improvement of performance. The same type of acquired memory mechanisms mediate individual differences in skilled activities in everyday life, such as text comprehension. (p. 803)

In the end, this debate may have no resolution, since however early in a person's experience his or her performance is gauged, someone can argue that it is due to prior practice—and someone else can rejoin that the ability to capitalize on prior practice was due to a previously existing innate talent. Some workers may nevertheless tend to side with Ericsson and Charnes in this debate on the grounds that the notion of *talent* tends to circularity: why does a person do well at a task? Because he has an innate talent for it. But why say he has an innate talent for it? Because he does well on the task. The advantage of the approach of Ericsson and Charnes, according to its supporters, is that they follow the principle that "the story is in the details". Only by looking at detailed aspects of the situation in which superior performance takes place can one truly identify the conditions underlying it. The alternative is to rely on ultimately circular logic rather than on, in the words of Ericsson and Charnes (1994), "careful observation and study of differences in the type of and amount of activities associated with the longitudinal emergence of abilities in performance in normal and 'very talented' children" (p. 804).

Parents and teachers have been found to play significant roles in deliberate practice. As noted by Ericsson and Charnes (1994), the majority of talented adults reached their skill level through an early start in instruction and intensive adult support. As will be shown later, parents and teachers greatly influence children's practice by *modeling the behavior in question, encouraging persistence to the point of mastery, facilitating mastery through coaching activities,* and *continuously rewarding the behavior* being practiced by the student.

Thus, prior practice, in the form of supervised rehearsal of knowledge and skills, can exert a significant impact on learning readiness. The way in which the instructor can use information regarding prior practice is by determining a) how much time the student typically spends on a daily basis practicing the types of skills or factual knowledge to be targeted in the teaching-learning effort and how long he or she has been doing so; b) in cases in which deficits are found, ascertaining the reason for the condition and estimating the amount of effort it would take to remediate it. In cases in which the amount of effort would exceed that which the instructor feels he or she can exert, he or she can seek help from others with the resources necessary to address the problem.

Prior Learning. While the concern with *prior practice* involves repetition and "fine-tuning" of specific cognitive, affective or physical behavior, the concern with *prior learning* involves acquired mental, affective or physical behavior or skill that is different from that at hand, but which may be necessary or useful for the mastery of new material. In work with college students, Scandura (1965) found that learning ability, far from being innate, depends on the amount of prerequisite learning already available; and in a review of research by educational psychologists on prior learning, Dochy (1988) reported that between 30 and 60 percent of the variance in study results can be explained by prior learning. Two forms of prior learning are considered in the following paragraphs: *Prior learning of rules,* and *prior learning of facts.*

Prior Learning of Rules. In their work on acquired mental skills as determinants of learning readiness, Siegler and Klahr (1982) demonstrated the relation between cumulative, existing rule knowledge or mastery and the acquisition of new information. They listed four principles they derived on the basis of their research on the interaction between existing knowledge, encoding processes and instruction:

1. Knowledge acquisition takes the form of rule mastery.

2. When two or more partially correct rules are used to master new material, they are ordered in terms of increasing correspondence with rules governing the new material

3. The effectiveness of a learning experience is largely determined by the degree to which the experience discriminates between the rule the learner is using and the rule to be learned.

4. A major reason learners do not immediately adopt the correct rule for a given class of concepts is their limited encoding of the correct rule's dimensions. This failure can be due to lack of knowledge of the dimension's importance, lack of salience of the rule in the context in which it is to be applied, or lack of ability to hold the relevant information in memory.

According to Siegler and Klahr (1982), their rule mastery approach to prior learning helps to eliminate a certain redundancy inherent in the concept of learning readiness:

> These concepts and analytic procedures have greatly increased our ability to deal with such notions as "readiness" and "the match". They suggest a way out of the circularity of these venerable and intuitively plausible concepts, and enable us to propose well-defined

instructional sequences that increase the probability of learning. (p. 207)

This author takes issue with Siegler and Kahlr's first principle of acquired mental skills, since it seems to him apparent that some learned material involves memorization of simple facts rather than the acquisition and understanding of abstract rules. For this reason, he deems it important to consider non-rule-related facts, the next form of knowledge proposed to be involved in prior learning.

Prior Learning of Facts. It seems obvious that possession of certain factual knowledge is necessary in order to grasp new factual information. For example, to understand the message "my telephone number is 2223", a person must know what a telephone is, that there exists a system of electronically connected telephones, and that the system is organized in such a away that each phone is assigned a number which a person can "dial" in order to reach it. The above statement does not convey the same information to a person lacking this prior knowledge as it does to a person possessing it. On work on acquired factual knowledge as a determinant of learning readiness, Reigeluth (1980) posited six kinds of prior factual information with potential impact on learning readiness:

1. Superordinate knowledge, including and subsuming the material to be learned.

2. Coordinate knowledge, closely related to the new material.

3. Subordinate knowledge, an instance or example of the new material.

4. Arbitrary knowledge, with no inherent relationship to the new material.

5. Analogic knowledge, outside of but similar to the content area of the new material.

6. Cognitive strategies, which are content-free skills used to facilitate learning and remembering. Obviously, deliberate practice, described above, can help in the mastery of such strategies.

Thus, prior experience, consisting of prior practice and prior learning, is an important factor influencing learning readiness. An instructor with information about his or her students' prior academic experience is in a better position to prepare for the teaching-learning effort than one lacking this information.

Relative to instruction, the way in which the instructor can use information regarding prior learning is by determining a) how much information or skill the student has already mastered relative to the material to be learned; and b) in cases in which the student lacks any necessary background information, estimating the amount of effort it would take to provide the student with it. In the case in which the amount of effort would exceed that which the instructor judges he or she can profitably exert, he or she can seek help from others with the resources necessary to address the condition.

Academic Self-Regulation. The third factor shown in Figure 1 hypothesized to influence learning readiness is academic self-regulation, one of the more powerful personal attributes found to differentiate between successful and unsuccessful students. Social cognitive theorists have made great strides during the past two decades in describing and studying academic self-regulated behavior.

Definition of Self-Regulation. Zimmerman (1989) described a self-regulated student as one who is motivated to accomplish some task, sets realistic goals for himself or herself relative to the task, uses specific strategies to pursue these goals, self-monitors to check for strategy effectiveness, and adjusts his or her strategy usage behavior as necessary to ensure the likelihood of success.

In his *Triadic Model of Self-Regulated Learning*, Zimmerman (1989) proposed that in order to study self-regulation, it is necessary to consider three factors of the learning setting: *The environment, a student's cognitive processes* and *the student's behavior*. This model has an important contextual component, concern with which can be highlighted with two quotations from Zimmerman's work:

> Self-regulated learning is not determined merely by personal processes; these are assumed to be influenced by environmental and behavioral events in reciprocal fashion. For example, a student's solution response to a subtraction problem such as "8 - 4 = ?" is assumed to be determined not only by personal (self) perceptions of efficacy, but also by such environmental stimuli as encouragement from a teacher and by enactive outcomes (i.e., obtaining a correct answer to previous problems). This reciprocal formulation also allows that such self-regulative responses as self-recording can influence both the environment ... and various personal processes. (p. 330)

Moreover,

> Reciprocity does not mean symmetry in strength or temporal patterning of bidirectional influence. Environmental influences may be stronger than behavioral or personal ones in some contexts or at certain points during behavioral interaction sequences. (p. 330)

Thus, a self-regulated student is one who is in constant interaction with his or her surroundings as he or she attempts to accomplish some task. This interaction takes the form of attempts at mastery and attention to environmental feedback regarding task success, and it is followed by modification of task-related behavior on the basis of environmental feedback.

Academic Self-Regulation and Learning Readiness. Zimmerman and Martinez-Pons (1986, 1988) developed and tested a model of student academic self-regulated learning strategies. They showed that high achieving students displayed significantly greater use of 13 forms of self-regulated learning strategies than did lower-achieving students. These strategies, which differentiated between the two groups with 93 percent accuracy, are displayed in Table 6.

Table 6. Self-Regulated Learning Strategies found to Differentiate Between High- and Regular-Track High School Students. From Zimmerman and Martinez-Pons (1986).

1. Reviewing tests
2. Organizing and transforming
3. Goal setting and planning
4. Seeking information
5. Keeping records and monitoring
6. Environmental structuring
7. Self-consequences
8. Rehearsing and memorizing
9. Seeking assistance from peers
10. Seeking assistance from teachers
11. Seeking assistance from adults
12. Reviewing notes
13. Reviewing textbooks

On the basis of the work of Zimmerman and Martinez-Pons (1986) and Zimmerman (1989), Martinez-Pons (1999) developed a measure of academic self-regulation addressing the five self-regulation areas of motivation, goal setting, strategy usage, self-monitoring and strategy adjustment. He found a substantial correlation between this measure of self-regulation with teachers' ratings of student academic achievement (this finding is discussed in some detail below under *Parental, Teacher and Peer Influences on Academic Self-Regulation*). In addition, Lindner and Harris (1993), working with 160 college students, found that self-regulated learning explained the majority of differences in academic performance in this population.

The role of self-regulation in school success described above involved attainment in cognitive areas of learning. But self-regulation in the school has also been shown to be relevant in achievement in the *psychomotor domain*, that area of learning involving hand-eye coordination and coordination of body movement to achieve some goal (the psychomotor domain of instruction is described in Chapter 3). In the area of school sports, for example, Zimmerman and Kitsantas (1997) found that high school students who used goal setting, self-monitoring and strategy adjustment in the acquisition of a complex motor skill surpassed those who failed to do so in this area.

Standardized Measures of Academic Self-Regulation. Aside from the experimental procedures described above to assess academic self-regulation, a number of standardized, commercially available instruments exist addressing various aspects of this key contributor to learning readiness. The *Surveys of Problem-Solving and Educational Skills* (Meltzer, 1987) is a set of standardized, individually administered procedures for assessing key aspects of self-regulation. It consists of student self-reports and observations of student behavior involving such key areas of self-regulation as strategies used, strategy awareness, self-monitoring, and error correction. Meltzer, Solomon, Fenton and Levine (1989) reported that the *SPES* accurately differentiates between high- and low-achieving students in elementary and middle schools.

As another example of a standardized test addressing aspects of academic self-regulation, Weinstein and Palmer (1998) developed the *Learning and Study Strategies Inventory (LASSI)*, an instrument designed to assess such areas of study behavior as *motivation for study, attitudes toward learning, time management, control of test anxiety, concentration, information-processing skills, selecting main ideas, study aids*, and *test-taking skills*. The *LASSI* exists in high school and college versions. Shanley, Martinez-Pons and Lopez-Lubal (1999) found scores on the *selecting main ideas* and *test anxiety* subscales of the college version of the *LASSI* to statistically significantly explain college student performance on the New York State teacher certification exam, the *Liberal Arts and Science Test (LAST; $r = .57$, $p < .05$, and $r = -.53$, $p < .05$*, respectively); together, their explanation of *LAST* performance was $R = .66$, $p < .05$.

It is clear from the above findings that academic self-regulation is an important determinant of the likelihood of a student's benefiting from the educational experience. Of special importance in this regard is SR's adaptive quality. There is nothing in self-regulation theory that stipulates this attribute to be a fixed mode of behavior. In fact, the self-regulatory behavior Zimmerman (1989) stipulates in the *Triadic Model of Self-Regulated Learning* is highly adaptive to situational demands and in this way promotes learning readiness regardless of the situation at hand.

The way in which the instructor can use information gained through self-regulation (SR) assessment is by a) deciding on a student's SR level; and b), in the case of a student with a low level of academic self-regulation, estimating the amount of effort it would take to remediate the condition. In the case in which the amount of effort would exceed that which the instructor feels he or she can exert, he or she can refer the student to school personnel with the resources necessary to address the problem.

Parental, Teacher and Peer Inducement of Academic Self-Regulation. The behavior of parents, teachers and peers has been found to significantly influence students' academic self-regulation.

Parental and Teacher Inducement of Academic Self-Regulation. Martinez-Pons (1996) developed a model in which student self-regulation is hypothesized as a function of parental modeling of self-regulatory behavior—and of parental encouragement, facilitation and rewarding of the self-regulatory behavior of their offspring. This model, entitled the *Parental Inducement Model of Academic Self-Regulation (PIMASR)* appears in Table 7.

Table 7. Parental Inducement Model of Academic Self-Regulation (PIMASR). From Martinez-Pons (1996).

Parental Behavior	Student Self-Regulation				
	Motivation	Goal Setting	Strategy Usage	Self-Monitoring	Strategy Adjustment
Modeling					
Encouraging					
Facilitating					
Rewarding					

Of particular interest in this model are the *modeling* and *facilitating* components of parental behavior. As noted in Chapter 3, Bandura (1986) has shown that modeling is the principal way in which people learn in social systems, and that a number of important elements of modeling are involved in the effective occurrence of this process. The aspect of facilitation emphasized by Martinez-Pons (1996) in the PIMASR was that of *apprenticeship learning* (Collins, Brown & Newman, 1989; Pressley & McCormick, 1995). In this approach to facilitation, after demonstrating the behavior in detail and explaining its finer points to the child, the adult offers feedback and suggestions on the basis of the child's attempts to replicate the behavior; encourages the child to "talk his or her way through" the behavior to develop a better understanding of it, to compare his or her performance to that of others, and to go beyond the behavior mastered and explore ways of applying it to other areas of his or her life.

The researcher surveyed 105 students in grades 5 through 8 in a public school in a large metropolitan area to test the power of the PIMASR in predicting self-regulation (SR) and academic achievement. He used the *Parental Inducement of Academic Self-Regulation Scale (PIASRS)* an experimental instrument derived from the PIMASR, and the *Multidimensional Scale of Self-Regulation (MSSR)* to generate the information (copies of these questionnaires appear in Appendix B), and he used path analysis to examine the data. As shown in Figure 8, parental SR inducement predicted academic self-regulation ($\beta = .50$, $p < .05$) in adolescent pupils, and academic self-regulation in turn predicted academic achievement ($\beta = .44$, $p < .05$) on the part of these students.

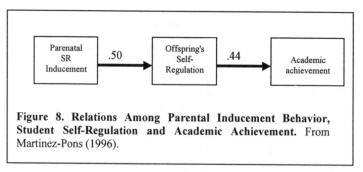

Figure 8. Relations Among Parental Inducement Behavior, Student Self-Regulation and Academic Achievement. From Martinez-Pons (1996).

In a second study, Martinez-Pons (1999a) examined the relative effects of parental and teacher behaviors on student academic self-regulation. The researcher used 187 9th and 10th grade students, their parents and teachers, drawn from schools in Shanghai, China; and in public schools in the New York Metropolitan Area. As shown in Figure 9, the relation of teacher inductive behavior with student self-regulation was $r = .69, p < .05$, which dropped to $\beta = .58, p < .05$ when the qualifying effect of parental behavior was statistically controlled. The correlation of parental behavior with self-regulation was $r = .55, p < 05$, although it dropped to $\beta = .16, p < .05$ when the qualifying effect of teacher behavior was controlled statistically.

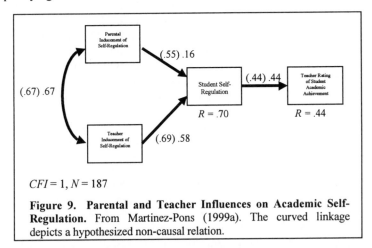

$CFI = 1, N = 187$

Figure 9. Parental and Teacher Influences on Academic Self-Regulation. From Martinez-Pons (1999a). The curved linkage depicts a hypothesized non-causal relation.

Peer Influences on Academic Self-Regulation. Under laboratory conditions, Schunk and Hanson (1985) studied the influence of peers in engendering student academic self-regulation. The researchers examined the comparative effects of peer and teacher models on the academic self-regulation of school-age children. They used two types of peer models: mastery models who verbalized statements reflecting strong confidence of being able to solve subtraction problems correctly and reflecting high self-efficacy and ability, low task difficulty and positive attitudes; and coping models who made numerous initial errors working on the math problems. They verbalized negative statements followed later by coping statements such as "I need to pay attention to what I'm doing". The researchers found that, while students observing peer models increased self-efficacy and skill better than did those observing the teacher and those observing no model, students observing peer coping models outperformed the other two groups. Improved self-efficacy resulted in improved attitudes and greater involvement, and these processes in turn produced improved skills. On the basis of the outcomes, Schunk and Hanson (1985) concluded that the children tended to emulate models they perceived to be like them (e.g., other children trying to cope with a difficult task) more readily than they did models they perceived to not be like them (e.g., teachers or peers who do not experience difficulties in early attempts at mastery).

The influence of peers on students' self-regulation was also investigated experimentally by Orange (1999). In her study, participants in an experimental group watched a videotape in which low-achieving students are addressed by a self-regulated peer portrayed as previously low-achieving. The peer explained a 12-step action plan for becoming more self-regulated. The experimental group made a commitment in writing to use the action plan. Orange found that the difference in pre- and post-test scores on a measure of self-regulation was statistically significantly greater for the experimental group than for a control group not receiving the treatment. The mean (M) for the former was 8.55 and the standard deviation (SD) was 18.27 (see Frame 3 for a discussion of the mean and standard deviation and related concepts); for the control group, $M = 1.88$, $SD = 34$. The findings lent support to the proposition that peer models can exert an important influence in the development of self-regulatory behavior.

Thus, self-regulation, consisting of motivation to accomplish some task, goal setting relative to the task, strategy usage in pursuit of these goals, and self-evaluation and strategy adjustment as necessary, is an important factor influencing learning readiness. Parents, teachers and peers can influence academic self-regulation through their modeling of self-regulated learning behavior. In addition, research has shown that teachers and parents can further promote the student's self-regulation through encouragement to persist at attempts at mastery of the behavior, facilitation efforts, and rewarding of the student's self-regulated learning behavior when it occurs. An instructor with information about his or her students' level of self-regulation—and about the students' parents', teachers' and peers' influences in this area—is in a better position to prepare for the teaching-learning effort than one lacking such information.

The way in which the instructor can use information gained through peer influence assessment relative to academic self-regulation (SR) is by a) deciding on the quality of peer behavior that may influence the self-regulatory behavior of the student; and b), in the case in which the influence is negative, estimating the amount of effort it would take to remediate the condition. In the case in which the amount of effort would exceed that which the instructor deems he or she can

exert, he or she can seek help from others with the resources necessary
to effectively address the problem.

Frame 3. The Mean and the Standard Deviation and Related Concepts

The mean (M) is the average of a set of scores; it is calculated by
dividing the number of scores (N) into the sum of the scores, like this:

$$M = \text{Sum} / N$$

The standard deviation (represented by s for a sample or σ for a
population) is a measure of the differences that exist among a group of
scores; it is calculated as a special average of the degree to which the
scores differ from the group's mean. First, the square of the difference
between each score and the mean is calculated, and then the square
root of the mean of these squares is calculated, like this:

$$s = \sqrt{\frac{\Sigma (X - M)^2}{N}}$$

The symbol Σ is an instruction to sum all squared differences
between the scores and the mean. Without the square root, the value
generated by the formula is termed the *variance*, represented by s^2 for
a sample or σ^2 for a population.

s is useful in a number of ways. For example, it can be used to
estimate the effect of some intervention. In the study by Orange
(1999) cited above, s for the control group was about twice as large as
it was for the experimental group, showing that the intervention
reduced differences among the members of the experimental group.
Another way in which s can be of use is in determining the degree to
which a particular score differs from overall group performance. It can
be used to this end by dividing it into the difference between the score
and the mean to yield a *z-score*, like this:

$$z = (X - M) / SD$$

The *z*-score provides an indication of the number of standard
deviations above or below the mean a particular score lies.

Mental Ability. The fourth factor appearing in Figure 1 assumed to impact on learning readiness is mental ability. Mental ability, mental acuity, or intelligence, is one of the more controversial concepts found in the social sciences and education. One reason for the controversy is the multitude of ways in which it has been described (Biehler and Snowman, 1986). A second reason is the way in which the matter has been studied—an approach leading to increasingly abstract formulations and culminating with the concept of g, whose correlational manner of derivation renders it virtually sterile as a theoretical construct. According to Jensen (1985),

> All potential speculation [concerning the nature of g] so far, has been quite lacking in the heuristic power needed to get on with the empirical job of hypothesis testing, which is the *sine qua non* of theory building. At present, it seems safe to say, we do not have a true theory of g or intelligence. (p. 25)

The reservations concerning the concept of intelligence range between cautionary and dismissive, and in the view of this author, they also range in tenability between valid and invalid. In the final analysis, from this writer's perspective, the more realistic reservations concerning the intelligence concept involve Type a (cautionary, valid) issues, pointing to the need for better approaches to the description and investigation of the phenomenon. In fact, as shown below, when approached from a certain paradigmatic stance, it is possible to infuse the notion with some degree of theoretical and heuristic power. At any rate, while controversy exists surrounding the concept of mental ability, educators continue to use it with great frequency, lending the notion of intelligence, according to Gage and Berliner (1984), a certain degree of legitimacy.

Definition of Mental Ability. This author (see Martinez-Pons, 1998) argued that in order to be of any use to educators, any definition or description of mental ability must adhere to the following criteria:
1. It must be intuitively appealing to educators, and in particular, to school teachers. As already noted, Jensen (1965) criticized the correlational nature of the traditional approach to theory-building in the area of intelligence, which has culminated with the notion of g, seen as theoretically sterile and intuitively unappealing to teachers. To be acceptable, any definition of intelligence must be able to overcome this limitation.
2. It must be amenable to observation and measurement.
3. It must be relevant to learning.

4. At the same time that it is relevant to learning, it must be *separate* from academic achievement.

5. It must be amenable to manipulation to maximize performance. As noted earlier, traditional positions on talent have held that mental ability is innate and fixed. However, as also noted, Ericsson and Charnes (1994) have found that what differentiates talented from non-talented individuals is deliberate practice under expert supervision, usually for long periods of time. Any definition of intelligence must be able to capitalize on this fact in order to be of any practical use to educators.

6. It must have theoretical appeal for workers in the field of cognitive science.

Through *grounded theory research* (see Frame 4 for a discussion of grounded theory research), the researcher developed a teacher-oriented model of intelligence adhering to the above criteria. The model consisted of three major components: *speed of acquisition* (*SA*), or the amount of information a person can acquire within a given period of time; *effectiveness of retention* (*ER*), or the amount of material a person can effectively retain over a given period of time; and *extent of utilization* (*EU*), or the amount of new information a person can generate within a given period of time. The model for this conceptualization of intelligence appears in Table 8.

The researcher tested the sequential nature of the SA, ER and EU model by determining the degree to which it met Guttman's (1953) criteria for sequential structures. According to Guttman, in order to empirically establish the sequential structure of models such as that of intelligence entertained here, one must show that correlations exist between adjacent components, and that zero or statistically non-significant correlations exist between non-adjacent components. In terms of these criteria, in order for the present model of intelligence to be truly sequential, correlations must emerge *only* between SA and ER; and between ER and EU; but not between SA and EU. The method the researcher used to test the sequential structure of the model was path analysis (see Frame 2 for a discussion of path analysis). The analysis outcomes, appearing in Figure 10, showed that the model met the Guttman criteria for sequential structures and thus supported the idea of intelligence as a sequence of mental processes involving acquisiton performance, retention performance and utilization performance.

The author tested this model's *discriminant* and *convergent* validity by *factor analyzing* (see Frame 5 for a discussion of factor analysis and convergent and discriminant valitidy) SA, ER and EU measures, along with a more traditional measure of intelligence (i.e.,

The Quick Test; Ammons & Ammons, 1962) and national percentile scores on mathematics and reading achievement.

Frame 4. Grounded Theory Research

Grounded theory is a method of research through which the investigator begins with a minimum number of assumptions concerning the nature of the thing being investigated, letting the facts of the matter emerge in the course of his or her observations. Pressley and McCormick (1995) summarized this method in terms of the following steps:

1. Collection of qualitative data through observation or unstructured survey or interview methods.

2. Identification of regularities or categories among the qualitative data.

3. Checking for category credibility and elaboration of categories through more focused surveys or interviews.

4. Organization of categories into a cohesive theoretical structure.

5. Construct validation of the theoretical structure through the use of statistical methodology.

Thus, grounded theory research combines the so-called qualitative and quantitative methods of research into one seamless process enabling the researcher to a) minimize his or her pre-conceived notions about the topic at hand, and b) use sophisticated mathematical methodology to examine the dynamics at hand with a degree of precision sufficient to afford explanation and prediction of the phenomenon at hand.

The researcher reasoned that if SA, ER and EU truly form parts of intelligence, then scores on these attributes should load on the same factor as *Quick Test* scores; and that scores on math and reading tests would load on a factor separate although related to the intelligence factor. The results of the analysis appear in Table 9. Loadings in this table accompanied by asterisks are statistically significant beyond the .05 level (Stevens, 1996) and can thus be accepted as supportive of the theory. As evidenced by these outcomes, the intelligence measures loaded on one factor and the academic achievement measures loaded on a separate factor. The two factors proved to be correlated ($\phi = .53$), supporting the hypothesis that intelligence, although distinct from academic achievement, is related to it. Thus, the path and factor analysis findings supported the idea of intelligence as composed of the speed with which one acquires information, the effectiveness with which one retains it, and the extent to which one can utilize it.

Table 8. Three-Component Model of Intelligence. From Martinez-Pons (1998).

Component	Performance Dimensions		Summary
	Amount	Time	
Acquisition	How much material is learned	How long it takes to master the material	How much material is learned within a given period of time
Retention	How much material is retained	How long the material is retained	How much material is retained over a given period of time
Utilization	How extensively the retained material is used	How quickly the retained material is used	How much new information is generated within a given period of time

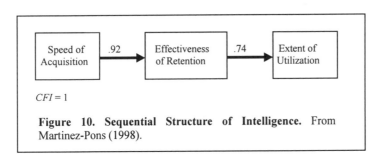

CFI = 1

Figure 10. Sequential Structure of Intelligence. From Martinez-Pons (1998).

Standardized Measures of Mental Ability. Aside from the experimental procedure developed to test the three-component model of mental ability described above, standardized tests exist designed for the assessment of intelligence. Anastasi (1982) listed a variety of individually- and group-administered tests designed for the purpose. Some of the more widely known of these tests are the *Stanford-Binet Intelligence Scale*, the *Wechsler Adult Intelligence Scale (WAIS-R)*, the *Wechsler Intelligence Scale for Children (WISC-R)*, the *Wechsler*

Preschool and Primary School Scale of Intelligence (WPPSI), the *Miller Analogies Test*, and the *Progressive Matrices Test (Raven)*.

Frame 5. Factor Analysis, Convergent Validity, and Discriminant Validity

Factor Analysis

Factor analysis is a statistical procedure used to determine the common things, or factors, associated with a set of measures—and the degree of association between each measure and each factor.

Typically, the analysis begins with a relatively large number of measures on the basis of the correlations that emerge among them, the procedure tests whether they address a fewer number of factors. For example, a test of anxiety may contain 40 items, and factor analysis may disclose that items 1-20, being highly correlated with one another, reflect a factor that can be characterized as *trait* anxiety; and that items 21-40, highly correlated with each other, reflect a factor that can be characterized as *state* anxiety (factors are named or characterized by ascertaining the things that highly correlated items share in common).

In *exploratory* factor analysis, the researcher leaves it to the analysis to determine the number of factors involved and the degree of association of each measure with each factor (the index of degree of association between a measure and a factor is termed a *factor loading*). In *confirmatory* factor analysis, the researcher specifies in advance what he or she believes to be the factors and loadings at hand, and the analysis confirms or disconfirms these stipulations. According to Stevens (1996), loadings of .40 or above can be considered high enough to be empirically meaningful.

Convergent and Discriminant Validity (CV and DV)

CV refers to an instrument's items loading on factors on which they are hypothesized to load, and DV refers to an intrument's items *not* loading on factors with which they are *not* hypothesized to load. Thus, in the above example, if the researcher who developed the test of anxiety hypothesized in advance that items 1-20 would be measuring trait anxiety but not state anxiety; and that items 21 to 40 would be measuring state anxiety but not the trait anxiety, then the instrument can be said to possess convergent and discriminant validity.

Table 9. Construct Validation of a Model of Mental Ability: Factor Analysis Outcomes. The factors were correlated, and hence, the rotated pattern matrix shown was used for interpretation. From Martinez-Pons, 1998.

	Factor 1	Factor 2	Communality
Quick Test	.59*	.45	.39
Acquisition Performance	.95*	.39	.89
Retention Performance	.94*	.38	.89
Utilization Performance	.85*	.38	.73
Reading	.33	.87*	.75
Mathematics	.47	.86*	.75
Eigenvalue	3.38	1.02	
% of Variance Explained	56.40	17.10	
Total Variance	73.40		

*$p < .01$, 2-tailed test (Stevens, 1996). $\phi = .53$.

Arguing that traditional standardized tests of intelligence (that is, IQ tests) fail to provide the type of information needed to help in the planning of instruction, Bolig and Day (1993) developed the *Dynamic Assessment of Giftedness (DAG)* test as a viable alternative. According to Bolig and Day (1993), an important feature of the *DAG* is its measurement of training responsiveness, involving what proves to be speed of acquisition, effectiveness of retention and extent of utilization. They report having used the procedure successfully to address the educational needs of gifted students, and there seems to be no reason to assume that the methodology cannot be profitably used with other classes of students as well.

Relevance of Mental Ability to Learning Readiness. Although controversial because of the way in which it has been described and assessed, it is clear that intelligence is a construct with relevance to the likelihood of a student's benefiting from instruction:

1. As shown in Table 9, it is a construct distinct from but substantially related to academic achievement.

2. When seen as speed of acquisition (SA), effectiveness of retention (ER) and extent of utilization (EU), it has intuitive appeal for educators, and more specifically, for teachers. As shown in Figure 11, representing a "hybrid model" (Kline, 1998) of *path analysis with factors* (see Frame 6 for a discussion of path analysis with factors), the correlation between intelligence (as SA, ER and EU) and academic

achievement (as math and reading performance) was .53, the same as for the factor analysis shown in Table 9, but with the *Quick Test* measure excluded.

Frame 6. Path Analysis with Factors

Path analysis with factors (PF) is a statistical procedure used to test path models in which relations are stipulated among unobserved variables (i.e., factors composed of any number of elements). The procedure works in two phases. First, it performs what is essentially a confirmatory factor analysis for each factor stipulated in the model. Then, using these factors as single variables, the procedure performs a path analysis in the usual way. Single-measure variables as well as multiple-measure factors can be included in such an analysis. As in path analysis using single-measure variables exclusively, PF performs a test of the degree to which the model fits the data when not all possible linkages among variables and factors are stipulated. The *Comparative Fit Index (CFI)* is used to test the fit of the model. A *CFI* equal to or greater than .90 is indicative of a good fit. PF models can include both factors and single-measure variables.

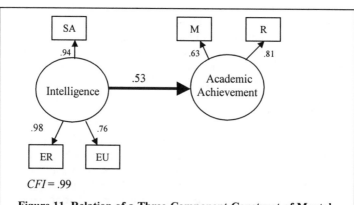

$CFI = .99$

Figure 11. Relation of a Three-Component Construct of Mental Ability with Academic Achievement

---

3. Intelligence has been shown to be, up to a point, amenable to manipulation for the purpose of enhancing learning readiness. Of particular interest in this regard is the work of Ericsson and Charnes (1994), discussed earlier, on deliberate practice. This work shows that,

far from being innate, talent is largely a function of the amount of practice that has gone into the development of a particular skill, and there is no reason to assume that practice of skills related to speed of acquisition, effectiveness of retention and extent of utilization cannot have a significant impact on mental ability defined in this way. In fact, research has shown this to be the case. Regarding acquisition, such strategies reported by Dasenrau (1979) as *concentration management* to engender a mood for concentrating when reading a text, and *networking* for organizing the material in ways meaningful to the individual have shown encouraging results with college students experiencing difficulties with the acquisition of printed material.

Regarding retention, success with such strategies as the use of attention-getting devices to improve sensory register functions, rehearsal and chunking techniques to improve short-term memory, and imagery and verbal encoding to improve long-term memory have been reported in the literature (Webster, 1981; Biehler & Snowman, 1982). Finally, regarding utilization, research by Jampole (1990) on higher-order thinking skills has shown that how well and how extensively students utilize learned material can be dramatically improved.

For these reasons, in the view of the present writer, the continuing interest in the topic of mental ability has merit—and when seen as SA, ER and EU, diagnostic targeting as the basis of attempts at its enhancement holds promise for the promotion of learning readiness.

Thus, mental acuity, mental ability, or intelligence, can be defined as the speed with which a student can acquire new knowledge or skill, the effectiveness with which he or she can retain the material or skill, and the extent to which he or she can utilize that which he or she has acquired and retained. One advantage of this conceptualization of intelligence is that it allows for maximization through deliberate practice. An instructor with information about his or her students' mental ability level is in a better position to prepare for the teaching-learning effort than one lacking such information.

The way in which the instructor can use information gained through speed of acquisition (SA), effectiveness of retention (ER) and extent of utilization (EU) assessment is by a) deciding on the level of SA, ER, and EU for a particular class of tasks; and b), in the case of a student with deficits in these areas, estimating the amount of effort it would take to remediate the condition to the point where SA, ER and EU can serve to promote readiness to learn. In the case in which the amount of effort would exceed that which the instructor feels he or she can exert, he or she can refer the student to educational personnel with the resources necessary to address the problem.

The above treatment of mental ability relates to *rational* intelligence. But some scholars have suggested that there is also such a thing as the ability to manage one's emotions, an attribute that has come to be known as *emotional intelligence* (EI), and that EI influences the degree to which people in general succeed in life—and more specifically, the degree to which students succeed in school. EI is the fifth major element appearing in Figure 1 hypothesized to impact on student learning readiness.

Emotional Intelligence. The EI notion was introduced by Salovey and Mayer (1989) with their article *Emotional Intelligence*, appearing in the professional journal *Imagination, Cognition and Personality*, and was popularized by Goleman (1995) in his trade book *Emotional Intelligence*. Since then, the concept has taken hold in the thinking of many social scientists and educators, and it appears to be gaining a place in the psychological lexicon. Before discussing the concept of emotional intelligence it may be worthwhile to examine some aspects of the dynamics attending emotional processes.

Emotional Dynamics. Relative to emotional intelligence, the nature of emotional dynamics can be understood by looking at the anatomy of an emotion and by looking at the nature of emotional dysfunction.

The Anatomy of an Emotion. An emotion is a complex of psychological processes involving assessment of some situation relative to one's values or personal well-being, physiological arousal in response to this assessment, and channeling of arousal into potential for some course of action. Figure 12 shows an abbreviated view, compiled from Goleman (1995), LeDoux (1992) and Reber (1995), of the mechanism of an emotional response. In this figure, a set of sensations (sound, sight, touch, smell, taste) is transmitted to the *thalamus*, that part of the brain in which sensory information is transformed into perceptual wholes interpretable by other parts of the brain. From the thalamus, the information is simultaneously relayed to the *hippocampus*, that part of the brain in which the information is reviewed for familiarity; to the *cortex*, that part of the brain in which the information is rationally examined for meaning and in which response alternatives to the perceived situation are considered; and to the *amygdala*, that part of the brain in which judgements are intuitively made concerning the perceptions' significance for the person's value system or well-being—and from which response activation is triggered in other parts of the system (e.g., the *hypothalamus*, which secretes a hormone that activates the body's responses to threatening situations; and the brainstem's *locus ceruleus*, which secretes a hormone that increases the acuteness of the brain's sensory centers). Reciprocal activity is possible between the thalamus, hippocampus, cortex and amygdala.

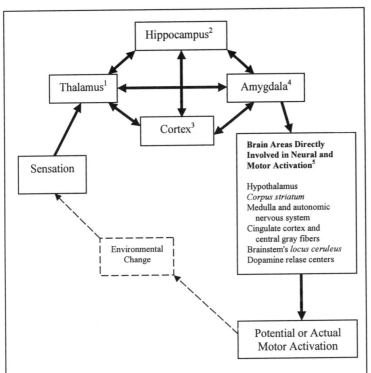

Thalamus[1]

Hippocampus[2]

Cortex[3]

Amygdala[4]

Sensation

Environmental Change

Brain Areas Directly Involved in Neural and Motor Activation[5]

Hypothalamus
Corpus striatum
Medulla and autonomic
nervous system
Cingulate cortex and
central gray fibers
Brainstem's *locus ceruleus*
Dopamine relase centers

Potential or Actual Motor Activation

[1]Sensory data is received and transmitted to other parts of the brain
[2]Sensory data is evaluated for familiarity
[3]Detailed analysis is carried out for meaning and appropriate response
[4]Evaluation of information relative to one's well being; activation of
response mechanisms
[5]Secretion of hormones for neural and motor activation

Figure 12. The Mechanism of an Emotion. Compiled from Goleman (1995), LeDoux (1992) and Reber (1995).

Finally, motor activity generated by amygdala-induced neural and motor activation can bring about environmental changes registered as new sensations by the individual—and the emotional response process has an opportunity to begin anew.

Emotional Dysfunction. If the cortex has a chance to rationally assess what appears to be an adverse condition and to examine the relative merits of a variety of possible response alternatives, the person has an opportunity to undertake well-considered adaptive behavior that can maintain or promote his or her and others' well-being. However, as already noted, sensory data is sent directly from the thalamus to the amygdala as well as to the hippocampus and cortex—and this can happen before the cortex has a chance to rationally assess the situation at hand—or to evaluate alternative responses the person can make to the situation. In such a case, the probability rises that the person will react to the situation "emotionally", "irrationally", in response to "blind", unexamined interpretations and commands originating in the amygdala. Under such conditions, the person, who in extreme cases is said to be experiencing an "emotional highjack" (Goleman, 1995), is unable to exert full rational control over his or her actions—and the consequences, particularly in social situations, can prove detrimental to the person's and others' well being—either adding to the deleterious effect of an adverse condition or creating an adverse condition where none before existed.

According to Salovey and Mayer (1989), a person with a high level of emotional intelligence is better able to deal with personally challenging events and is better able to minimize the likelihood of the occurrence of "emotional hijacks" than is a person possessing a lower level of emotional intelligence.

Definition of Emotional Intelligence. Gross (1997) defined emotional intelligence as the ability to guide one's thinking with information inferred from one's and others' moods and emotions, and Salovey and Mayer (1995) posited three central components of EI: Being in touch with one's moods and emotions, sorting out one's moods and emotions and regulating one's emotions and moods.

Suggesting that managing one's moods and emotions is not possible unless one has sorted them out and that sorting out one's moods and emotions is not possible unless one is in touch with them, Martinez-Pons (1997-1998) argued that in order for the Salovey et al. (1995) notion of emotional intelligence to be considered tenable the model must exhibit this sequential structure. Using the *Trait Meta-Mood Scale* (Salovey and Mayer, 1989), he tested this property of their model with 108 adults in a large metropolitan area; through path analysis techniques, he found the model to exhibit this sequential structure. The findings appear in Figure 13. In this figure, correlations emerged between adjacent components of EI, but not between non-adjacent components—demonstrating the sequential structure of the central elements of the EI construct.

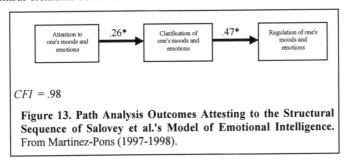

CFI = .98

Figure 13. Path Analysis Outcomes Attesting to the Structural Sequence of Salovey et al.'s Model of Emotional Intelligence. From Martinez-Pons (1997-1998).

Emotional Intelligence as a Self-Regulatory Process. Martinez-Pons (2000a) developed a *Self-Regulation Model of Emotional Intelligence (SRMEI)* on the basis of the work on EI and the work on self-regulation that has appeared in the literature. The model appears in Table 10.

Table 10 . Self-Regulation Model of Emotional Intelligence. From Martinez-Pons (1997-1998).

Self-Regulation	Emotional Engagement		
	Being in touch with one's moods and emotions	Sorting out one's moods and emotions	Managing one's moods and emotions
Motivation			
Goal Setting			
Strategy Usage			
Self-Evaluation			

In Table 10, the *Self-Regulation* (SR) column contains motivation, goal-setting, strategy usage and self-evaluation (SE) components posited by Zimmerman (1989), and the *Emotional Engagement* (EE) column contains emotional intelligence elements posited by Salovey and Mayer (1989): *being in touch with, sorting out* and *managing* one's moods and emotions. On the basis of the twelve cells representing the intersections of the SR and EE categories, the author developed the *Self-Regulation Scale of Emotional Intelligence (SRSEI)*, an experimental instrument assessing emotional intelligence as a self-regulatory process. The scale appears in Appendix C.

The construct validity of the *SRSEI* was demonstrated when the model's hypothesized sequential structure,

Motivation → Goal Setting → Strategy Usage → Self-Evaluation,

was supported through path analytic findings (Frame 2 discusses path analysis methodology). The outcomes are shown in Figure 14. In addition to attesting to the model's sequential structure as a self-regulatory process, this figure shows the relation of emotional intelligence with affective states such as depression, positive affect and life satisfaction.

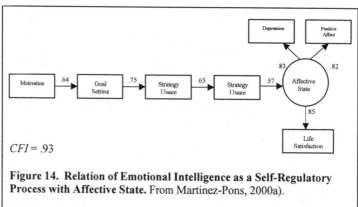

Figure 14. Relation of Emotional Intelligence as a Self-Regulatory Process with Affective State. From Martinez-Pons, 2000a).

Relevance of Emotional Intelligence to Learning Readiness. The perceived importance of emotional functioning in the school became clear following a school needs assessment that was described earlier in this chapter. In open-ended focus group interviews conducted in an elementary school, panels of parents, teachers and administrators uniformly cited the need for positive outlets for students to resolve negative feelings; and, as shown in Table 3, structured survey questionnaire responses by the school's parent, teacher and administrative populations ranked this matter among the top concerns for students in their school.

A review of the literature supports this concern. A report by the Federation of Families for Children's Mental Health (Huff, 1999) shows that upward of 20 percent of children in the US suffer from diagnosable mental, emotional or behavioral disorders; and Kelleher, McInerny, Gardner, Childs, and Wasserman (2000) found that the problem more than doubled between 1979 and 1996, and reported that this finding held even after they controlled for improved ways of identifying emotional dysfunction. Emotional disorders, of which the more debilitating are depression (feelings of helplessness, low self-esteem, lack of interest in normal activities, loss of energy, difficulty concentrating) and anxiety disorders (phobias, separation anxiety, and academic apprehensions such as math and test anxiety) contribute to hyperactivity-attention deficit disorder and decline in school performance (Kovaks & Bastiens, 1994; Huff, 1999). On the positive side, Martinez-Pons (1998) found that students with high levels of emotional intelligence also displayed high levels of *task orientation* ($r = .70, p < .05$), an attribute, discussed below, associated with academic performance (Roedl, Schraw & Plake, 1994).

Given the growing problem of emotional disorder among children, as well as the relevance of emotional intelligence to academic achievement, Woitaszewski, Aalsma and Gridley (1998) called for school programs that teach emotional awareness: "Given the nature of the evidence, we believe that emotional literacy must become a priority for all children" (p. 77).

Assessing Emotional Intelligence. Aside from the experimental questionnaire described above developed to test the *Self-regulation Model of Emotional Intelligence (SRMEI)*, a large number of assessment instruments have been developed to assess EI. Schutte and Malouff (2000) published a compendium of measures of emotional intelligence and related constructs. Among the more widely known included in their book is the *Trait Meta-Mood Scale*, mentioned earlier, a 30-item questionnaire developed by Salovey, Mayer, Goldman, Turvey and Palfai, (1995) in their pioneering work on EI. Through factor analytic techniques, the authors found the three factors encompassing the central element of EI discussed above: being in touch with, sorting out and regulating or managing one's moods and emotions.

Issues Regarding the Concept Emotional Intelligence. In their editorial article appearing in the journal *Intelligence*, Mayer and Salovey (1993) addressed some criticisms that have been leveled at the notion of emotional intelligence. The following are two of these criticisms and the responses to them given by Mayer and Salovey:

1. The authors originally conceived of emotional intelligence as part of intelligence proper, along with the verbal-propositional and spatial-performance elements found through factor analytic studies of traditional intelligence test scores. Relative to this position, critics have argued that intelligence is not an appropriate metaphor for the construct Mayer and Salovey propose, since the intelligence concept has always been understood to refer to *rational* ability (Cronbach, 1960). In fact, some workers have begun using the term *emotional self-regulation* (Fox, 1996; Gross, 1997), leaving out the term *intelligence,* to refer to what is essentially the same phenomenon addressed by Salovey and Mayer.

Mayer and Salovey argued, in effect, that this is a Type *i* (dismissive, invalid) issue by pointing out that there has always appeared to be a third factor in addition to the verbal-propositional and spatial-performance factors derived through factor analysis of IQ scale scores: *Social intelligence.* Thorndike (1920) defined this factor as "the ability to understand and manage people" although, as he noted at the time, whether the factor truly existed remained to be conclusively demonstrated. Mayer and and Salovey argued that the reasons for the inconclusive findings concerning this factor may be that social intelligence has been measured using test items loaded heavily with reading comprehension, and that *emotional intelligence* may be more clearly identifiable as a distinct factor of intelligence if it is measured specifically as involving the manipulation of emotions and emotional content.

2. According to critics of emotional intelligence theory, while the notion of intelligence implies *ability*, there are no important, unique abilities connected with emotions. Mayer and Salovey argued, in effect, this to be a Type *h* (dismissive, debatable) issue; EI, as they conceive it, constitutes mental aptitude because it is in fact the *ability to manipulate emotions and emotional content*—an ability which actually seems to assist intellectual processing.

The responses of Mayer and Salovey to the above criticisms may seem speculative in nature, since—at least to this writer's knowledge—no definitive work has been reported factor analyzing EI scores and IQ subscale scores to test the construct of EI as an integral component of general intelligence.[2] On the other hand, in the view of Mayer and Salovey, the fact remains that the major objections to the notion of emotional intelligence have themselves been highly speculative, and have not been persuasively presented.

It is the opinion of this writer that, although some Type *d* (questioning, valid) issues remain to be resolved regarding the relation of emotional intelligence with mental ability, enough evidence has accumulated to date pointing to the construct's cohesiveness and predictive power of academic-related behavior, psychological well being and social functioning to merit its consideration as a diagnostic target in the pre-engagement phase of instruction.

Thus, emotional intelligence is the ability to guide one's thinking with information inferred from one's and others' moods and emotions, and its central elements involve being in touch with, sorting out and regulating one's emotions and moods. EI has been found to be strongly related to *goal orientation*, a process, as shown next, that in turn influences academic achievement. An instructor with information about the emotional intelligence of his or her students is in a better position to prepare for the teaching-learning effort than one lacking such information.

The way in which the instructor can use information gained through emotional intelligence assessment is by a) deciding on the level of functioning for each of the 12 cells of the SRMEI; and b) in the case of low-standing students, estimating the amount of effort it would take to remediate the condition to the point where functioning in these 12 areas can serve to promote learning readiness. In the case in which the amount of effort would exceed that which the instructor feels he or she can exert, he or she can refer the student to school personnel with the resources necessary to address the problem.

---

[2] While Davies, Stankov and Roberts (1998) did report on a series of studies which failed to show a common factor of various EI measures and measures of crystalized or fluid intelligence, they noted that the EI instruments used lacked the level of reliability necessary to provide conclusive results. Hall (2000) found that, although highly correlated with measures of crystallized intelligence (CI), measures of verbal emotional perception nevertheless loaded on a factor separate from the CI factor. However, as noted by Hall, these findings are only suggestive of the relation between EI and cognitive intelligence, because her study targeted a part of EI addressing only the emotions of *others*, leaving out that part of EI involving one's own emotions.

Parental Inducement of Emotional Intelligence. Using the social cognitive concepts of modeling, encouragement, facilitation and rewards that he used to explore parental inducement of academic self-regulation, Martinez-Pons (1999a) showed the influence of parental behavior on the emotional intelligence of their offspring. The model he developed to study this effect appears in Table 11. The correlation between the parental inducement measure and student emotional intelligence proved to be $r = .44, p < .05$.

Table 11. Parental Inducement Model of Emotional Intelligence (PIMEI). From Martinez-Pons (1998-1999).

Parental Behavior	Emotional Engagement		
	Being in touch with one's moods and emotions	Sorting out one's moods and emotions	Managing one's moods and emotions
Modeling			
Encouraging			
Facilitating			
Rewarding			

The way in which the educator can use diagnostic information regarding parental inducement of emotional intelligence is as follows: for students rating low or very low in parental inducement of EI, workshops can be offered to their parents to improve their modeling, encouragement, facilitation and rewarding behavior relative to emotional intelligence on the part of the students. In the case in which parental participation cannot be secured, or in which parental participation results in low gains, the educator or educators who work with the student may have to compensate by increasing their own EI inducement behavior in a concerted effort to improve the student's emotional intelligence.

Goal Orientation. The last process appearing in Figure 1 hypothesized to contribute to learning readiness is goal orientation.

Definition of Goal Orientation. Goal orientation has been proposed by Dweck and Elliott (1983; also see Dweck and Leggett, 1988) as the existence of two diametrically opposed tendencies: *learning orientation,* or concern with task mastery and personal improvement; and *performance orientation,* or "a desire to look good and receive favorable judgments from others or *not* to look bad and receive unfavorable judgments" (Ormrod, 1999, p. 436). Dweck and Leggett (1988) posited that the former is conducive to adaptive processes such as strategy shifting and higher goal attainment in daily functioning, while the latter leads to maladaptive forms of behavior such as lack of persistence and learned helplessness (learned helplessness is described in some detail in Chapter 4).

Assessing Goal Orientation. Roedl, Schraw and Plake (1994) developed the *Goals Inventory,* a 25-item questionnaire designed to measure goal orientation. Through factor and correlational analysis techniques, they found the questionnaire to possess a high degree of convergent and divergent validity and to be reliable over time. Roedl et al. (1994) found that learning orientation is positively associated with high academic self-efficacy and low test anxiety, while performance orientation is negatively associated with these attributes. They suggested that as a placement measure,

> the Goals Inventory may help to identify students at risk for maladaptive behaviors in the classroom... Used diagnostically, it may clarify the type of beliefs and behaviors that contribute to low performance or low self-esteem (p. 1020).

It is important to note that while goal orientation is seen as a factor impacting on learning readiness, it is in turn closely related to emotional intelligence. As noted earlier, Martinez-Pons (1998) found a correlation of $r = 71$, $p < .05$ between emotional intelligence and learning orientation.

Thus, goal orientation was proposed by Dweck and Leggett to influence a student's readiness to benefit from the teaching-learning effort. It is assumed that an instructor with information concerning his or her students' goal orientation is in a better position to meet their educational needs than one lacking such information.

The way in which the instructor can use information gained through goal orientation assessment in the pre-engagement phase of instruction is by a) deciding on a student's levels of learning orientation (LO) and performance orientation (PO); and b) in the case of a low-standing student, estimating the amount of effort it would take to remediate the condition to the point where goal orientation can function to promote learning readiness. In the case in which the amount of effort would exceed that which the instructor feels he or she can exert, he or she can seek assistance from others with the resources necessary to address the problem.

The preceding pages considered student learning readiness as a key contributor to the success of the teaching-learning effort. They also considered six contextual factors found to impact on the learning readiness of students: environmental influences, prior experience, self-regulation, mental ability, emotional intelligence, and goal orientation. However, these processes represent only half the story concerning the likelihood of the success of the teaching-learning effort. The other half involves the matter of instructor effectiveness. This matter is addressed next.

Instructor Effectiveness

The second major diagnostic target in the pre-engagement phase of instruction involves instructor characteristics that may impact on the success of the teaching-learning effort. Two major teacher characteristics related to instructional success and considered in the following pages are *teacher efficacy* and *teacher commitment to teaching*.

Teacher Efficacy

Crow and Crow (1954) reported the results of a survey in which college students were asked to state what they felt constitutes teacher efficacy. The top 10 skills that emerged making up teacher efficacy, which seem as pertinent today as they did nearly 50 years ago, are as follows:

1. Systematic organization of subject matter
2. Speaking ability
3. Ability to explain clearly
4. Ability to encourage thought
5. Sympathetic attitude toward students
6. Expert knowledge of subject
7. Enthusiastic attitude toward subject
8. Fairness in grading tests
9. Tolerance toward student disagreement
10. Pleasing personality

The degree to which teachers feel they possess skills characterizing a good instructor is termed *teacher self-efficacy* (*TSE*).

TSE is widely held to influence various aspects of teacher functioning. For example, Rich, Lev and Fischer (1996) posited that teacher self-efficacy "has a significant effect on the nature and quality of teachers' work and subsequently on student functioning" (p. 1015). Research has provided strong evidence of the effect on TSE of such school processes as staff development and organizational characteristics (Rich, Lev & Fischer, 1996). In addition to the influence exerted on it by organizational factors, TSE has been consistently shown to be influential on student motivation in general (Woolfolk & Hoy, 1990), and in particular, motivation of students with behavioral disorders (Kauffman & Wong, 1991). In fact, as shown in the following paragraphs, together these last two processes have been found to be related to teacher commitment to teaching.

Teacher Commitment to Teaching

Teacher commitment to teaching can be generally defined as a desire to remain in the field of education; and, more specifically, as the time and effort a teacher is typically willing to devote to his or her craft, and the time and effort he or she is willing to devote to overcome difficulties encountered in the course of teaching. Research has shown a number of variables to be influential of teachers' commitment to teaching: a) Job satisfaction (Fresko, 1997), b) self-efficacy (Coladarci, 1992), and c) teacher perceptions of the degree to which administrators and other school staff provide professional support (Bess, 1979). In addition, Woolfolk, & Hoy (1990) reported a corrrelation between teacher commitment and student academic behavior.

To test in one comprehensive model the assumptions that key relations exist among school processes, teacher self-efficacy, teacher job satisfaction, teacher commitment and student behavior, Martinez-Pons (2000c) used data from the 1990 follow-up of the National Educational Longitudinal Study (NELS:88; this study was briefly described in Chapter 2). The researcher used a sample of 15,908 teachers from the 1990 NELS:88 follow-up effort. The variables used in this analysis appear in Figure 15, and the items used to assess each variable, as described in the NELS:88 electronic codebook, appear in Appendix D. Path analysis outcomes of the variables involved (see Frame 2 for a discussion of path analysis) appear in Figure 15. In this figure, Pearson correlation coefficients appear within parentheses, and path coefficients, in the form of standardized regression weights (β), appear without parentheses. As shown in this figure, processes beginning with *quality of principal's leadership* lead to *teacher self-*

efficacy, and from there to *job satisfaction* and *commitment to teaching*. The relevance of these processes to the success of the educational enterprise was suggested by the strong relations that emerged of *teacher self-efficacy, job satisfaction* and *commitment to teaching* with *student academic-related behavior*.

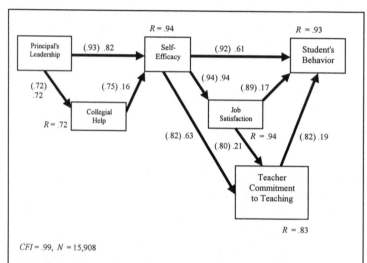

$CFI = .99$, $N = 15,908$

Note: Pearson correlation coefficients appear enclosed in parentheses, and path coefficients, in the form of standardized regression weights (β), appear outside parentheses. All coefficients are statistically significant beyond the .05 level.

Figure 15. Path Analysis Outcomes of School Influences on Teacher Self-Efficacy, Job Satisfaction and Commitment to Teaching. From Martinez-Pons (2000c).

Thus, an instructor equipped with high levels of teaching efficacy and teaching commitment—important determinants of the likelihood of the success of the teaching-learning effort—is in a better position to embark on the teaching-learning enterprise than one with lower levels in these areas. School-related processes such as principal's leadership and help by others as the teacher attempts to develop or improve his or her teaching skills exert an influence on teacher self-efficacy.

The way in which the instructor can use information gained through self-assessment of commitment to teaching is by a) deciding on his or her level of self-efficacy, job satisfaction and commitment to teaching; and b) in the case in which he or she finds low levels in these areas, ascertaining the school-related factors involved, and taking steps to remediate or compensate for the problem.

The preceding pages discussed the gathering of information in the pre-engagement phase of instruction concerning students and instructor, information relevant to the success of the teaching-learning effort. Learning readiness was the topic discussed concerning students, and efficacy and commitment to teaching were the topics discussed concerning the instructor.

SUMMARY

In summary, in the information-gathering part of the pre-engagement phase of instruction, the educator gathers information that he or she can use in the planning of the teaching-learning effort. Through needs assessment methodology, the instructor ascertains what interested parties see as the needs to be addressed through the instructional effort, and through diagnostic activities the educator ascertains the student's learning readiness in terms of such processes as environmental influences, mental ability, emotional intelligence, and self-regulation. Through diagnostics procedures, the instructor also clarifies for himself or herself the impact on his or her teaching efficacy and commitment exerted by key aspects of the educational setting.

The instructor who embarks on the teaching-learning effort with information in these areas about his or her students and about himself or herself is in a better position to succeed in the teaching-learning effort than one lacking such information. The *Student Learning Readiness Diagnostic Form* appearing in Table 12 can be used to record a) a student's learning readiness in terms of the areas covered in this chapter, and b) an estimate of the amount of effort it would take to help the student in overcoming whatever difficulty he or she may be experiencing in any of these areas.

The *Diagnostic Form of Factors Influencing Teacher Commitment and Job Satisfaction* appearing in Table 13 can be used to record a) a teacher's self-efficacy, job satisfaction and commitment to teaching, as well as factors impacting on these two attributes; and b) an estimate of the amount of effort it would take to rectify or compensate for deficiencies in any of these areas.

Table 12. Student Learning Readiness Diagnostic Form

Area	Status					Projected effort required to aid the student in this area			
	Very low 1	Low 2	Moderate 3	High 4	Very high 5	Low 1	2	3	High 4
Health									
Prior practice									
Prior learning									
Academic self-regulation (SR)									
Mental acuity *acquisition*									
retention									
utilization									
Emotional functioning									
Goal orientation *task mastery*									
competitiveness									
Parental influences *general*									
academic SR									
emotional intelligence									
Peer influences *academic SR*									
emotional intelligence									

Table 13. Diagnostic Form of Factors Influencing Teacher Commitment and Job Satisfaction

Area	Status					Estimated effort required to correct or compensate for problem in this area			
	Very low 1	Low 2	Moderate 3	High 4	Very high 5	Low 1	2	3	High 4
Quality of administration's leadership									
Support from school staff									
Self-efficacy *knowledge of subjecs taught*									
pedagogical skills									
Student school behavior									
Job satisfaction									
Commitment to teaching									

Once he or she has gathered valid and reliable information about a) what students should learn and b) student and instructor characteristics relevant to the instructional needs to be addressed, the educator can proceed to structure the way in which the needs are to be satisfied. This task, considered in the next chapter, forms the second part of the pre-engagement phase of instruction.

POSTSCRIPT: LEARNING STYLE THEORY

The notion of learning style (LS) has drawn much attention during the past several decades, and numerous theoretical formulations and assessment procedures have been developed during this time for the study and diagnosis of learning style preference. The concept has drawn criticism, although it is still used by a number of theorists in addressing diagnostic aspects of the pre-engagement phase of instruction. Because the notion is still in use, it is important for the educator to be conversant with its definition and proposed makeup, as well as with reservations that have been voiced concerning it.

Definition of *Learning Style*

During the 1970's, a task force was convened by the National Association of Secondary School Principals to develop a comprehensive definition of *learning style*. The group generated the following definition: a learning style is "the composite of characteristic cognitive, affective and physiological factors that serve as relatively stable indicators of how a learner perceives, interacts with, and responds to the learning environment" (Keefe, 1979). According to learning style theorists, LS is an important student diagnostic target because instruction that is tailored to a student's learning style is more likely to succeed than instruction that ignores this student attribute.

Learning Style Theories

A number of LS theories have been proposed ranging in complexity from the relatively simple to the comparatively elaborate. At a relatively simple level, Witkin (1950) proposed the notion of *field dependence/field independence*, a two-category construct involving the ability to disembed key elements from their surroundings (persons who can do this are said to be field-independent, and persons who cannot are said to be field-dependent); and Beatrice (1999) proposed a model of LS involving three categories of learning preference: *Visual, auditory* and *kinesthetic*.

　　　　Many other LS theories at more complex levels have been proposed—so many, in fact, that Curry (1987) saw a need to use some classificatory scheme to facilitate their study and discussion. He developed the following four-category taxonomy for the purpose: *personality theories, information-processing theories, social interaction theories*, and *multidimensional theories*.

Personality Theories of Learning Styles (PTLS)

PTLSs address the influences of basic personality traits on preferred approaches to acquiring and integrating information. A prime example of a PTLS is that of the model developed by Myers and Myers-Briggs (Myers, 1978) on the basis of Jung's theory of personality. According to Myers and Myers-Briggs, there are sixteen types of learning styles, derived by classifying individuals along Jung's four bipolar descriptors of *introversion vs. extroversion, sensing vs. intuitive, thinking vs. feeling,* and *judging vs. perceiving.* Felder and Solomon (1999) developed a similar model, also consisting of four bipolar descriptors, with the following dichotomies: *active vs. reflective, sensing vs. intuitive, visual vs. verbal, sequential vs. global.*

Information-Processing Theories of Learning Styles (IPTLS)

IPTLSs address an individual's preferred intellectual approach to assimilating and working with information. An example of an IPTLS is Kolb's (1984) cyclical model of experiential learning. This model consists of four sequentially occurring stages: *planning the learning experience, undergoing the learning experience, reflecting on what happened,* and *reflecting on the theory underlying the learning experience.* In this model, completion of one cycle is followed by the beginning of another cycle with planning of the next learning experience. A second example of an IPTLS is that proposed by Race (Percival, Ellington, & Race, 1993), who, dissatisfied with the level of complexity reached by many LS formulations, decided to develop a model easily interpretable by educators. Race termed this model the *"Ripples" Model of Learning (RML).* The *RML* consists of four elements functioning in an integrated, reciprocal manner: *a need or want to learn (motivation), learning by doing (practice, trial and error), feedback (seeing the results and other people's reactions)* and *digesting (making sense of what has been learned).*

Social Interaction Theories of Learning Styles (SITLS)

SITLSs hold that the manner in which students interact in the classroom is an important determinant of learning readiness. An example of an SITLS is Reichmann and Grasha's (1974) model of learning style, which posits various social interaction learning styles: *independent, dependent, collaborative, competitive, participant,* and *avoidant.*

Multidimensional Theories of Learning Styles (MDTLS)

MTDLSs involves combinations of features found in other LS theories. They include the *Learning Style Model* of Dunn and Dunn (1978) and the *Human Information Processing Model* of Keefe (1989). Of particular interest is the Dunn and Dunn model—probably the most influential work in the field of learning style (Krause, 1996)—which stipulates that *environmental, emotional, sociological, physical,* and *psychological preferences* of an individual must be taken into account in order to accurately determine his or her learning readiness.

Assessing Learning Style

Five widely used learning style instruments are noted below. The first three are based on the multidimensional learning style theory of Dunn and Dunn (1978), the fourth is based on the personality learning style theory of Myers and Briggs (Myers, 1978), and the fifth is based Witkin's (1950) field dependence-independence learning style model.

The *Learning Style Inventory—Primary Version* (Perrin, 1981) is a pictorial questionnaire designed for use with children in kindergarten through grade. The *Learning Style Inventory* (Dunn, Dunn, & Price, 1985) is a self-report 104-item questionnaire designed for use with students in grades 3 to 12. It enables the respondent to indicate preferences related to psychological, environmental, sociological and physical, aspects of his or her life. The *Productivity Environmental Preference Survey* (Dunn, Dunn, & Price, 1982) is a 100-item self-report questionnaire designed for use with adults. It enables the respondent to express his or her preferences for a variety of learning and working conditions. The *Myers-Briggs Type Indicator* (Myers, 1978) consists of a number of dichotomous scales measuring extroversion versus introversion, sensing versus intuition, thinking versus feeling, and judging versus perception. Finally, the *Embedded Figures Test,* the *Children's Embedded Figures Test,* and the *Group Embedded Figures Test* were developed by Witkin, Otman, Reskin and Karp (1971) to assess field dependence/independence for various age groups under a variety of conditions.

Issues Concerning the Notion of Learning Style

There is a certain amount of controversy surrounding the concept of learning style (Reynolds, 1997). Among the more salient issues raised regarding the LS concept are the following:

1. Not all situations allow the learner to use his or her preferred style to master instructional material. Under many, if not most, circumstances, a student may have no choice but to adapt to the demands of the situation at hand in his or her learning behavior, and the teacher may have no choice but to attend to situational demands in the

planning of instruction—a possibility, according to Sneider (1992), ignored by learning style theory: "This approach considers the characteristics of the learner and the teaching method but does not consider the nature of the task" (p. 6).

In point of fact, learners seem to intuitively recognize the need to attend to task demands in their learning activities. In research conducted by Westman, Alliston and Theriault (1997), students indicated that their analysis of task demands, rather than their learning style preferences, determined their use of learning modality. In the words of Westman et al. (1997), "for the time being, how best to present materials seems to depend on students' assumptions about the tasks to be done. Students behave in accordance with the demands of the task rather than their own preferences" (p. 737).

2. The quality of the research supportive of learning style theory has been questioned. According to Krause (1996),

> Previous work on learning styles, whether in sciences or other academic course areas, have been limited to small populations, and rarely have been carefully controlled and statistically rigorous. For that reason, many educators have been justified in stating doubts of the validity of the whole concept of differences in how people learn. (p. 10)

For example, although Dunn, Griggs, Olson, Beasley and Gormann (1995) cited 35 studies pointing to the benefit to academic achievement of matching instruction to learning style, Kavale, Hirshoren and Forness (1998) questioned the quality of the studies reviewed and the interpretation of the findings. On the basis of their review of the work of Dunn et al. (1995), Kavale et al. (1998) concluded that the Dunn and Dunn learning style model has not truly been validated. Finally, Curry (1987, 1990) noted a number of external threats to the validity of studies supportive of LD theory: for example, many such studies often use control and experimental groups selected on the basis of extreme scores and hence become subject to the phenomenon of *regression toward the mean* (see Frame 7 for a discussion of regression toward mean), biasing the interpretation of results. In addition, many such studies fail to control for reactive effects to pre-testing of learning style that may sensitize the students to the purpose of the study.

3. Research exists tending, in the opinion of some writers, to disconfirm LS theory. For example, in work conducted with 292 subjects, mostly college students, Cornwell and Manfredo (1994) found no support for the validity of the Kolb model of learning style

preference. Additionally, in a study carried out with 79 medical students, Leiden (1990) found no correlation of course performance with efforts to accommodate instruction to scores on learning style preference tests.

Frame 7. Regression toward the Mean

The term *regression toward the mean (RTM)* was given wide circulation by Sir Francis Galton (1889), who noted that very tall parents tend to have very short offspring, and that very short parents tend to have very tall offspring. RTM involves the observation that when a person obtains an extreme score on some measurement, he or she is likely to later obtain a score in the opposite direction on the same measure (the less reliable the measure, the greater the change in the opposite direction). In research, when experimental and control subjects are selected because of their extreme (very high or very low) scores on a pretest, the responses of the two groups will tend to be closer to the mean on the second testing: The group high on the pretest will tend to score lower on the posttest, the group low on the pretest will tend to score higher on the posttest, and these changes will occur independently of the experimental interventions. RTM is considered a major threat to the external validity of any experiment—that is, to the legitimacy of concluding that the study's results are due to the interventions rather than to external factors such as extreme sample pre-test scores.

---

4. In a related issue, the validity of measures of LS that have been used in work supporting LS theory has been questioned (test validity and reliability are discussed elsewhere in this text). As one example, Krause (1996) posited that many of the items included in the *Myers-Brigs Type Indicator (MBTI)* are ambiguous, as in the case of the following item from the *MBTI*: "Which mistake would be more natural for you: (a) To drift from one thing to another all your life, or (b) to stay in a rut that didn't suit you?" (Myers, 1978). In addition, regarding the use of many such measures, Curry (1990) noted that

> The tendency among the learning styles researchers, however, has been not to pursue the necessary iterative pattern of hypothesis-investigation-modification but rather to rush prematurely into print and marketing with very early and preliminary indications of factor loadings based on one data set. This haste weakens any claim of valid interpretation from the test scores (p. 51)

Ruble and Stout (1998), commenting on Kolb's *Learning Styles Inventory (LSI),* posited one example of this tendency:

> Although the *LSI* has been very popular, extensive evidence available in the published literature indicates that both the original and revised versions of the *LSI* are deficient in reliability and construct validity. It is concluded that the *LSI* does not provide adequate measures of learning styles and that its use in research should be discontinued. (p. 1)

5. In addition to questions of validity and reliability concerning them, the instruments used to assess learning style have typically addressed *style preference,* tending to ignore *style skill.* This approach has been defended on the grounds that there are no right or wrong learning styles—that from the educator's point of view, in developing instruction the important matter to take into account is a student's preferred style. But it seems possible for a student to prefer some sort of learning modality at which he or she is not efficient, and through adherence to it to insure continued failure at mastery of whatever he or she is trying to learn.

One exception to the trend in attending to learning style preference rather than to skill is the *Embedded Figures Test (EFT)* of Witkin, Ottman, Raskin, and Karp (1971), a test of cognitive style ability found to load statistically significantly on the analytical factor of the *Wechsler Adult Intelligence Scale* and the *Wechsler Intelligence Scale for Children* Witkin et al. (1971). At the same time, it is worth noting that performance on the *EFT* is not related to the verbal or attention-concentration factors of intelligence as measured by the Wechsler tests. In the words of Witkin et al. (1971),

> One cannot say that persons who are field independent on the EFT are superior in *general* intelligence, as reflected in the Wechsler, since they may show wide variations in the other two IQ factors. (p. 7)

Aside from the restriction of the *EFT* to the assessment of analytical ability, a new issue arises when, as in the case of field independence, style ability rather than preference becomes the focus of attention in instructional planning: What would it mean to say that the educational effort must be geared to ability level in field independence? Would it mean that if a student is, say, low in FI, instruction must be geared to his or her low FI functioning level? But if so, and mastery of the material at hand is dependent on high FI ability, then it seems that in the end the approach would deny the possibility of the student mastering the material—rendering self-contradictory the idea of tailoring instruction to a student's learning style ability to help him or her to attain mastery. If FI theory has any relevance to instruction, it must be, as in the case of intelligence theory in general, in terms of *remediation* in the case of low-functioning students. Here, the objective would have to be to *modify* learning style rather than to choose the best style from an existing repertory, or to adapt instruction to a given style—an orientation different from that espoused by most learning style theorists. At any rate, adherence to this interpretation of FI theory requires that methodology be brought to bear on the task of raising FI performance level when needed; as of this writing, this author was unaware that any such methodology had been developed or validated.

6. As shown above, learning style theories are many and varied, and they continue to proliferate—a state of affairs that an educator may find daunting as he or she attempts to use LS theory to learn something about his or her students to help in the planning of instruction (Curry, 1990).

Given the limitations noted by critics of learning style theory, it may be that the only way in which the LS concept can assume any real value in instruction is if workers in this field successfully undertake the following tasks:

1. Develop a definitive taxonomy of learning styles on the basis of the material that has been written so far on the topic, in much the same way that Euclid developed his geometry on the basis of all that had been said on the subject up to his time. Whether such a feat is possible given the seemingly endless possibilities of learning style lists that can be generated is open to question.

2. Develop a comprehensive taxonomy of the conditions under which the teaching-learning process takes place—including conditions involving task demands—and of the *combinations* of learning modalities typically most conducive to learning success under each conditions—in much the same way that Gagné (1985) developed his *conditions of learning* framework. Whether such a taxonomy is any more feasible than one addressing learning styles alone is also open to question.

3. Develop valid and reliable methodology for ascertaining the typical *combination* of learning styles a person uses under the learning conditions described by the above taxonomies—and for assessing style skill as well as preference in this regard.

4. Develop effective methodology for maximizing student learning style efficacy given the instructional conditions and task

demands at hand. This step is particularly important in view of the possibility that, as argued by Krause (1996), "no one method will be best for all learners, that what works best must be a variety of methods, an appropriate mix of strategies to meet the needs of a variety of individual learners" (p. 10).

Some may argue that until such sweeping measures are taken, learning style theorization will remain, at best, a set of well-meaning but highly speculative and sketchy attempts to aid in the teaching-learning process. At worst, from a certain perspective, it may provide a false sense of direction as educators try to identify relevant student attributes in preparation for the teaching-learning effort.

Given these considerations, whether the above reservations concerning learning style theory are judged to be Type d (questioning, valid) or Type g (dismissive, valid) issues depends on the perceived feasibility of the four suggested steps proposed above. Some may be less than fully optimistic regarding the prospects for success of such broad undertakings, and for this reason they may tend to see the reservations expressed about learning style theory as representing Type g issues.

Proposing that at present the concept of learning style is too broad to be of real value for instructional planning or for the explanation or prediction of learning performance, Reynolds (1997) argued for the alternative concept of *learning strategy*—a notion which, because of its reference to specific task-related behavior, is seen as having greater power in explaining and predicting academic achievement. The concept forms an integral part of the theory of self-regulation being espoused by an increasing number of scholars as an alternative to the concept of learning style and discussed earlier in this chapter.

Chapter 3

Planning

INTRODUCTION

In the first part of the pre-engagement phase of instruction, the educator conducted an assessment of student educational needs to be addressed through the educational enterprise; the instructor also performed a diagnostic assessment of student readiness to benefit from efforts addressing these needs and the instructor's own readiness to embark on the teaching-learning enterprise. In the second part of the pre-engagement phase of instruction, the educator uses information gathered through needs assessment and diagnostic activities to plan for the engagement of the student in the teaching-learning process.

The importance of planning for the effective management of the teaching-learning effort was demonstrated by Anderson (1979), who in a year-long study of 28 third-grade teachers collected data describing their classroom management practices. The investigator compared the seven most effective and the seven least effective teachers to determine which dimensions of management discriminated between the two groups. Teachers who qualified as "better managers" were characterized as follows:

1. They had a firm idea of desired student behaviors.

2. They structured their classroom in such a way as to actively discourage intolerable behaviors and promote desired behaviors.

3. They were skilled in dividing instructional tasks into simpler tasks to facilitate planning of the teaching-learning effort.

4. They had expertise in efficiently coordinating teacher and student activities.

These are key elements in the planning of instruction, and they, among others, will be discussed in this chapter. The first step in the planning facet of the pre-engagement phase of instruction involves the grouping of students according to diagnostic findings.

GROUPING OF STUDENTS ON THE BASIS OF DIAGNOSTIC FINDINGS

Definition of *Grouping*

The term *grouping* is employed loosely to refer to the use of information about student commonalities to plan the teaching-learning effort. The purpose in grouping on the basis of diagnostic outcomes is not so much to physically segregate students on the basis of the findings as it is to enable the instructor to identify those interventions students can share given common learning readiness profiles. In fact, there is no reason why students differing dramatically in areas of readiness to learn cannot be found in the same classroom: it is not physical separation that constitutes grouping, but the decision concerning which students will receive which classes of interventions. Grouping thus refers to the different instructional approaches the educator uses and the identification of students for whom these interventions are to be carried out in the teaching-learning effort.

An important area of concern regarding grouping involves the matter of homogeneity. The assumption when a group is formed for the purpose of instruction (in, say, reading) is that the individuals comprising it have something in common based on which instruction can be planned. A misconception regarding this assumption can be that the goal in any grouping effort is to generate a completely homogeneous group in which the members are alike in every respect. But such a goal is untenable, since any given group will most likely be both homogeneous in terms of one set of criteria (e.g., reading entry level) and heterogeneous in terms of some other set (e.g., learning disability)—and such differences can render a particular instruction intervention appropriate for some group members but not for others. In this respect, the question concerning group composition is whether those attributes on which the group's members differ can interfere with instruction methodology addressing the group's commonality. If it can, then the group may have to be subdivided to accommodate the discrepancy; if not, then there is no reason why the grouping scheme cannot function for the instructional purposes at hand, even given strong dissimilarities in other areas among the group's members.

Traditional Grouping Practices

The literature on grouping has tended to concentrate on academic ability, and the focus concerning grouping practice has been on differentiating between *ability grouping* and *ability tracking*. According to Loveless (1998), elementary schools tend to use ability grouping in reading, with instruction designed to address group reading level; and middle and high schools use tracking to group students between classes, offering courses in academic subjects that reflect differences in students' past achievement. According to Loveless (1998), "Today, schools assign students to tracks for particular subject areas based on proficiency" (p. 1).

Loveless' review of research on grouping by ability level suggests that when high ability students are placed in accelerated curricula their academic achievement improves, but that the same is not true when different ability groups are exposed to the same curriculum.

Criticisms of Traditional Grouping Practices

A number of criticisms have been leveled at traditional grouping practices:

1. Even though educators may in principle value the idea of providing low- and high-track students with the same quality of instruction, in practice the instruction given to low ability students is inferior to that given to high ability pupils (Oakes, 1985).

2. Differences in the quality of instruction eventually widens the differences in achievement for the two tracks (Loveless, 1998).

3. When students are separated on the basis of academic differences, they also tend to be separated on the basis of socioeconomic characteristics (Oakes, 1990).

4. Low tracks often emphasize good behavior and menial skills, while high tracks offer preparation for college. These differences

in learning environments tend to depress the academic achievement of poor and minority students (Loveless, 1998).

5. In the past, tracking has been rigid and deterministic, and students who have been placed in a given track have had little or no chance or moving to a different one (Loveless, 1998).

The findings of a 2-year study of 92 honors, regular and remedial students in secondary schools conducted by Gamoran, Nystrand, Berends and LePore (1995) tend to render the first three of the above criticisms Type *a* (cautionary, valid) issues. Regarding the first criticism, the authors reported that the quality of instruction is higher in honors classes in terms of discussion time allotted; relative to the second criticism, they reported that discussion time engenders achievement inequality because only honors students tend to benefit from discussion. In addition, honors students tend to spend more time on task and to turn in assignments more often than do students in remedial tracks, and these additional differences contribute to higher achievement levels on the part students in honors classes. Regarding the third criticism, Gamoran et al. (1995) concluded on the basis of their findings that

> Ability grouping divides students on social as well as cognitive characteristics, so by magnifying achievement inequality it contributes to overall achievement inequality among social groups. (p. 709)

According to Gamoran et al., the way to deal with the problem is by raising the quality of instructional content and level of student participation in both regular and remedial classes. In general, according to the authors, in addressing the first three of the above criticisms leveled at grouping practices,

> the practice of ability grouping must be reconsidered, and if it is not replaced with other organizing principles...the quality of experiences in regular and remedial classes must be improved—as clearly indicated by the results of this study. (p. 708)

The last two criticisms of traditional grouping practices also appear to represent Type *a* (cautionary, valid) issues, and, in this writer's view, they can be addressed if the basis for grouping is expanded beyond ability to include the other contributors to learning readiness discussed in Chapter 2. Such an approach is discussed next.

Alternative Grouping Practices

Two grouping forms alternative to traditional practice are discussed next. The first involves grouping on the basis of diagnostic findings of student background and attributes such as those covered in Chapter 2: *environmental influences, prior academic experience, self-regulation, mental ability, emotional intelligence* and *goal orientation.* These are areas in which effort beyond the particular instruction at hand may have to be exerted in order to raise a student's general learning readiness to desired levels, and in which the effort may have to take place at a time and in a setting different from that in which regular instruction occurs. This grouping form serves the purpose of *remediation*, apart from the normal instructional effort (Loveless, 1998).

The second alternative grouping practice entertained here involves classification of students according to entry level relevant to the objectives of instruction, an approach that works well within the setting in which instruction takes place. Before taking this alternative approach, it is necessary first to work out a set of *instructional objectives* and *task analysis* addressing the ends to be pursued through the teaching-learning effort and then to pre-test the students to determine their standing relative to these goals. Following instructional objectives-based pre-testing, the students can be grouped in various ways according to similarities in their test results.

Before the alternative grouping practices suggested above can be implemented, it is necessary to formulate the objectives that instruction is to serve. This is the next topic discussed regarding the planning facet of instruction.

INSTRUCTIONAL OBJECTIVES

There are three major theorists historically associated with the topic of instructional objectives: Mager (1962), Gronlund (1978) and Gagné (1985). While Mager conceptualized instructional objectives in strictly behavioral terms, Gronlund argued that, particularly when the objectives involve mastery of such unobservable things as concepts and values, it is necessary to refer to these abstract entities as well as to their observed manifestations in order to make clear the universe of discourse that instruction is to serve. The way Gronlund suggested the instructor do this was by first looking at long lists of observable objectives such as those prescribed by Mager and then, based on what the objectives appear to share in common, formulate *general* objectives, or goals, from which the ones in the original list can be deduced; and finally, under each general objective, derive up to five *specific* terminal behaviors using action verbs.

Gagné contributed the idea that once an instructional objective has been formulated, it is important to identify the skills necessary to attain it; he termed this process of identification *task analysis*. Both instructional objectives and task analysis will be discussed in the following pages.

Definition of *Instructional Objective*

An instructional objective is a statement of behavior the instructor wants the student to be able to enact following instruction.

The Multifaceted Nature of Instructional Objectives: the Instructional Domains

Human behavior can take one of three major forms: cognitive, affective and psychomotor—and it is possible for the teaching-learning effort to address any of these three psychological modalities. Educational theorists have developed taxonomies of instructional objectives for each of these domains; the most widely known of these taxonomies will be discussed in the following pages.

The Taxonomy of Instructional Objectives for the Cognitive Domain

The cognitive domain of instructional objectives involves mastery of material involving rational thinking. Bloom, Engelhart, Furst, Hill and Krathwohl (1956) developed a widely known taxonomy of instructional objectives for the cognitive domain. This scheme, known as "Bloom's taxonomy", consists of a hierarchy of cognitive processes ranging from relatively simple (knowledge or memorization) to highly complex (evaluation), with mastery at each level necessary before mastery at a higher level can be attained. The following paragraphs consider two aspects of Bloom's taxonomy: the levels of the cognitive domain and issues that have been raised concerning it.

The Levels of Bloom's Taxonomy of the Cognitive Domain. These are the six levels Bloom's taxonomy for the cognitive domain:

Knowledge. At the knowledge level of the cognitive domain, the instructor's objective is to enable the student to memorize facts and procedures that the student can later repeat on demand. Examples of knowledge in this sense are being able to repeat the multiplication table, knowing one's home address, and being able to tell the year in which Columbus first arrived in the Western Hemisphere.

Comprehension. At the comprehension level of the cognitive domain, the instructor's objective is to enable the student to understand the reason for a rule or event, or to mentally grasp the implications of some formulation. An example of an instructional objective at the comprehension level is, "The student will be able to describe in his or her own words the rule for deriving the least common denominator, and state the rationale behind this rule".

Application. At the application level of the cognitive domain, the instructor's objective is to enable the student to use rules, ideas, and procedures in situations other than those in which the student has learned them. An example of an instructional objective formulated at the application level is, "Having learned the rule for adding fractions, the student will be able to carry out operations such as $1/2 + 1/4 = ?$ and $3/4 + 1/8 = ?$".

Analysis. At the analysis level of the cognitive domain, the instructor's objective is to enable the student to decompose an idea, object or process into its component parts. An example of an instructional objective formulated at the analysis level is, "A student will be able to analyze a piano sonata in terms of the work's exposition, development and recapitulation".

Synthesis. At the synthesis level of the cognitive domain, the instructor's objective is to enable the student to combine separate elements into meaningful structures. An example of an instructional objective formulated at the synthesis level is, "Having performed a review of the research literature on child abuse, the student will be able to arrange the variables encountered in the various studies into one comprehensive, cohesive model of the causes and effects of child abuse".

Evaluation. At the evaluation level of the cognitive domain, the instructor's objective is to enable the student to assess the degree to which something satisfies previously stated criteria. For example, "Having learned the criteria for a well-developed theoretical models [e.g., structural integrity and instrumental strength as described in

Chapter 1] the student will be able to assess the strength of a research proposal submitted by another student".

Issues Related to Bloom's Taxonomy for the Cognitive Domain. At least two issues have been raised concerning Bloom's taxonomy. The first concerns the taxonomy's *cohesiveness,* or the intuitive appeal of the way the model's components are hypothesized to relate to one another. The second concerns empirical support for the sequence stipulated among the taxonomy levels.

Model Cohesiveness. Concerning cohesiveness, Furst (1981) questioned the hierarchical order stipulated among the taxonomy's components: for example, he argued that to say that knowledge occurs *before* comprehension overlooks the fact that in many cases the acquisition of new knowledge is impossible without the comprehension of prior knowledge.

Empirical Support for the Sequence Stipulated Among the Taxonomy's Levels. The empirical support of the stipulated sequence among the taxonomy's levels was studied by Miller, Snowman and O'Hara (1979) (also see Madaus, Woods and Nuttall, 1973; and Seddon, 1978). Miller et al. used data generated by Kropp and Stoker (1966) on intelligence and taxonomy level data for students in grades 9 through 12 ($N = 1,128$) in ten Florida schools. Miller et al., using a subset ($n = 247$) of this sample, empirically tested the taxonomy's sequential structure in several ways. The major criteria they used were those posed by Guttman (1953). As noted in Chapter 2, according to Guttman, in order to empirically establish the sequential structure of hierarchical models (such as Bloom's taxonomy), one must show that correlations exist between adjacent components, and that zero or statistically non-significant correlations exist between non-adjacent components. In terms of these criteria, in order for Bloom's taxonomy to be truly hierarchical, correlations must emerge *only* between knowledge (K) and comprehension (C), between C and application (AP), between AP and analysis (AN), between AN and synthesis (S), and between S and evaluation (E).

The principal procedure Miller et al. (1979) employed to test the taxonomy's structure was path analysis, a method discussed in Frame 2 and, as noted earlier, used to test the sequential relations stipulated among components in hierarchical structures. The method is especially suited for testing the justification in omitting any set of linkages from such models. Miller et al. (1979) tested the taxonomy's structure by including the measure of intelligence collected by Kropp and Stoker. The present author reanalyzed the data omitting the intelligence measure, and he used the comparative fit index (*CFI*) to test the justification in leaving out linkages between non-adjacent taxonomy levels. As noted in Frame 2, in path analysis a *CFI* above .90 is indicative of a "good fit"—that is, of the statistical justification for omitting such linkages—and a *CFI* lower than .90 is indicative of a poor fit. As shown in Figure 16, path analysis of the data addressing Bloom's taxonomy yielded a *CFI* of .58, disconfirming the hierarchical structure of the taxonomy stipulated by its authors.

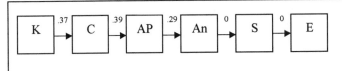

CFI = .58

Note: The coefficients shown are path coefficients in the form of standardized regression weights.

Figure 16. Path Analysis Test of the Hierarchical Structure of Bloom's Taxonomy

To round out the sequential test of the taxonomy, the present writer determined the best fitting model among the formulation's six components. This model, disclosing a *CFI* of .99, appears in Figure 17. As evidenced by an examination of this figure, there is nothing in the model that resembles the single-path hierarchical sequence stipulated by the taxonomy's proponents. Although the structure somewhat approximates the sequential stipulation for knowledge (K), comprehension (C) and application (AP)—an approximation only, because of the statistically significant and substantial path coefficient that emerged between the theoretically non-adjacent K and APP levels—the rest of the structure does not exhibit the taxonomy's stipulated hierarchy. Of particular interest is the path coefficient of β = .41 that emerged between the non-adjacent C and AN elements and those that emerged among other non-adjacent components; and the zero coefficients of AN with S, of S with E, and of K with AP, S and E. These outcomes disconfirm the sequential structure stipulated among the taxonomy's levels.

Given the taxonomy's manifest theoretical and empirical limitations, some authors have urged caution in its use for the purpose of instructional planning. For example, noting that since Synthesis and Evaluation are independent of the hierarchical structure as originally stipulated, Madaus, Woods & Nuttall (1973) argued that

> Given the widespread use of the taxonomy in formulating objectives in a multitude of curricular areas, for various types of students at differing levels of education, further investigation of the Taxonomy's assumptions would not be without considerable practical value. (p. 262)

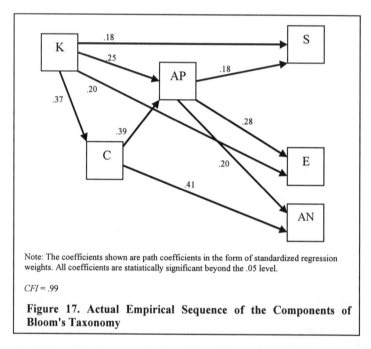

Note: The coefficients shown are path coefficients in the form of standardized regression weights. All coefficients are statistically significant beyond the .05 level.

CFI = .99

Figure 17. Actual Empirical Sequence of the Components of Bloom's Taxonomy

Despite its theoretical and empirical limitations, other authors (e.g., Gage and Berliner, 1984; Davis, 1983; Biehler and Snowman, 1986) have argued for the use of Bloom's taxonomy for the development of instructional objectives, even if restricted to the K, C and AP levels.

At least one alternative to Bloom's taxonomy of educational objectives for the cognitive domain has been proposed. Gagné (1964), combining cognitive, affective and psychomotor learning outcomes into one single conceptual framework, posited a five-component model of the objectives of instruction: *Verbal information* (facts, processes, etc.), *intellectual skills* (discrimination, classification, rule application), *cognitive strategies* (ways of learning and remembering new things), *attitudes* (values, fears, self-concept), and *motor skills* (writing, operating computers and using tools). In Gagné's work, for each of these objectives it is possible to determine the prerequisite skills the student must have before beginning work toward the outcome in question. *Task analysis* is the term Gagné gave to the process through which the instructor makes this determination. This aspect of Gagné's work, along with issues that have been raised concerning it, will be discussed later.

The Taxonomy of Instructional Objectives for the Affective Domain

The affective domain of instructional objectives, involving values, attitudes and feelings, addresses the degree to which a student is willing to become involved in the topic or process at hand. Krathwohl, Bloom and Masia (1964) developed what is probably the most widely known taxonomy for the affective domain. Like that of the cognitive domain described above, this taxonomy is arranged in a hierarchy, with the lowest level involving the least amount of commitment to some idea or course of action and the highest involving the greatest degree of commitment. Successful traversal of one level is necessary for the successful traversal at higher levels. These are the levels of Krathwohl et alia's taxonomy of the affective domain:

Attending. At this, the lowest level of the affective domain, the instructor's objective is to ensure the student's willingness to receive information. An example of an instructional objective for the affective domain stated at the attending level is "The student will listen to a movement of Beethoven's Ninth Symphony without protest or signs of discomfort".

Responding. At this level in the affective domain, the instructor's objective is to induce the student's willing involvement in the proceedings at hand. An example of an instructional objective for the affective domain stated at the responding level is "The student will respond to questions regarding the structure of a movement from Beethoven's Ninth Symphony".

Valuing. At this level in the affective domain, the instructor's objective is to induce the student to commit to, accept, or prefer the value of the thing being addressed. An example of an instructional objective for the affective domain stated at the valuing level is "The student will defend the worth of Beethoven's Ninth Symphony in a debate regarding the symphony's 'quality'."

Organizing. At this level of the affective domain, the instructor's objective is to induce the student to integrate valuing of the thing being considered with other values into a coherent system. An example of an instructional objective for the affective domain stated at the organizing level is "The student will state how he or she perceives the relative positions of *equality* and *freedom to excel* in a democratic system of values".

Characterizing by a Value or Value System. At this level in the affective domain, the instructor's objective is to induce the student to accept the thing being considered into his or her way of life. For example, "The student will make allowance in his or her daily routine for listening to classical music, will seek others to share his or her enjoyment of classical music and will regularly attend classical music concerts".

Some may see a limitation in the way in which Krathwohl et al. approached the matter of affect in the development of their taxonomy. As in the case of the taxonomy for the cognitive domain, Krathwohl et al.'s framework may seem too "behavioristic" in nature, addressing only processes that can be observed at a very low level of abstraction. But the term *affect* connotes processes that underlie directly observable behavior—processes involving feelings such as anxiety, depression, anger and euphoria—and often it is necessary to address such processes as targets of instruction (in connection to emotional intelligence, the reader will remember the calls for curricula for education on emotional intelligence discussed in Chapter 2). As noted earlier, Gagné, integrating affective and cognitive concerns into one general scheme, stipulated values, fears and self-feelings along with cognitive processes as key targets in the planning phase of the teaching-learning effort—and critics of Krathwohl et al.'s model may argue that such key elements are lacking in this taxonomy.

The Taxonomy of Instructional Objectives for the Psychomotor Domain

Instructional objectives for the psychomotor domain address the learning of coordinated body movement. At least two taxonomies for the psychomotor domain have been proposed. One was developed by Simpson (1972) and the other by Kibler, Barker and Miles (1970). The taxonomy of Kibler et al., considered here, consists of four levels:

Gross Body Movement. At this level in the psychomotor domain, the instructional emphasis is on strength and speed in using upper limbs (e.g., throwing a ball), using lower limbs (e.g., running across a room) or using two or more body units (e.g., a running throw of a football).

Finely Coordinated Movements. At this level in the psychomotor domain, the emphasis is on coordination of movement patterns, i.e., riding a bicycle.

Nonverbal Communication Sets. At this level in the psychomotor domain, the emphasis is on wordless communication, e.g., making facial expressions, gestures and bodily movement.

Speech Behavior. At this level in the psychomotor domain, the emphasis is on the production of speech, e.g., vowel and consonant sounds, complete words, projection of sound so as to be heard, using gestures to enhance a verbal message.

Criteria for Evaluating Instructional Objectives

Three major criteria have been proposed for the evaluation of instructional objectives, regardless of the domain involved (Gage and Berliner, 1984). These are *observability, conditions of performance* and *performance criteria.*

Conditions of Performance

The conditions under which the behavior stipulated in the instructional objective is to take place should be specified. For example, "Given a printed pencil and paper multiple-choice test..."

Observability

The terminal behavior specified in the instructional objective should be stated in action words, since actions can be observed. For example, "the student will place a pencil mark next to the correct answer for each question"

Performance Criteria

Objectives should specify the criteria that will be used to judge whether the objective has been met. For example, "...for at least 80 percent of the questions."

A fourth criterion, one proposed by this author, is the *time frame* within which the student should be able to meet the objectives.

Issues Across Domain Related to the Use of Instructional Objectives

A number of reservations have been expressed concerning the use of instructional objectives, regardless of the domain in question. Three of the more frequently stated are the following:

1. The more important goals in education (e.g., "self-actualization", aesthetic growth, the spiritual aspects of life) cannot be stated in observational terms. As with the objection concerning needs assessment discussed in Chapter 2, this seems to be a Type *i* issue (dismissive, invalid). It seems dismissive because it does not allow for the possibility that instructional objectives can address these aspects of life; it seems invalid because it does not seem reasonable to demand that something be accurately addressed which cannot be described in observable terms to begin with.

2. Objectives restrict student learning by narrowing the learning possibilities about some topic. What if the student notices some aspect of the topic that he or she would like to pursue? To meet the stated objectives, he or she would have to ignore such enriching detail. This appears to be a Type *a* issue (cautionary, valid), because it points to a real need to allow for students' exploration of unexpected areas that emerge in the process of learning.

3. Objectives engender conformity and interfere with the development of one's individual humanity. This appears to be a Type *b* (dismissive, debatable) issue, since it is not clear what is meant by "conformity" or "humanity".

Melton (1978) noted three things that an instructor can do to ensure that instructional objectives serve to promote the success of the teaching-learning effort:

1. Induce the students to work toward the stated objectives by motivating them and ensuring that they understand them.

2. Ensure the objectives are clear and unambiguous.

3. Set the objectives at the proper level of difficulty for the students involved.

In summary, instructional objectives describe the behavior the instructor wants students to be able to enact following instruction. Instructional objectives can be stated in one or more of three psychological domains: cognitive, involving rational mental behavior; affective, involving values and attitudes; and psychomotor, involving coordinated body movement. Each of these domains consists of a taxonomy of psychological processes occurring at varying levels of complexity, mastery at each level requiring earlier mastery at lower levels. The success of the teaching-learning effort is partly dependent on the specificity with which the taxonomy level, conditions of performance, and performance criteria for the terminal behavior are described.

TASK ANALYSIS

Definition of *Task Analysis*

Task analysis involves the decomposition of the terminal behavior stipulated in an instructional objective into sub-behaviors that can be individually taught. The purpose of the decomposition is to enable the student to reach the goal of instruction by completing relatively simpler tasks, each of which can often facilitate the undertaking and completion of a subsequent, relatively more complex task. In this way, the sub-tasks identified through task analysis lead logically to the terminal behavior stipulated in the instructional objective.

Two methods of task analysis exist: *technological* and *psychological*. In the technological method, a description of the components of the thing to be taught is sought along with the relations that exist among the components. In the psychological approach, the educator is concerned with the sub-skills the learner must master before he or she can master the terminal behavior stipulated in the instructional objective. It is the psychological approach to task analysis that will be discussed in this chapter.

Psychological task analysis involves working backward from the terminal behavior stipulated in an instructional objective, determining the immediately preceding sub-skill to be learned in order to be able to master the skill at hand. The procedure is repeated until the point is reached at which the identified sub-skill is already part of the student's repertory. This already mastered sub-skill is termed the *entering skill.* For example, assume that the terminal behavior stipulated in an instructional objective is being able to divide whole numbers. A task analysis of this objective might take the following form:

1. Knowledge of numbers
2. Ability to add
3. Ability to subtract
4. Ability to multiply
5. **Ability to divide**

Item 5, appearing in bold face, refers to the terminal behavior stipulated in the instructional objective, and items 1 to 4 refer to the skills necessary to reach the terminal behavior. To ensure that the student reaches the terminal behavior in item 5, the instructor would first ensure that the student can function at level 4, level 3, and so on. Whichever of sub-skills 1 through 4 the student already possess is the entry level for this student, and any sub-skill the student lacks is one that he or she must be taught before he or she can reach the instructional objective at hand. Thus, according to Derry and Lesgold (1998, pp. 787-788), task analysis serves the instructional process by enabling the instructor to:

1. Analyze the domain knowledge into a hierarchy of tasks or "atoms", each of which is either a very small piece of knowledge or a relatively simple combination of previously specified atoms.

2. Sequence the atoms for instruction so that a combination atom is not taught until its component atoms are taught.

3. Design an instructional approach for each atom in the sequence.

Characteristics of a Properly Executed Task Analysis

Anderson and Faust (1973, p. 83) summarized a number of criteria for an effective task analysis. The following are six of these criteria:

Completeness

Completeness refers to the matter of whether every important sub task has been identified in the analysis.

Amount of Detail

Amount of detail refers to whether the number of sub tasks into which the terminal behavior has been decomposed is optimal. Insufficient sub tasks can defeat the purpose of the analysis by making it difficult for the student to traverse the sequence between the entry and terminal behaviors; too many sub tasks can create a minutiae of detail that can prevent the student from "seeing the forest for the trees".

Specificity

The question of specificity refers to whether the skills involved (and the relations among them) have been described in enough detail to be of any use in the instructional effort.

Signaling Cues

Signaling cues are signals that indicate to the student the timing for carrying out each task in the analysis.

Definition of Mastery

As in the case of the terminal behavior stipulated in an instructional objective, it is necessary to describe what one means by mastery of a sub-skill. This need can be met by using the criteria of observable terminology, the conditions of performance and the criteria for acceptance applied to instructional objectives.

Hierarchy that May have to be Mastered Among the Sub-skills

Typically, the sub-skills identified in a task analysis can be arranged in a hierarchy, in which the mastery of one sub-skill is necessary before mastery of another sub-skill can be attempted— although it is possible that some skills can appear parallel rather than subordinate or superordinate to others. The hierarchy is typically identified in the process of working backward from the terminal behavior.

Issues Related to the Method of Task Analysis

Writers have pointed out that the theoretical work conducted during the 1960s and 1970s on task analysis was designed to address skills at the lower levels of the cognitive domain but not to address learning outcomes involving higher cognitive skills or skills in the psychomotor or affective domains. According to Derry and Lesgold (1998), the problem with these limitations is that they prevent task analysis methodology from addressing modern concerns with instructional objectives:

> Many educators now believe that beyond intellectual skills and verbal knowledge, higher order thinking capabilities are the most important goals for schooling. As traditional instructional design theory does not address these types of learning outcome, it is not capable of addressing the challenges associated with the winds of corporate and educational reform that are sweeping our country today. (p. 788)

For example, in traditional task analysis-based instruction, if the skill being taught consists of individual "atoms", or sub-skills, of knowledge (e.g., symbol-sound associations), each sub-skill is individually taught and practiced with trivially simple material until the sub-skill has been mastered. Only then are all the sub-skills brought together to form more complex and meaningful behavior. The problem with this approach is that, for example in the case of reading, slower learners miss opportunities to work with complex meaningful material while they practice with trivial information:

> Over the primary years—or even the elementary years—slower children, ironically, would then receive less practice in "reading for meaning". Although some might argue that these children "aren't ready" for more complex reading activities, the reality remains that the time available for education is not totally elastic, and often only the units at the top of the hierarchy, and hence the end of a course sequence, have real external or motivational value. (p. 790)

Moreover, according to Derry and Lesgold (1998), a key assumption in developing a hierarchy of skills leading to some terminal behavior is that whatever scheme the educator generates will be applicable and comprehensible to the learner. But it is possible for two persons to arrive at the same terminal behavior through different steps—and left to his or her own devices, the student may construct a path different from that of the educator—and the educator's path may prove ineffective for a student, while the student's may prove appropriate for his or her learning needs. For this reason,

> From the point of view of task analysis, it is critical that the means whereby knowledge is acquired and described be mappable onto the experience of the student. (p. 802)

These seem to be Type *a* (cautionary, valid) reservations concerning the practice of task analysis because they call attention to the need to take into account the domain level of the instructional objective, the condition of performance and the student's own understanding of the task breakdown. To address this need, Derry and Lesgold (1998) developed a *process of successive approximation* to enable educators to overcome the limitations of early forms of task analysis. This method includes the following steps:

1. Observing the way in which an expert enacts the behavior in question and questioning him or her regarding behavioral details.

2. Constructing a tentative representation of the expert's knowledge.

3. Observing expert performance that can be enacted by the task analyst and critiqued by the expert.

4. Repeating the process with the task analyst taking the place of the expert, and the student taking the place previously taken by the task analyst. This method involves

> some give and take, dialectic, between the task analyst and the expert. Further...knowledge acquisition by the student must also involve this negotiation of meaning. Consequently, it is critically important that the outcome of knowledge engineering be not only the meaning finally understood by the task analyst but also a process for negotiating meaning with the student that can lead to the student's having a functionally similar body of knowledge after learning. (p. 802)

This process is similar to the method of *apprenticeship learning* (Collins, Brown & Newman, 1989) described in Chapter 2 and discussed in greater detail below. Through the process of successive approximation, the task analyst learns to reflect in his or her own thinking the behavior of the expert; and, through a dialogue with the task analyst, the student learns to reflect in his or her own thinking the analyst's thinking—and indirectly, the expert's behavior.

Just as important as the potential problem regarding independence from the student in task analysis, the sub-skills, or "atoms of knowledge", generated by traditional task analysis have been shown to be often excessively abstract, making it difficult for the learner to determine the specific conditions under which they can be profitably used. For this reason, suggesting that all cognitive activity is in fact socially and physically situated, Derry and Lesgold (1998) argued that

> When we teach only the verbalizations about a body of knowledge, or even the abstracted principles behind situations to which that knowledge applies, we may not be providing the learner with accessible, real-life knowledge, nor may we be taking full advantage of the power of situations to provide an experiential grounding for those abstractions. (p. 794)

Considerations of a) the learner as an active participant in the development of a task analysis and b) the social and situational elements of terminal behavior form a radical departure from classical task analysis methodology, and make the process more challenging than that originally formulated by Gagné: "This is clearly a tougher assignment than the classic task of specifying the target knowledge independent of the task situation or the student's prior knowledge" (p. 802).

Thus, task analysis involves the decomposition of the behavior stipulated in an instructional objective into simpler, component behaviors that the student must master before he or she can undertake mastery of the terminal behavior stipulated in an instructional objective. Task analysis can take one of two forms: Technological and psychological. In psychological task analysis, the instructor endeavors to ascertain the skills the learner must master before being able to enact the behavior stipulated in the instructional objectives. While earlier versions of task analysis tended to rely entirely on the instructor's own notion of how the terminal behavior can be decomposed into necessary sub-skills, modern versions of the theory stipulate inclusion of the learner as active participant in the analysis, and, often, inclusion of an expert whose behavior is to be used as a model for instruction. They also stipulate the social and contextual conditions under which the terminal behavior is to take place.

Once he or she has determined what he or she wants the student to be able to do following instruction, the educator must decide how he or she will determine whether the student can indeed do it. At this point the instructor becomes concerned with the assessment method he or she will use for the purpose.

ASSESSMENT METHODOLOGY

A misconception is possible that assessment is something in which the instructor becomes interested following instruction. Actually, assessment becomes an area of concern even before the instructor begins development of a lesson plan or module. The reason is that following development of instructional objectives and completion of the task analysis for instruction, the instructor knows everything he or she needs to know concerning what to test for following instruction. Waiting until other aspects of the pre-engagement phase of instruction have been addressed or until the instruction itself has been carried out runs the risk of taking attention away from the objectives as the basis of test development.

The Need for Instructor Familiarity with Assessment Methodology

Recognizing the importance of familiarizing teachers with the matter of assessment in instruction, in 1987 the American Federation of Teachers, the National Council on Measurement in Education and the National Education Association appointed a committee of scholars to develop standards for teacher competence in the assessment of students "out of concern that the potential educational benefits of student assessments be fully realized" (Sanders, 1990, p. 1). In 1990, the committee completed its work following reviews of earlier drafts by measurement specialists, teachers, and teacher preparation and certification professionals. The committee proposed the following seven standards:

1. Choosing assessment methods appropriate for instructional decisions.
2. Developing assessment methods appropriate for instructional decisions.
3. Administering, scoring and interpreting the results of both externally-produced and teacher-produced assessment methods.
4. Using assessment results in decisions about individual students, planning teaching, developing curriculum, and school improvement.
5. Developing valid and reliable pupil grading procedures which use pupil assessments.
6. Communicating assessment results to students, parents, other lay audiences, and other educators.
7. Recognizing unethical, illegal, and otherwise inappropriate assessment methods and uses of assessment information.

The Use of Assessment in Instruction

There are many uses to which assessment can be put. Dwyer and Stufflebeam (1996) summarized the major uses as follows: a) Assessment for the purpose of instructional improvement, usually conducted by trained evaluators; b) assessment for the purpose of professional accountability and development, usually conducted by teachers themselves in the form of records of performance which they present to interested parties; c) assessment for the purpose of administrative supervision, usually conducted by school principals through in-class observations; d) assessment to examine the relations of student performance with classroom processes, usually conducted by university researchers; e) assessment for the purpose of protection of student interests such as employability and college readiness, usually conducted by independent observers; and f) assessment for the purpose of the awarding of merit pay to teachers or individual schools, usually taking the form of supervisor evaluations and student achievement. Dwyer and Stufflebeam (1996) provide an extensive literature review regarding these uses of assessment.

These assessment uses are thought to relate to teacher evaluation. However, they can also come into play in the evaluation of school administrators and school systems. All of the various assessment uses identified above are associated in some way with the process of instruction; those emphasized in this text have to do with the improvement of classroom teaching, teacher or administrator professional development, and research into the relations among classroom processes and student achievement.

To use assessment productively, the instructor must be familiar with types of tests he or she can use in his or her work as well as with certain properties that tests must possess in order to be of any use in the teaching-learning endeavor.

Types of Assessment Instruments

There are many kinds of assessment instruments—so many, in fact, that some sort of classificatory scheme is necessary to facilitate their discussion. One useful three-category framework, developed by Fox (1969) will be used below to discuss the various types into which assessment instruments can be divided: *questioning tools, observation tools,* and *measurement tools.*

Questioning tools are assessment instruments raw responses to which are taken at face value and used as the information of interest.

Respondents either construct their answers in their own words or select their answers from a list of response alternatives. Questioning tools include *individual* and *focus group interview schedules*; *questionnaires* and *checklists*; and *critical incident queries*, in which the respondent is asked to judge others about some critical aspect of behavior such as teaching skills. Observation tools yield information about the frequency, duration or intensity of behavior

While the information gathered with questioning and observation tools is used in its original form, that gathered with measurement tools is interpreted on the basis of some frame of reference or standard. Measurement tools are designed to assess constructs such as achievement, intelligence, self-concept, personality and depression. They can take the form of *tests*, used to evaluate performance by reference to some set of criteria; *projective techniques*, used to elicit a respondent's thoughts or feelings by the use of ambiguous cues, responses based on which the investigator can deduce something about the subject's personality; *inventories*, used to provide indications of whether or not any number of attributes are true of the respondent; *sociometric* techniques, in which members of a group are asked to indicate with which group members they would want to interact in various ways, enabling the instructor to ascertain the group's overall cohesiveness; and *scaling* techniques, used to elicit indications of judgment of magnitude concerning some set of stimuli.

Table 14, adapted from Martinez-Pons (1996), summarizes the forms of assessment instruments available to the educational researcher, their subtypes, the way in which they are used, and their typical assessment targets.

The type of measurement tool known as a *test* is of particular interest in this chapter because of its prevalent use in instruction. Two features of tests are worth noting at this point: their *reference* and their *source*. Concerning the former, a test can be *criterion-referenced* or *norm-referenced*. Criterion-referenced tests are developed to assess the degree to which specific instructional objectives have been met, and norm-referenced tests are tests developed to compare students' performance with that of others.

In addition to its *reference*, a test's *source* is an important consideration for the instructor preparing to embark on the teaching-learning effort. There are two major sources of tests used in education: *internal*, in which the instructor himself or herself develops the instrument, typically for use with his or her own students; and *external*, in which the test is developed by someone other than the teacher, typically for use by more than one instructor with more than one group of students.

Table 14. Types of Assessment Instruments and Their Use.
From Martinez-Pons (1996).

Instrument Attributes	Instrument Type		
	Questioning	Observation	Measurement
Subtypes	Interviews Questionnaires Checklists Critical incident reports	Systematic Random	Tests Projectives Inventories Sociograms Scaling techniques
Approach	Information provided by an informant is usually taken as given	Information obtained directly, without the aid of an informant, is used as the data	Information provided by an informant or through direct observation is interpreted according to some standard
Typical Assessment Target	Opinions Demographics Social processes Attitudes Motivation	Social processes Individual behavior Grounded theory research	Intelligence Academic achievement Personality Depression

Combinations of the reference and source categories can produce four different kinds of tests available to the instructor. Table 15 shows the combinations possible between the reference and source categories of assessment instruments.

The cell values in Table 15 show the proximity of each type of test to instructional objectives. Well-developed criterion-referenced teacher-produced tests (Cell 1) are more likely to "map on" to the objectives of some instructional effort than are tests with higher cell numbers, criterion-referenced externally-produced tests (Cell 2) are more likely to "map on" to the instructional objectives than are tests with higher cell values, and so on. On the other hand, the cell values going from highest to lowest show the relevance of test types to assessing student performance *by reference to a population.* For example, well-developed norm-referenced externally produced tests (Cell 4) are more likely to provide a realistic comparison of a teacher's class with student populations at the national level than are test types with lower cell values.

Table 15. Forms of Tests by Reference and Source

Reference	Source	
	Teacher-Produced	**Externally-Produced**
Criterion	1	2
Norm	3	4

Types of assessment instruments and procedures other than those considered above exist, falling under the rubric of *authentic assessment.* Because at present great interest (and no small amount of controversy) surrounds these approaches to assessment, they will be considered in some detail in the *postscript* at the end of this chapter.

Test Development

Martinez-Pons (1996) proposed the following steps in the development of any assessment instrument:

1. Determine the skill, behavior or value the student is to manifest following instruction
2. Determine the instrument type to use
3. Generate the instrument's items
4. Design the instrument's layout
5. Develop an initial draft of the instrument
6. Develop the administration procedures
7. Develop the scoring and interpretation protocols
8. Conduct pilot testing and make instrumental modifications as necessary
9. Validate the instrument (see below for a discussion of validity)
10. When the instrument is to be used as a norm-referenced tool, develop the instrument's norms.

Callahan, Clark and Kellough, (1998), Childs (1989) and Williams (1991) have written clear, easy to follow texts on the construction of teacher-produced tests.

Properties of Acceptable Assessment Instruments

An assessment instrument must possess two principal properties in order to be considered appropriate for use in education: it must be valid and it must be reliable.

Validity

Validity refers to the question of whether an assessment tool assesses what it is supposed to assess. The literature on this topic is broad, with some disagreement among writers concerning the nature of validity. While some writers differentiate between *face validity* (the degree to which a lay person can tell whether an instrument's items address what the instrument is said to address), *content validity* (the degree to which the instrument's items represent the theoretical model of the construct being addressed), *criterion validity* (the degree to which the test measures the same thing that similar, previously validated tests measure) and *construct validity* (the degree to which the instrument reflects the nature of the construct in question), others hold that first, face validity is really not validity at all, and that second, content and criterion validity are actually part of construct validity (Anastasi, 1982). Martinez-Pons (1996) treats these issues under one comprehensive validity model and describes the manner in which construct validity is determined through the use of modern statistical methodology.

In addition to the matter of *construct* validity, the instructor must consider the matter of *objectives-related* validity (ORV) in his or her use of assessment to ascertain student mastery of instructional objectives. When developing or identifying a test to determine whether a given instructional objective has been met, it is necessary to ensure that the test meets three important criteria: to be valid for a particular instructional effort, a test must assess performance *in the domain (cognitive, affective or psychomotor)* and *at the domain level* stipulated in the instructional objectives. In addition, to be valid for a particular instructional effort, a test's makeup must be such that it adheres to the conditions of performance stipulated in the instructional objectives. Finally, to be valid for a particular instructional effort, a test's grading instructions must adhere to the performance criteria the objectives have stipulated.

Reliability

Reliability refers to the consistency with which an assessment instrument assesses what it assesses. Such forms of reliability exist as *test-retest reliability* (the degree to which an instrument assesses its target across time), *interjudge reliability* (the degree to which different persons agree on their assessment of some behavior or process), and *internal consistency* (the degree to which all the items in an instrument address the same thing). Martinez-Pons (1996) discusses in detail these forms of reliability and describes the manner in they are tested through modern statistical methodology. The most common measure of internal consistency reliability, to which reference will be made later in this text, is Cronbach's *coefficient alpha* (α). This coefficient can range between 0 and 1. An *alpha* coefficient of 0 indicates that each item in the instrument addresses something totally unique to it, and a coefficient of 1 indicates that all the items in the instrument address exactly the same thing. In general, a coefficient equal to or greater than .70 indicates a high degree of consistency among the instrument's items.

Additional desired qualities in assessment instruments were proposed by Linn, Baker and Dunbar (1991): *test score interpretation that has consequences for instruction, cultural fairness, transfer and generalizability of scores to achievement more broadly defined than that which the test covers, cognitive complexity at the higher levels of the cognitive domain, content consistent with the best existing knowledge in the area, comprehensiveness through representative sampling of the different features of the topic at hand, use of problems and tasks meaningful to the examinee,* and *administration efficiency and manageable cost.*

Research Design in Testing

Research design in testing in instruction involves the manner in which test data is generated so as to ensure the credibility of findings. The following paragraphs briefly discuss research design in the assessment of student performance following instruction.

Assume that the objectives of an instructional module stipulate passing a pencil and paper multiple-choice test with at least 80 percent accuracy, and that none of the students in the class performs below this level on a post-instruction test. Given this outcome, the question arises, "Should one be satisfied that instruction has been successful in enabling the students to reach the objectives?" The answer to this question, involving consideration of matters involving *pre-testing* is "It depends on how well the students performed before instruction": were pre-test scores to disclose that no member of the class performed with less than 85 percent accuracy on an exam covering the same information as the one after instruction, then one may have to conclude that the objectives had already been met *before* instruction, and that in fact, instruction had little or nothing to do with performance on the post-test.

Now assume that the pretest shows that no one in the class scored higher than with 85 percent accuracy before instruction and that in a post-test no one scores lower than with 85 percent accuracy. Can one now be satisfied that instruction has been effective in enabling the students to reach the objectives? The answer still has to be prefaced with the statement "It depends". The matter now becomes one of *control group utilization* in research design. Assume that a control group not receiving the instructions at hand is used for comparison. Assume also that while no one in this group scored at or above 85 percent in a pre-test, no one in the group scores below 85 percent in the post-test. In the face of these findings, one may have to conclude that while something happened between the pre-test and the post-test to improve student performance in the instruction group, it is likely that something other than the instructional experience was the change agent—possibly the same agent which brought about gains in the control group.

Now a third concern regarding research design in testing arises: it is possible that when the control and instruction groups perform at the same level in the pre- and post-tests, it is due to the fact that simply taking a test twice enables a person to perform better on it the second time. This research *artifact* or confounding condition is termed *test-retest effect*.

The ideal way to control for test-retest effects is to use a second instruction group and a second control group, neither of which receives the pre-test but both of which receive the post-test. The research design using this approach appears in Table 16. In this table, O stands for "observation" or testing, and X stands for "experimental intervention" or instruction. This design is termed the *Solomon pretest, posttest multiple group design* (Campbell & Stanley, 1963), and is the most sophisticated of the research designs available to social scientists and educators. In this design, even if test gains made by the first instruction and control groups are close enough to be indistinguishable, one can conclude that the instruction has been effective if comparisons yield the following results:

$O_2 = O_5$, and $O_4 > O_6$.

Table 16. The Solomon Pretest, Posttest Multiple Group Design

	Pre-Test	Instruction	Post-Test
Experimental Group 1:	O	X	O
Control Group 1:	O		O
Experimental Group 2:		X	O
Control Group 2:			O

Under ideal conditions, students are assigned to each of the groups at random, and when randomization is used the design is termed an *experimental* design; when randomization is not used, the design is termed a *quasi-experimental* design.

Because the design appearing in Table 16 requires the employment of two separate experimental groups and two separate control groups, its use may not be feasible in most instructional efforts. Nevertheless, it is important to emphasize that, particularly in the case of quasi-experimental plans, the degree to which the design for a given evaluation task approximates that of the SPPMGD is the degree to which the evaluation findings can be considered credible. When randomization is limited, as it is in the typical instructional effort, the most restricted version of this design retaining any degree of credibility is one, shown in Table 17, using single experimental and control groups. The use of this restricted research plan will be assumed for the remainder of this discussion of summative evaluation.

According to Campbell and Stanley (1963), when the investigator uses one control and one experimental group and administers a post-test but no pre-test, as shown in Table 18, no threat occurs to the internal validity of the findings if he or she randomly assigns the students to the control and experimental groups.

Thus, in preparing to assess the effectiveness of his or her effort, the instructor must consider the credibility of the information to be generated through testing. Valid research design in testing in modern instruction requires the use of pre- and post-tests, control groups, and ideally, randomization of group assignments.

Table 17. Pretest, Posttest Control Group Research Design

	Pre-Test	Instruction	Post-Test
Experimental Group:	O	X	O
Control Group:	O		O

Table 18. Reduced Pretest, Posttest Control Group Research Design

	Instruction	Post-Test
Experimental Group:	X	O
Control Group:		O

Following pre-testing, the task of the instructor becomes the grouping of students according to their entry level on the skill hierarchy for the instructional objectives generated through task analysis.

GROUPING ON THE BASIS OF PRE-ASSESSMENT FINDINGS

The Purpose of Grouping on the Basis of Pre-Assessment Findings

A misconception is possible that the purpose in grouping on the basis of pre-test scores is to enable the instructor to set different objective levels according to group membership. Actually, the instructional objectives remain the same for everyone regardless of diagnostic or pre-test findings. What is different is the manner in which each group is addressed in helping its members to reach the objectives. Thus, while the instructional objectives are the same for everyone regardless of entry level, different groups may begin at different levels in their move toward the common terminal behavior stipulated in the set of instructional objectives at hand.

Grouping Levels

In some respects, the most favorable teaching situation involves the teacher and student working in a one-on-one setting, in isolation from outside distractions. At the other extreme is the situation in which an instructor works in a classroom with 30 to 40 students (in some introductory college courses, there can be up to 200 students in a class, usually conducted in a larger auditorium). A compromise between the two extremes is that of grouping students according to diagnostic or pre-test findings and then giving as much focused attention to each group as possible.

Once he or she has formed the groups for instruction, the educator can proceed to consider the instructional methodology, or student engagement procedure, that he or she will use for each group involved.

DEVELOPMENT OF THE STUDENT ENGAGEMENT PROCEDURE

As he or she develops the procedure for engaging the student in the teaching-learning effort, it is important for the instructor to keep in mind important principles governing the way in which people go about learning. The likelihood of the success of any method designed for student engagement depends on the degree to which it attends to such principles. Learning theory attempts to identify and describe such learning principles, and for this reason it is important for the instructor to have some familiarity with current learning theory.

Attention to Learning Processes: Learning Theory

In his review of theories of learning, White (1989) examined seven conceptual frameworks that seem to have held sway in education during the past twenty or thirty years: Pavlov's (1927) *conditioning theory*, Gagné's (1985) *task-cognitive theory*, Piaget's (1951) *cognitive development theory*, Skinner's (1968) *operant conditioning theory*, Houston's (1981) *information-processing theory*, White's (1976) *psychology of pedagogy theory* and Bandura's (1977a) *social learning theory*. Gage and Berliner (1984) provide comprehensive summaries of *operant conditioning* and *information-processing* theories, and White (1989) discusses these and other salient theories of learning in some detail.

After examining the relative merits of the seven learning theories he reviewed, White concluded that, while methods and reinforcement strategies have dominated the pedagogical work of the

'70s and '80s, principles of learning and pedagogy based on social cognitive and information-processing theories (SCT and IPT, respectively) "should occupy the stage of importance in the decade of the '90s" (p. 1). This shares White's endorsement of SCT. In addition, although the present author agrees with critics who point to certain limitations in information processing theory, he generally agrees with White's endorsement of IPT as guide in the development of the engagement procedure to be used in the teaching-learning effort. The following pages will discuss these two theories of human learning.

Information Processing Theory

Rather than being a single theory, IPT is more of a general approach to the study of the sequence in which cognitive processes take place (Schunk, 1991). Two major forms of the information processing perspective exist: the *dual memory model,* and the *levels of processing model.*

The Dual Memory Model. The model appearing in Figure 18 is a composite of dual memory models offered by Atkinson and Shiffrin (1968), Houston (1981) and Schunk (1991).

In Figure 18, through the physical input represented by Linkage 1, information enters the *sensory register* (SR) and quickly decays (usually within a period 1 to 4 seconds) unless it is passed on to a more permanent storage area. From there, through the process of *attention* represented by Linkage 2, information from SR is transferred to short term memory (STM), in which about seven individual items of information can be held for about 15 seconds before the data begins to decay (with adequate rehearsal, information can remain in STM indefinitely). STM has limited storage capacity; and to ensure retention, it is usually necessary to transfer information from STM to a memory storage area with greater capacity.

In the next phase of learning the information is transferred from STM to long term memory (LTM), where storage capacity is virtually unlimited. According to Houston (1981), the process through which this transfer takes place is that of *rehearsal,* represented by Linkage 3. When needed, the information in LTM can be retrieved through the process of *encoding,* represented by Linkage 4, into short term memory for temporary usage. The *executive control processes* of the dual memory processing model are those mental acts through which the person decides what information to allow into the sensory register and in which of the memory banks the information is to be placed.

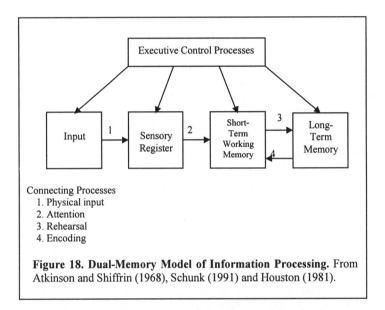

Connecting Processes
1. Physical input
2. Attention
3. Rehearsal
4. Encoding

Figure 18. Dual-Memory Model of Information Processing. From Atkinson and Shiffrin (1968), Schunk (1991) and Houston (1981).

The Levels of Information Processing Model (LIPM). LIPM was proposed by Craik and Lockhart (1972) as an alternative to the dual memory model. The major components of LIPM are three levels of information processing: physical, or surface (e.g., spelling of the word *car*), the level closest to the "surface"; acoustic (e.g., the sound of the word *car*), the next level in depth; and semantic (e.g., the meaning of the word *car*), the deepest level of processing.

Information processing becomes more complex or elaborate the deeper the level in which it occurs, with surface processing the least elaborate and semantic processing the most elaborate, like this:

Depth: *Lowest*   *Moderate*   *Greatest*

Level: Surface   Acoustic   Semantic

In contrast to the dual memory model, the LIPM does not postulate a sequence among the information processing components. Instead, the LIPM holds that the mind processes information simultaneously at the three information processing levels.

Issues Surrounding IPT. As noted earlier, a number of limitations have been noted regarding information processing theory (IPT). Some of the more salient are the following.

Addressing earlier versions of IPT, Neisser (1976) argued that the computer is too limited a metaphor to enable IPT to fully address these key processes in human learning behavior. In using the computer as its model for thinking about how people learn, IPT tends to ignore two fundamental aspects of human learning that differentiate it from computer information-processing: a) the social influence on human learning behavior involved in modeling, encouragement, facilitation and rewarding processes; and b) the emotional component involved in learning, without which rational thought is unlikely to begin or to persist (Mayer & Salovey, 1997).

In addition, Schunk (1991) noted a number of limitations that apply to each of the two IPT models described above:

1. The theory does not fully address information processing of non-verbal material.

2. The theory fails to take into account the learner's purpose for learning some material, or the learner's use and adaptation of strategies for learning.

3. The executive control process of the dual-memory model is too sketchy to fully explain how information moves from one component to another.

4. Also concerning the LIPM, objective measures of level are rare or non-existent, making it impossible to determine how level processing affects learning (Baddeley, 1978, as cited by Schunk, 1991).

Finally, work exists showing the two major information processing models to lack a certain degree of comprehensiveness. Discussing brain research that has led to current knowledge about memory, Schooler (1998) noted that although theorists in this area differ in exactly how they view the divisions of memory, there are numerous distinct memory types beyond those labeled *short-* and *long-term.* On the basis of her review of the literature, Sprenger (1999) expounded on such memory forms as semantic, episodic, procedural, automatic and emotional. Writing on their relevance for instruction, the author described ways of enhancing these five memory types as well as ways of enhancing short- and long-term memory. Acceptance of these additional classes of memory in turn leads to a recognition of the need to examine ways in which IPT can be expanded to include them in order to offer a more comprehensive account of human information processing than that offered to date.

These appear to be Type *d* (questioning, valid) issues because they point to the need for further theoretical work to address important questions about information processing by humans. Still, despite its present limitations, IPT provides a useful metaphor for thinking about the efficiency with which people go about acquiring new information, the effectiveness with which they retain it, and the extensiveness with which they can utilize it. IPT was used in Chapter 2 as the basis of the discussion of the approach to mental ability propounded by the present writer.

Implications of Information-Processing Learning Theory for Instruction. The way in which the instructor can use IPT as a frame of reference for instructional module development is as follows:

1. Create conditions that minimize distractions and focus attention on the material at hand.

2. Allow time and opportunity for rehearsal to ensure the permanence of information in long-term memory.

3. Encourage the development of clear frames of reference within which new information can be meaningfully placed in LTM.

Social Cognitive Theory

Social cognitive theory was introduced by Bandura (1977a) with his book *Social Learning Theory*, and later expanded in his book *Social Foundations of Thought and Action* (Bandura, 1986). Later, in order to emphasize the cognitive aspects of social learning, Bandura changed the theory's name to *Social Cognitive Theory*. Two central aspects of social cognitive theory are discussed in the following paragraphs: *social cognitive learning principles* and the *social cognitive learning mechanism*.

Social Cognitive Leaning Principles. The following are the social cognitive principles of learning expounded by Bandura (1986):

1. Rewarded behavior is likely to be repeated, and punished or unrewarded behavior is unlikely to be repeated.

2. Learned behavior is enacted *in anticipation* of rewards. What determines whether the person does something that manifests learning is the person's expectation of being rewarded for the behavior rather than the simple fact that the behavior has been previously

reinforced. In this respect, social cognitive theory differs from operant learning theory, which holds that learning occurs following reinforcement.

3. People learn by watching others. Bandura (1986) termed this phenomenon *modeling*.

4. People learn to expect reward or punishment by watching others being rewarded or punished. Bandura (1986) termed this phenomenon *vicarious motivation.*

The Social Cognitive Learning Mechanism. The mechanism through which vicarious learning takes place is complex, requiring satisfaction of certain conditions for it to occur. It involves the sequentially occurring processes of *attention, retention, reproduction, motivation* and *self-regulation.*

1. In order to learn from a model, a person must *attend* to the model's behavior. But whether a person attends to the behavior of the model is a function of the latter's *status* (how attractive or important the model seems to the person) and *salience* (how noticeable to the person the model's behavior is) and *similarity* (how similar to the model the learner perceives himself or herself to be, and how likely the learner believes it is that he or she may be called upon to perform the behavior being enacted by the model).

2. In order to successfully emulate the model's behavior, the learner must be able to retain it in memory. But whether the person retains in memory the behavior enacted by the model is a function of a) the degree to which the person succeeds in encoding the behavior, either verbally or in terms of images that he or she can later recall for enactment, and of b) the degree to which the person mentally rehearses the behavior.

3. In order to eventually reproduce the behavior from memory, the learner must accurately formulate the behavioral, cognitive or affective algorithmic sequences comprising it. This formulation can come about in one of two ways: Through *discovery*, in which the person figures out as best he or she can the behavioral sequence of behaviors enacted by the model; and through *coaching*, in which an expert guides the person in the formulation of the sequence. Coached formulation is more powerful than discovered formulation in enabling the person to accurately reproduce the sequence.

4. In order to enact the behavior, the learner must feel *motivated* to do so. But whether the person is motivated to enact the behavior is a function of his or her *self-efficacy*, or confidence in being

able to do it successfully; and *outcome expectation*, or his or her expectation of positive or negative consequences of success or failure.

5. Finally, assuming success in these four processes, the learner can eventually reach the point at which he or she is able to enact the behavior independently of external social influences. This condition is termed *self-regulation*, or the person's self-directed motivation, goal setting, strategy usage, self-monitoring, and strategy adjustment in enacting the behavior.

Implications of Social Cognitive Theory for Instruction. It is clear that modeling is a powerful tool at the instructor's disposal during engagement. However, it is also clear that in order for modeling to serve its function a number of conditions must be satisfied. First, the instructor must be in some way attractive to the student, and the student must be able to take notice of the instructor's behavior. Second, it is best to coach the student in his or effort to encode or mentally formulate the behavior modeled by the instructor. Third, the instructor must make provisions in the preparation facet of the instructional process to enable the student to feel confident in being able to enact the behavior (self-efficacy) and perceive an advantage in successfully doing so (positive outcome expectations).

In summary, in his or her planning of instruction, it is important for the instructor to attend to general principles that underlie human learning. Two modern learning theories can be of help in this respect: Information-processing theory and social cognitive theory. In this writer's view, the two theories are complementary, the former addressing the dynamics involved in the acquisition, retention and utilization aspects of learning and the latter addressing the contextual and social factors impinging on these processes as well as the mechanisms underlying these relations.

Classroom Structuring

In developing the method he or she will use to engage the student in the teaching-learning effort, the instructor considers the manner in which he or she will structure the learning setting. Three elements of classroom structure have received special attention during the past several decades: the degree of structure, classroom sitting location, and class size.

Degree of Structure. The degree of a classroom's organization can range from unstructured to highly structured. An example of a low-structure classroom is the *open education environment* (Silberman, 1973), in which students do not sit at an assigned desk but move as they like from one activity area or small group to another. Activity and group areas are designed to accommodate student interest. In a highly structured classroom, students sit at their desks and, typically as a class, cover academic material in a specific, universal sequence. After comparing different forms of classroom structure, Morrison (1979) concluded that highly structured classrooms ensure the greatest amount of work involvement on the part of students.

Classroom Sitting Location. The relation between classroom sitting location and academic performance has been studied by a number of investigators (Sommer, 1967; Axelrod, Hall & Tams, 1979), and studies have consistently shown an apparent relation between the two variables. For example, McCroskey and McVetta (1978) noted that in a traditional, rectangular sitting configuration, different locations appear to engender different levels of interaction between teachers and students. Their findings are shown in Figure 19. In this figure, the value of 1 denotes a sitting location least conducive to positive teacher-student interactions, and the value of 3 denotes a sitting location most conducive to positive interactions between teacher and student.

Questions have been raised concerning the definitiveness of findings regarding classroom seating. For example, Wulf (1976) found that while university students who *chose* to sit in the preferred areas interacted more with the instructor and performed better academically than students who sat elsewhere, students *assigned* to the preferred areas, taught by the same instructor, did not. These findings suggested that it was students who were self-regulated enough to actively seek favorable classroom sitting locations who gained from the experience. The implication for instructional planning that emerges from these findings is that since not all students in a classroom can occupy the more favorable sitting locations there, and since self-regulated students can find ways to compensate when they occupy less favorable locations, the instructor can probably make better use of his or her time if he or she takes steps to promote the academic self-regulation of his or her students than if he or she deliberates where in the classroom to sit them.

Class Size. Early research on the relation between class size and student performance yielded seemingly inconsistent findings. For example, in one effort examining 85 studies on class size prior to 1950,

Blake (1954) found that 35 indicated that small classes were better, 18 suggested that large classes were better, and 32 did not support either conclusion. Closer examination, however, revealed the inconsistencies to have been due to variations in the quality of the research. Blake reported that when controlling for the scientific rigor (sample adequacy, measurement of the independent and dependent variables, appropriateness of data analysis and conclusions) of the investigations, only 26 percent of the original 85 studies proved rigorous enough to merit credence. Of these, 73 percent favored small class size, 14 percent favored large class size, and 14 percent were inconclusive.

		Teacher		
2	3	3	3	2
2	2	3	2	2
1	2	3	2	*1*
1	*1*	3	*1*	*1*
1	*1*	2	*1*	*1*

1 = Low level of interaction
2 = Moderate level of interaction
3 = High level of interaction

Figure 19. Level of Teacher-Student Interaction by Classroom Sitting Location. From McCroskey and McVetta (1978). The value of 1 denotes a sitting location least conducive to positive teacher-student interactions, and the value of 3 denotes a sitting location most conducive to positive interactions between teacher and student.

Recently, Pate-Bain et al. (1997) reported on the effect of small class size on student achievement with over 6,000 Tennessee primary students during the years between 1985 and 1989, beginning at the K-3 level. They examined the comparative merits of three class size configurations: small, $N = 13\text{-}17$; regular, $N = 22\text{-}25$; and regular with full-time teacher's aide. The following are some of the study's more salient findings:

1. Students in small classes consistently scored higher on achievement and basic skills tests.

2. Inner-city, predominately minority children in small classes outscored their counterparts in both kinds of regular classes.

3. Students who were in small classes in the early grades continued to reap benefits as they moved into larger classes in high school.

4. The percentage of small-class students who had been held back before grade 10 was half that of their counterparts in the regular groups—17 percent versus 30 to 44 percent.

5. Students from small primary grade classes outscored the others in high school English, math, and science by more than 10 points.

6. Students in the small-class group had taken significantly more advanced courses, such as algebra II, calculus, advanced placement English and foreign languages, indicating they were more apt to be college-bound.

7. The small-class group had consistently fewer suspension days than did large-class students.

8. The small-class group had consistently fewer absences than the others as they moved through high school.

Although writers such as Mosteller (1995) have favorably commented on the rigorousness of the Tennessee project, others have expressed reservations concerning the study's findings. Hanushek (2000), for example, raised three major issues concerning the investigation:

1. The study's attrition rate was high, with as many as 50 percent of the pupils having left by the project's fourth year. According to Hedges (2000), this is in effect a Type *i* (dismissive, invalid) reservation because performance was higher for students in small classes even after the researchers controlled for attrition (the way the researchers controlled for attrition was by determining how well a student who withdrew had been performing before withdrawing).

2. The *effect size* (see Frame 8 for a discussion of effect size) ranged widely between .13 and .37, suggesting that something in addition to class size was at play in influencing student performance (according to Hanushek, 2000, one possible confounding factor varying across groups and not controlled for in the study was teacher effectiveness), bringing into question generalizations concerning the study's findings.

Hedges (2000), in effect arguing this to be a Type *h* (dismissive, debatable) reservation, responded that, after controlling for effect size at the Kindergarten level, ES did remain at .37 three years later—and that while it would have no doubt been informative to have controlled for such additional factors as teacher efficacy, the results nevertheless strongly suggest a positive influence exerted on academic performance by small class size. The literature would seem to support Hedge's contention. Pate-Bane et al. (1997) reported that when controlling for a host of possible confounding variables, consistent findings across studies have been that, under the right conditions, small class size can be beneficial, especially for students experiencing academic difficulties. According to Pressley and McCormick (1995), "Virtually all reviewers of the literature on class size conclude that smaller classes boost achievement, particularly for weaker students" (pp. 337-338).

Frame 8. Effect Size

The term *effect size (ES)* refers to the *strength of relation* between two sets of variables. *ES* is calculated in different ways for different research conditions. For a correlational study, it is depicted by an index of association such as the Pearson correlation coefficient, represented by *r*, discussed in Frame 2. For a study examining the difference between groups, *ES* can be calculated by dividing the total sample's standard deviation into the difference between any two means, like this: $ES = (M_1 - M_2) / SD_2$. This value can be interpreted as the number of standard deviations by which the two means differ. An effect size for two groups can be converted into a correlation coefficient through various methods (see Martinez-Pons, 1999a).

According to Cohen (1992), an *ES* coefficient lower than .20 can be interpreted as low, one of .20 of can be interpreted as low although not trivial, one of .50 can be interpreted as substantial, and one of .80 or above can be considered high.

---

3. Even assuming findings supportive of small class size, the implications for policy-making are less than clear-cut because the cost of maintaining small-sized classes can be prohibitive—somewhere around $20,000 per class per year—due to the greater number of teachers required. To this writer, this appears to be a Type *a* (cautionary, valid) reservation, calling for some sort of compromise between the often experienced need for small classes and the need to control for educational costs. One way to address this issue is by focusing on the reason class size is assumed to promote student performance. In this writer's view, the reason has to do with the level of

individualized attention the teacher can devote to each student—attention that decreases in direct proportion to class size.

A compromise between the need to control for cost and the often felt need to maximize individualized attention can be worked on the assumption that while direct teacher-to-pupil contact is important in some circumstances, it is not necessary or even useful in others. For example, it has been found that under the right conditions, students can learn as much if not more from one another than they can directly from a teacher. Workers such as Brown and Palincsar (1989); Johnson, Maruyama, Johnson, Nelson and Skon (1981); and Slavin (1985) have shown that in small group collaborative learning activities, students can a) jointly develop ideas and understanding more sophisticated than they can under other conditions; b) develop higher levels of self-efficacy and its accompanying motivation to learn and to persist to the point of mastery; c) model effective learning behavior and higher level thinking skills for one another by "thinking aloud" during small group work; and d) overcome risk of academic failure when it arises. One way to reach a compromise between the need to control for cost and the need to at some point provide individualized instruction is to design engagement methodology using small-group collaborative activities, and to then attend individually to students still in need of help following the small group learning interventions. Such an approach was proposed in a document released by the Educational Research Service (1980), which suggested that efficient instructional planning and class management can be used to offset the potentially deleterious effect of large class size.

Reservations concerning the use of small classes have been expressed in addition to those voiced by Hanushek (2000). As noted in the aforementioned Educational Research Service (1980) document, although smaller classes can have positive effects on pupil achievement in the early primary grades for low-ability or economically disadvantaged pupils, larger classes may be justified in areas in which pupil achievement is minimally affected. This seems to this writer to be a Type *a* (cautionary, valid) issue, because it alerts the instructor against generalizing the benefits of small class size for low-achieving students to students at all levels of achievement.

Given what is now known about class size, it seems safe to say that, assuming an appropriate level of teacher effectiveness, small classes, where economically feasible, are beneficial for students experiencing academic difficulties. In the case in which a small class is desirable but a large one unavoidable, the instructor preparing to teach can attempt to approximate the benefits of the former by designing small-group collaborative learning activities followed by individualized instruction for those students still experiencing difficulties following the small-group interventions.

Engagement Procedure

The term *engagement procedure* refers to that set of activities the instructor designs to enable the student to fill the gap between a task-analysis-related entering skill and the terminal behavior stipulated in a set of instructional objectives.

Engagement Methods

In the view of some writers, while a large number of student engagement methods exist, little is known about their relative merit. As far back as 1973, Anderson and Faust wrote,

> Research attempting to answer the practical questions—e.g., whether the discovery method is better than the expository method, whether televised lectures are superior to live lectures, etc.—has been almost uniformly inconclusive...Neither the *discovery method,* the *learner-centered method* or the *tutorial method* has proved consistently more effective than alternative methods with which they have been compared. (pp. 4-5)

This state of affairs has prevailed to present times. For example, Woolfolk and Hoy (1990) noted that researchers have found little consistency between what teachers do in the course of engagement and student academic achievement; and Miller (1999) referred to the "fad-like" quality of teaching methods in existence, noting that in one study examining the research basis for 24 "whole school" teaching programs, the research supporting only 3 proved to be rigorous enough to merit confidence. For reasons such as these, according to Gage and Berliner (1984), the research that has accumulated during the past 30 or 40 years on teaching methods can enable educators to draw only very rough conclusions or generalizations concerning the approaches' relative merits.

It is noteworthy that what holds true for instructional *methods* such as the lecture and discussion holds true as well for instructional *media* such as television and computer assisted instruction. According to Owston (1997), "after more than 50 years of research on instructional media, no consistent significant effects from any medium on learning have been demonstrated" (p. 29).

According to Anderson and Faust (1973), there are several reasons for the inconclusive nature of research on the effectiveness of teaching methods. First, different methods may be best for different students, different purposes and different conditions, and no frame of reference has been developed or validated to match these elements of the teaching-learning setting. Second, there has been confusion about what is meant by a given teaching method. While different workers use the same terminology to refer to their instructional methods, close examination of what actually goes on typically reveals too many differences and idiosyncrasies to render the methods "the same" in all cases. Gage and Berliner (1984) shared this observation: "Lectures vary greatly, and so does teaching by the discussion, humanistic, individualized, and classroom methods" (p. 447). In addition, each method emphasizes a few processes and features of instruction but ignores others. One reason is that different methods can be based on different theories of learning that may emphasize different instructional outcomes—rendering any attempt to ascertain the methods' relative effectiveness a futile undertaking to begin with.

In a related matter, no study (to this author's knowledge) comparing instructional methodology has reported on the levels of efficacy or commitment the teachers involved have brought to bear on the methods compared. But it seems possible that regardless of the method used, lowered teacher effectiveness can in turn lower the likelihood of success of the instructional effort—or that regardless of the assumed ineffectiveness of a given method, high adaptive skill, enthusiasm and commitment on the teacher's part will raise the likelihood of success.

Gage and Berliner (1984) argued that despite the inconsistent findings regarding teaching methods, it may nevertheless be worthwhile to try to get some idea of the conditions under which existing approaches can be most profitably employed. They undertook the task by thinking in terms of the relation between instructional *methods* and instructional *objectives*. To this end, they developed an objectives-method matrix consisting of the cognitive, affective and psychomotor domain taxonomies described earlier in this chapter and the following methods of instruction: the *lecture*, in which the instructor expounds on some topic and the students listen and take notes (more than 40 students are typically involved in the lecture method of instruction); the *discussion*, in which 2-20 students exchange ideas while the teacher guides the exchange; *individualized instruction*, in which one student works alone or with the teacher on a one-on-one basis; and *classroom teaching*, in which the instructor orchestrates lecture, discussion and individualized instruction activities within one class session (between 20 and 40 students are typically involved in the classroom teaching method of instruction).

Looking for those areas in which research findings have shown at least minimal consistency, Gage and Berliner (1984) attempted to arrive, through a certain amount of conjecture, at the best estimate concerning the applicability of the various teaching methods to the different forms of instructional objectives. The authors rated each method using a four-point letter scale (A = excellent...D = poor). Only group discussion and individualized instruction earned a rating of A in any of the domains of instructional objectives. Group discussion was rated A for the application-to-evaluation levels of the cognitive domain; the receiving-to-valuing levels of the affective domain; and the coordinated movement and speech behaviors of the psychomotor domain. Individualized instruction received an A rating for the knowledge-to-synthesis levels of the cognitive domain, the receiving level of the affective domain, and the gross body movement of the psychomotor domain. Neither the lecture nor classroom teaching methods proved to be, in the view of Gage and Berliner (1984), optimal for instruction; each received ratings below B.

A General Structure for the Engagement Effort

In teacher observations the present writer has conducted at the elementary school, college and graduate school levels during the past 15 years, he cannot recall one case in which an instructor he considered successful used one "method" exclusively in his or her teaching. The writer has noticed instead that instructors successful in maintaining student engagement and in helping students to master instructional material have been those who, in addition to having a clear idea of what they have wanted their students to be able to do following instruction, have used a certain general structure in their teaching effort (the structure is general, although as shown below, the details can vary considerably according to subject matter and instructional context). The structure seems relevant regardless of the instructional objectives at hand or the instructional method or methods used.

This structure, which the author has found useful in his own teaching activities, seems to accord with principles of *apprenticeship learning* (Collins, Brown & Newman, 1989; Pressley & McCormick, 1995), introduced in Chapter 2, and addressed in some detail in the following paragraphs; with principles of *modeling* (Bandura, 1986; Rosenthal & Zimmerman, 1978); with principles of *appropriate practice* (Popham & Baker, 1970); and with principles of *deliberate practice* (Ericsson & Charnes, 1994). The approach is best described in terms of the following seven steps: *introduction, exposition, clarification, enactment, feedback, transfer,* and *deliberate practice.*

Introduction. In the introductory part of engagement, the instructor describes to the students the objectives of the session and motivates the students to become involved in the learning activities to follow. Since instruction can occur in the cognitive, affective or psychomotor domains, the same criteria apply to the introductory part of engagement that apply to testing: it is important at this point that the instructor inform the students of a) the domain in which instruction is to take place, b) the taxonomy level targeted for instruction, and c) the criteria for acceptable performance. The motivational part of the introduction occurs mainly in the affective domain, and in its design it is important for the instructor to have a clear idea of the affective level (attending, responding, valuing, etc.) at which he or she wants the students to be involved during and after instruction.

Exposition. In the expository part of engagement, the instructor demonstrates in detail the working of the idea, process or value at hand, and explains the material's subtleties to the students. It is in the expository part of engagement that principles of modeling (Bandura, 1986; Rosenthal and Zimmerman, 1978) and apprenticeship learning (Collins et al., 1989) begin to come into play. Two important questions that arise in the planning of the expository part of engagement are, what is it that is to be modeled, and what is it that is to be apprenticed?

Increasingly, theorists are coming to the view that how exposition is conducted is largely a function of the subject matter at hand. Although in the past the emphasis in educational psychology regarding exposition has been on the development of grand theories of instruction applicable across subject matter (for example, Judd, 1916, 1936; Gagné, 1985), work has been accumulating suggesting that different subject areas (e.g., mathematics, history, literature) require different expository approaches. Shulman and Quinlan (1998) argued that

> the capacity to teach, therefore, is not composed of a generic set of pedagogical skills; indeed, teaching effectiveness is highly dependent on both content knowledge and pedagogical content knowledge, on how well one understands the subject matter and on how well one

understands ways of transforming the subject matter into pedagogically powerful representations. (p. 409)

In fact, the matter of subject-specific exposition is today considered so important that upward of six chapters were devoted to the topic in the *Handbook of Educational Psychology* (Berliner & Calfee, 1998): Work was presented in that book on the unique psychology of learning and teaching of *history* (Wineburg, pp. 423-437), *science* (Linn, Songer & Eylon, pp. 438-490), *mathematics* (De Corte, Greer & Verschaffel, pp. 491-549), *literacy* (Hiebert & Raphael, pp. 550-602) and *second language learning* (Hakuta & McLaughlin, pp. 603-621). One who reads this work is impressed with the unique expository form attending each of the subject areas addressed by the authors. A succinct discussion of the unique psychological and expository processes attending subjects taught in the schools today was provided by Ormrod (2000); Table 19 summarizes this work.

Although at present the study of subject-specific exposition has not reached the point where it can be said to offer a well-defined, coherent theoretical framework, according to Shulman and Quinlan (1998), "contemporary educational psychology is attempting to combine rigor and relevance as it reinvents a psychology of school subjects" (p. 401). The following statements summarize what has emerged so far from work in this area:

1. There is no such thing as one comprehensive, universal method of exposition that transcends all subject matters.

2. An effective instructor is one who is an expert in the *subject matter* (mathematics, history, science, etc.) he or she is preparing to teach.

3. An effective instructor is one who is an expert in the unique *pedagogy* attending the subject matter in which he or she is preparing to engage the student; or one who, lacking this expertise, takes steps to acquire it before attempting to teach the material.

One implication of these principles of exposition is that before he or she embarks on the planning facet of the process of instruction, the educator must have acquired expert knowledge of the content as well as of the method of exposition suited to the subject matter at hand. The chapters in the *Handbook of Educational Psychology* cited above provide an overview of modern expository pedagogy for the major academic subject areas taught in the schools today.

Table 19. Key Psychological and Expository Processes Associated with Different School Subjects. Compiled from Ormrod (2000).

Subject Area	Key Psychological Processes	Some Expository Processes
Reading	1. Recognizing individual sounds and letters 2. Using word encoding skills 3. Using context cues to facilitate word recognition 4. Understanding the writer's intended meaning	1. Using everyday reading material other than "reading books" 2. Giving students reading choice 3. Using contexts that are meaningful in teaching reading 4. Generating discussions among students concerning what they read
Writing	1. Planning 2. Drafting 3. Self-evaluation 4. Revision	1. Assigning writing tasks on everyday matters 2. Offering students choices on what to write about 3. Using peer groups to promote writing skills 4. Promoting the use of word processing programs 5. Including writing assignments in all areas of the curriculum
Mathematics	1. Understanding numbers and counting 2. Understanding basic math concepts and principles 3. Encoding problem situations appropriately 4. Relating problem-solving procedures to math concepts and principles 5. Relating math principles to everyday situations 6. Developing effective metacognitive processes and beliefs	1. Having students tutor one another 2. Holding class discussions about math problems 3. Having students use calculators and computers
Science	1. Investigating natural phenomena objectively and systematically 2. Constructing theories and models 3. Revising theories and models in light of new evidence or better explanations 4. Applying scientific principles to real world problems	1. Engaging students in real-life scientific investigations 2. Using class discussions to promote conceptual change 3. Making use of computer technology
Social Studies	1. Understanding historical time 2. Drawing inference from historical documents 3. Identifying cause-effect relations among events 4. Recognizing that historical figures were real people	1. Choosing content that helps students discover important principles and ideas 2. Determining what students know and do not know about a new topic 3. Having students do their own research using primary sources

Clarification Through Questions and Answers. Following exposition, the instructor corroborates that what he or she thinks has been communicated to the students is in fact what has been communicated. To this end, in the planning facet of instruction the educator prepares questions that he or she can ask the students to ensure that they have understood the message; he or she also allots time to answer student questions to address any points they deem to be in need of clarification.

Student Enactment. In terms of apprenticeship learning, at this point in the engagement effort the instructor provides the student with an opportunity to enact the behavior or thought process covered in the exposition. In planning for this part of engagement, the instructor must keep in mind the instructional objectives driving the teaching-learning effort. He or she must plan for student enactment within the psychological domain (cognitive, affective or psychomotor) at the taxonomy level and level of proficiency stipulated in the instructional objectives.

Feedback and Correction. Here, in terms of apprenticeship learning, the instructor provides hints, feedback, and suggestions based on his or her observations of the student's attempts to enact the behavior in question. The instructor also encourages the student to reflect on his or her performance, and to compare it with that of others who are successful in enacting the behavior. In planning for this part of the engagement effort, the instructor pays special attention to the proficiency level stipulated in the instructional objectives. This information will enable him or her to gauge the students' performance, and will furnish him or her with a reference point for providing feedback relative to the students' efforts to replicate the behavior or thought process presented in the exposition.

Transfer. In terms of apprenticeship learning, at this point in the engagement effort the instructor encourages the student to go beyond the behavior or thought process taught and to explore ways of applying what he or she has learned. Thus, in planning for this facet of instruction, the educator in effect prepares to promote what has been characterized as the student's *transfer* of the material presented in the exposition. The matter of transfer is deemed important because, in the words of Davis (1983),

One of the central purposes of formal education is to teach knowledge, skills and values of future benefit to the learners and to society. School learning is intended to *transfer* to the world. (p. 207)

Problems with Transfer Behavior. Transfer, however, is not a simple matter, since the application of learned material appears to in many cases depend on existing similarities between the context in which the material has been learned and the context in which it is to be applied. After reviewing the research literature on transfer, Ceci and Roazzi (1998) concluded that

> Such findings show that thinking skills developed in one context often do not transfer to other contexts, so that cognitive abilities learned in one specific context may well have little impact on performance in connected areas. (p. 84)

And

> Our review of work that spans continents, social classes, and levels of formal education shows that the context in which learning occurs has an enormous influence on cognition, by serving to instantiate specific knowledge structures, by activating context-specific strategies, and by influencing the subject's interpretation of the task itself. (p. 98)

In fact, a name has been given to the theoretical stance holding that transfer is contextually bound: *situated learning theory* (Brown, Collins & Duguid, 1989; Light & Butterworth, 1992).

Some reasons have been advanced for the failure of learners to transfer acquired material to new situations. Pressley and McCormick (1995) summarized their review of the literature in this area as follows. First, although they may be able to transfer if given hints on how to do so, students may simply not recognize that knowledge gained in one context can be used in a different context. Second, at times, the student may realize that the knowledge gained is applicable to a new situation, but, confusing relevant and irrelevant information retained in memory, may use a jumbled strategy that proves ineffective. Third, the student may not enjoy carrying out the strategy or may not think that the benefits to be derived from the transfer are worth the effort.

A number of suggestions have been made for teaching to raise the likelihood that the student will transfer skills or information from the instructional context to other contexts. The following are five of the more commonly suggested methods (Davis, 1983; Gage and Berliner , 1984; Biehler and Snowman, 1986; Ormrod, 2000):

1. Explain how what the student is learning in a given lesson will be useful later to him or her.

2. Encourage specific transfer by arranging engagement conditions that are similar to conditions in which the information may have to be used.

3. Emphasize real understanding of the concepts and principles at an appropriate level of cognitive sophistication, and guide the student in general transfer by applying the extracted rule or principle to a variety of situations.

4. Combat *negative transfer* (e.g., skill gained in swinging a baseball bat interfering with learning how to swing golf club) by alerting the student to it and by providing the student with practice in differentiating between competing skills.

5. Provide a variety of examples when presenting a principle or generalization.

The notion that transfer is context-bound has its detractors. Anderson, Reder and Simon (1996), for instance, have argued that situated learning theory is too general in its claim that transfer is context-specific; the approach, according to these writers, fails to recognize cases in which transfer does occur regardless of contextual differences. For example, they pointed out, people transfer to everyday life reading and computational skills they have mastered in school. What is needed, according to critics of situated learning theory, is a theory that enables educators to predict when transfer will and will not take place. This sentiment is shared by Ceci and Roazzi (1998), who, while advocating situated learning theory, have asserted that in fact, at present the processes underlying difficulties in cross-contextual transfer are not fully understood:

> Although a large number of investigations (such as our own studies) have shown changes in performance as a function of changes in context, our understanding of the processes underlying such effects is far from complete. We have only a very limited knowledge of the nature of the interaction between context and performance or its development (p. 99)

A Social-Cognitive View of Transfer. In the final analysis, the limitations attending the notion of transfer may involve the way in which the phenomenon has been conceptualized: that is, as something that either is or is not successfully relocated from one setting to another, in much the same way that a teacup is removed from a cupboard and placed atop a dinner table—instead of as *part of a process* through which one tests the usefulness of combinations of previously acquired items of information or behavioral patterns as one attempts to adapt to a new situation.

Martinez-Pons (2000b) presented a point of view, based on social cognitive theory, in which the primary focus regarding transfer is not the amenability to generalization of a particular item of information or the transfer potential presented by a given expository technique, but the learner's adaptive behavior as he or she attempts to function in novel situations. From this alternative viewpoint, the matter of "transfer" resolves to one involving *self-regulatory behavior* as a person attempts to adapt to a new situation—partly by using combinations of previously and newly acquired information or skills.

A basic premise underlying Martinez-Pons' (2000b) position is that not all adaptive efforts are initially successful—that often, previously mastered material that the learner attempts to apply to a novel situation proves to be only partly applicable to the task (often, it may prove to be not at all applicable). In this view, it is because of the frequent original failure of attempts to adapt to novel conditions that self-regulation becomes an important concept in describing, explaining or predicting transfer behavior in terms of adaptive efficacy.

Self-Regulation. As noted earlier, Zimmerman (1989) described a self-regulated person as one who is motivated to succeed at some task, sets realistic goals regarding the pursuit of task completion, employs strategies to pursue completion of the task, *self-monitors* to gauge strategy effectiveness, and *replaces an ineffective strategy* or *adjusts his or her strategy usage behavior* as needed.

Self-Regulation and Transfer in Adaptive Behavior. In the present stance, successful adaptation to new situations partly by using previously learned material is primarily dependent, not on properties of the task at hand or even on the way material has been presented during instruction, but on the self-regulatory skills the person brings to bear on the task. In this view, the dynamics of adaptation, including transfer, have to do with a process of self-regulation through which a person enacts the following activities. He or she:

1. Perceives a state of affairs requiring some sort of adaptive behavior on his or her part.

2. Analyzes the situation in however much detail he or she deems necessary in order to determine how much of what he or she has in his or her cognitive, affective, or psychomotor repertories he or she can bring to bear on the situation at hand (area *a* in Figure 20), and how much the situation requires new learning on his or her part in order for the adaptive effort to succeed (area *b* in Figure 20).

3. Selects and combines elements of previously and newly acquired sets of information or behavioral patterns he or she estimates will best serve the adaptive effort.

4. Uses the information or enacts the behavioral sets identified in Step 3.

5. Self-monitors to ascertain the degree to which the activities of Step 4 promote the success of the adaptive effort.

6. *Modifies the effort as necessary to better accomplish the adaptive goal.* He or she performs this task through modification of the existing behavioral sets, inclusion of newly learned sets, or both.

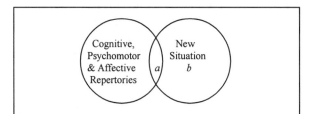

Figure 20. Relation Between an Individual's Psychological Repertory and a Novel Situation. From Martinez-Pons (2000b). Area *a* depicts elements of a person's psychological repertory applicable to a new situation and Area *b* depicts aspects of the situation requiring new learning for adaptation to take place.

The following are ways in which the social cognitive view of transfer behavior proposed by Martinez-Pons (2000b) differs from previous views of transfer. First, while for the latter the effort is seen as either successful or unsuccessful after one attempt, for the former initial failure is irrelevant. From a social cognitive perspective, what matters is the behavioral adjustment that follows when initial efforts at adaptation are less than fully successful. Second, while in the latter the assumption seems to be that transfer involves the application to new situations of intact items of information or skills, the social cognitive view holds that adaptive behavior often requires decomposition of prior items of information and their recombination into new items to meet situational demands. Third, while in the latter only prior learning is seen as relevant in efforts to adjust to new situations, the social cognitive view proposes that adaptation to new situations often requires mastery of new material, often "on the spot", for the adaptive effort to succeed. Finally, while in the latter transfer is seen as occurring automatically when the new situation is similar enough to that in which prior learning has occurred, in the social cognitive view the adaptive process served by transfer involves behavior that is goal directed and self-evaluative, with active modification of the adaptive effort as conditions demand. Thus, the social cognitive view of transfer recognizes the central role in the process of adaptation played by strategy planning, strategy usage, self-monitoring and behavioral adjustment—in contrast to previous views of transfer entertaining "one-shot", pass-fail attempts to apply single, intact items of information to novel situations.

Martinez-Pons (2000a) took the following steps to test the construct descriptive power of the social cognitive view of transfer he proposed. First, he developed the *Self-Regulated Transfer Scale (SRTS)*, an experimental seven-item instrument based on the six elements of adaptive behavior involving transfer described above. The *SRTS* appears in Appendix C. Next, the researcher administered the *SRTS* to 7th and 8th grade students in a public middle school in a large urban setting. He also administered the *Five-Component Scale of Self-Regulation (FCSSR;* Martinez-Pons, 1999a), a scale of academic self-regulatory behavior addressing academic *motivation, goal-setting, strategy usage, self-monitoring* and *strategy adjustment.* The *FCSSR* also appears in Appendix C. The author used factor analysis to test the convergent and discriminant validity of the model of self-regulated transfer. In addition, the researcher used SR and SRT to predict academic standing (AS; regular *vs.* honors track) with 111 of the students for whom achievement track information was available; he hypothesized that SRT would intervene between SR and AS.

Table 20 shows the rotated (pattern) factor matrix of the seven items of the *SSSR* and the four subscales of the *FDSSR*. While the two factors that emerged proved to be highly correlated ($\phi = .53$), only the *FDSSR* subscale scores loaded on the second factor, constituting a general self-regulation factor; and only the items scores of the *SRTS* loaded on the first factor, constituting a self-regulated transfer factor.

Figure 21 shows path analysis outcomes for the test of the SR→SRT→AS hypothesis ($N = 111$). Although both general academic self-regulation and self-regulated transfer behavior were related to academic achievement, only self-regulated transfer behavior proved to exert a direct effect on academic performance.

Thus, the social cognitive view of transfer proposes that when one says that "transfer has failed" one is in effect referring not so much to a failure in perfect transfer of an intact item of behavior or information, but to some failure in one or more of the six aspects of adaptive self-regulatory behavior described above.

From this point of view, training in self-regulation that uses combinations of information presented during engagement with information the learner acquires on his or her own may be more important to ensure his or her adaptation to new situations than the presentation of material in ever more involved ways so as to promote the learner's transfer of intact items of information or behavior. This approach differs from that of the 1920's in which general training in one area (e.g., Latin) was assumed, through some indirect process, to improve one's ability to adjust to situations in another area (e.g., mathematics). The present approach involves direct training of the behavior of interest: training in self-regulatory adaptive behavior is assumed to improve performance in self-regulatory adaptive behavior.

Table 20. Rotated (Pattern) Matrix of FDSSR and SRTS Scores for Middle School Sample. From Martinez-Pons (2000b).

	Factor		
	1	2	Communality
FDSSR Subscale Scores			
Motivation	-.10836	.82999*	.60510
Goal	.04313	.79871*	.67639
Strategy use	.03616	.86393*	.78086
Self-Evaluation	.38416	.59480*	.74409
SRTS Item Scores			
1	.72243*	-.05321	.48391
2	.81823*	.00952	.67787
3	.72830*	.02650	.55163
4	.72295*	.06428	.57615
5	.74072*	.01084	.55731
6	.84442*	-.08122	.64680
7	.48569*	.33513	.52110
Eigenvalue	5.55	1.27	
% of variance	50.40	11.60	
Total variance	62.00		
ϕ = .53			

*Empirically significant loading (Stevens, 1995)

In fact, in their review of the literature, Risenberg and Zimmerman, (1992) found experimental evidence that students trained in self-regulatory strategies improve their transfer performance in new situations. For example, Bielaczyc (1995) reported research integrating self-regulatory training with expository material. The author reported that the investigation "indicates that the particular self-explanation and self-regulation strategies in use contribute to learning and problem-solving performance" (p. 221). In other research, Lucangeli (1995) found that metacognitive (i.e., self-monitoring) strategy training enabled fifth graders with learning problems to perform better in a transfer reading task than did matched students in a control group.

Thus, in this part of the planning facet of the teaching-learning effort, the instructor considers ways in which he or she can promote the student's transfer of material to situations other than that in which learning takes place. Because of the obstacles to transfer often presented by contextual factors, successful application of learned material requires a certain form of self-regulatory behavior on the learner's part to adjust to novel situations—partly by using the material learned and partly by learning new material in the new context. Hence, in his or her planning of ways to promote application, the instructor must make provisions for student practice of self-regulatory strategies for cross-contextual transfer.

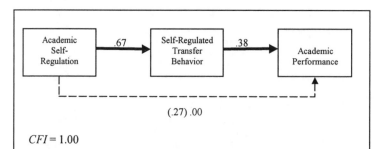

$CFI = 1.00$

Figure 21. Path Analysis Outcomes of Academic Self-Regulation, Self-Regulated Transfer Behavior and Academic Performance. From Martinez-Pons (2000b). The dashed linkage between academic self-regulation and academic performance is used to show that although the zero-order correlation between these two variables was $r = .27, p < .05$, the relation proved to be spurious ($\beta = 0$) when the intervening effect of self-regulated transfer behavior was statistically controlled.

Lesson Summary. There are two tasks that the instructor performs in a lesson's summary: he or she recapitulates what has been covered in the lesson, and he or she ensures the student's motivation to pursue the material beyond the teaching-learning setting.

Review. The purpose of the review is to encapsulate the main points presented in the exposition. Since during delivery, student enactment and feedback, much material will have been covered that is redundant or which approaches the same matter in different ways, it is possible for the student to begin to "fail to see the forest for the trees" in trying to grasp the gist of the exposition. The condition is similar to the construction of a building. Much scaffolding, equipment, and building material accumulates during construction, and at some point it becomes necessary to remove this extraneous matter in order to appreciate the building's structure in its final form. The process of review serves the purpose of clarifying the material in the student's mind free of the extraneous and repetitive information that has gone into the expository effort.

Motivation Maintenance. The instructor can promote motivation by reminding the student of how he or she can apply what he or she has learned in order to address any set of academic or personal problems or to reach and maintain any set of desired goals; but perhaps the most potent form of motivation maintenance occurs when the instructor models interest in and enthusiasm for the material covered in instruction. In any event, when planning to ensure the student's continued motivation to continue his or her involvement in the subject matter, it is important for the instructor to have a clear idea of the affective level (e.g. receiving, responding, valuing, etc.) at which he or she wants to maintain student involvement—and to model his or her own involvement at the affective level targeted.

Deliberate Practice. Engagement does not end upon completion of an instructional session; in fact, in a sense it is at this point that engagement truly begins, since it is only through continued rehearsal of the knowledge, value or skill the student has begun to acquire during exposition that mastery can actually develop. According to principles of apprenticeship learning described by Pressley and McCormick (1995), to be effective this practice must occur under some level of supervision on the part of the instructor:

> Apprentices practice the tasks that are expected [of them] although always being coached by the mentor...A good mentor "scaffolds"... his or her input, providing assistance when it is needed but not so

much that the student becomes dependent on it nor so little that the apprentice falters. (p. 233)

It is at this point that Ericsson and Charnes' (1994) method of deliberate practice comes into play. This principle, as noted in Chapter 2, holds that skill comes from prolonged focused practice under expert guidance. This notion has been specifically tailored to the process of instruction by Popham and Baker (1970) in their formulation of their *principle of appropriate practice.* According to Popham and Baker, it is important for the success of instruction for the teacher to provide the student with opportunities to rehearse the values, skills or knowledge constituting the terminal behavior of the instructional objectives. Thus, it is important for the educator at this point in the planning facet of instruction to design activities through which following exposition, the student can practice the material he or she acquires during the expository facet of instruction.

Engagement Plan Adjustments

Once the instructor has worked out the engagement module he or she will use in the teaching-learning effort, he or she can examine it to ascertain areas in need of adjustment. There are at least three ways in which the instructor can test the lesson plan he or she has developed: through review and feedback by other instructors, through comparison with a model plan, and through small-scale tryout.

Peer Review

In order to obtain their opinion concerning the likelihood of success of the module and to get their suggestions for improvement of the plan as necessary, the instructor can consult with peers who have had experience in instruction of the subject matter at hand.

Comparison with a Model Lesson Plan

A useful way of assessing the likely success of a lesson plan is to compare it to an existing plan found to have worked well in the past. This method is especially helpful for identifying elements of a good lesson plan that the instructor may have overlooked. In such cases, the instructor can use the information gained through comparison to round out the engagement plan at hand.

Small-Scale Tryout

In the absence of peers who can provide feedback concerning the quality of the lesson plan or of a model with which the lesson plan can be compared, the instructor can try out the lesson with a few students to identify areas in need of improvement. For example, he or she can assess the degree to which instructions are understandable to the students and the degree to which the students are able to keep up with the pacing of the presentation.

SUMMARY

In summary, key activities involved in the planning part of the pre-engagement phase of instruction are a) grouping on the basis of diagnostic findings, b) development of instructional objectives and task analysis, c) test utilization and testing design, d) grouping on the basis of pretest outcomes, e) attention to learning processes, f) classroom structuring and g) engagement module development and adjustment. Although issues have been raised concerning the way in which these tasks are approached, it is nevertheless true that the instructor must do certain things in order to prepare to effectively conduct the engagement phase of instruction. It may be suggested that even if some of the activities the instructor carries out in the pre-engagement phase of instruction do prove lacking in theoretical or even empirical rigor, it is better to begin with some plan that can be modified as the need for modification becomes apparent than to begin the engagement process with no plan at all.

POSTSCRIPT: AUTHENTIC ASSESSMENT

A form of assessment exists involving concepts, instrumentation and procedures different in key respects from those associated with the methods described earlier in this chapter. Generally known as *authentic assessment* (AA), the approach has gained in popularity during the past two decades, with the National Council on Education Standards and Testing calling in 1992 for examinations at the national level involving authentic assessment methodology. The wide attention given to AA was evidenced by an ERIC search, conducted at the time of this writing, which yielded 771 articles dealing in some way with the topic.

Since the seminal work of Archbald and Newmann (1988), who are credited with the introduction of the AA concept, other workers such as Darling-Hammond, Ancess and Falk (1995); Farr and

Tone (1994); Resnik and Resnik (1991); Gardner (1989); Brown, Collins and Duguid (1989); and Wiggins (1989a) have contributed to the development of authentic assessment theory and methodology. Burke (1999) wrote a text intended to serve as a practical guide for teachers in developing authentic assessment procedures.

AA grew out of a conviction that traditional objective tests (in particular, multiple-choice tests) "foster a one-right answer mentality, narrow the curriculum, focus on discrete skills, and underrepresent the performance of students from low socioeconomic backgrounds" (Hambleton and Murphy, 1991, p. 1)—and thus work against the fundamental purpose of assessment, which is to help manage student learning, monitor educational systems and evaluate students for institutional purposes. According to Hill and Larsen (1992), authentic assessment overcomes the limitations of traditional testing because AA

> (1) requires students to construct responses rather than select among existing options; (2) elicits higher order thinking in addition to basic skills; (3) uses direct assessment of holistic projects; (4) is integrated with classroom instruction; (5) uses samples of student work collected over an extended period of time; (6) is based on clear criteria of which students are made aware; (7) allows for the possibility of multiple human judgments; and (8) is more closely related to classroom learning. (p. 1)

In this way, in the view of Hill and Larsen (1992), AA can help educators to achieve the educational goals of strengthening curriculum and instruction, raising teacher effectiveness, and improving student performance through self-evaluation.

Authentic assessment actually consists of a number of different methods, of which the more widely known are *performance assessment* (PEA) and *portfolio assessment* (POA) (Bracey, 1993). Regardless of the form it takes, in the view of some workers certain issues remain unresolved regarding AA methodology. The following pages discuss the major AA forms involving PEA and POA and examine a number of issues that have been raised concerning them.

Authentic Assessment Forms

Performance Assessment

Definition of *Performance Assessment*. While the meaning of performance assessment (PEA) varies from writer to writer, a number of features seem to reoccur from account to account of PEA efforts (Swanson, Norman & Linn, 1995). In general, PEA emphasizes complex higher order thinking skills and knowledge, seeks to test for skills and knowledge in the real-world context in which are they are used, and uses open-ended tasks that require analysis and synthesis of information in the learner's possession.

Forms of Performance Assessment. PEA can take various forms. Four described by Swanson, Norman and Linn (1995) are *written simulations*, typically taking between 10 and 30 minutes, in which a progression of written scenario-oriented problems are presented to the examinee, and feedback is provided to the examinee's written responses; *computer-based simulations*, typically taking between 15 and 60 minutes, similar to written simulations, but with the added feature of high-resolution imagery, immediate feedback, and detailed instantaneous statistical analysis of examinee responses; *oral examinations*, typically taking between 30 minutes and 2 hours, in which a set of hypothetical cases are vocally presented to the examinee along with case materials and questions whose oral answers are evaluated according to previously established criteria; and *standardized patient*, taking between 10 and 30 minutes, in which the examinee interacts in a helping fashion with an actor trained to portray a patient, student, etc. experiencing some sort of difficulty or trying to achieve some objective.

Issues Regarding Performance Assessment. After examining the accumulated evidence regarding PEA in education, the health professions and public schools, Swanson, Norman and Linn (1995) drew a number of conclusions concerning the practice: First, they noted, performance-based assessment is above all, a simulation, regardless of how "realistic" it appears to be—and examinees behave differently in real life than they do under any simulated condition, so that claims that PEA overcomes the situational limitations of traditional assessment are not entirely accurate.

A second limitation of PEA is that, as the evidence shows, prediction of performance in one context on the basis of performance in another is poor, regardless of the assessment method used. In fact, due to the unique elements of the testing situation, the more detailed the assessment in a given context, the less predictive the findings usually prove to be.

A third limitation of PEA is that performance-based assessment methods are often involved and complex, and multiple test forms and test administrations are usually required to test large numbers of examinees. These properties of PEA pose "formidable equating and security problems" (pp. 9-10).

Finally, PEA cannot be expected to automatically lead to improved instruction and better learning outcomes. PEA's *usefulness* must itself be evaluated as an integral part of efforts to validate the approach: "Unfortunately, when new assessment procedures [such as PEA] are introduced, little effort is typically devoted by those involved to document unintended effects of the change." (p. 10). This was true of major PEA programs reviewed by Swanson et al. (1995).

Strong psychometric reservations concerning PEA have been expressed, particularly regarding its use in large-scale instructional programs, in addition to the reservations voiced by Swanson et al. For example, based on a study with 6,000 third and fourth grade students in a large school district, Crehan (1997) found low convergent and discriminant validity patterns of performance-based procedures used to assess student achievement. He concluded: "Results of this study may lead to questioning the value of performance assessments in a school district assessment program. It may be that the cost of preparing, administering, and scoring these assessments outweighs their benefits" (p. 1).

Portfolio Assessment

Definition of *Portfolio Assessment* (POA). A portfolio is a collection of student work used for such purposes as formative evaluation of the teaching–learning effort, summative evaluations of student typical and peak performance, teacher and student self-reflection, and simply the "global celebrations of students' accomplishments" (Herman, Gearhart & Baker, 1993, p. 202). As an alternative to traditional methods of student assessment, POA is said to offer a number of advantages. First, portfolios are, by their nature, integrated with classroom instruction—a feature that enables the teacher to clearly see the connection between what has been covered in class and what the student can do as a result. Second, they involve "authentic" student work that requires the use (and afford the assessment) of complex thinking skills. Third, they provide a more accurate portrait of students' strengths and weaknesses than do more traditional assessment methods. Finally, portfolios are said to encourage teachers and students to reflect on their progress and to adjust their efforts in the teaching-learning process accordingly.

There are a number of ways in which the method of POA is said to differ from traditional assessment methodology. First, portfolios usually involve classroom writing rather than responses to a standardized question or instruction. The teacher typically assigns a classroom writing task, and the student's written response becomes part of the portfolio.

A second way in which POA is said to differ from traditional assessment approaches is that the former affords the student manifold occasions to demonstrate competence across contexts and time periods. Thus, compared to assessment methods involving a single administration yielding a single "snapshot" of student performance, portfolios are said to be more like a series of film frames showing changes over time in student performance. In a related way, portfolio samples can represent the result of repeated revision, thus affording a chronology of progress made by the student over a given time period.

Finally, portfolio assessment differs from traditional assessment methods in that POA includes different subject areas such as mathematics, reading and social studies in a single task in such a way as to provide the student with an opportunity to integrate what he or she knows into holistic frameworks within which to respond to real-life tasks.

Issues Regarding Portfolio Assessment. The major issues raised regarding portfolio assessment have revolved around the question of the validity and reliability of the procedures involved. These matters have been studied by a number of researchers, and seemingly uniformly the findings have proven less than fully supportive of the psychometric quality of the approach. Herman, Gearhart, and Baker (1993) studied the reliability and validity of portfolio assessment in an elementary school. Three teachers and their classrooms in grades one, three and four participated in the study. The students maintained working portfolios with all writing work, including at least one monthly classroom narrative assignment. The rubrics, or scoring criteria, used by the teachers were designed to generate both holistic and analytic scores. The researchers found that although the teachers scored the portfolios consistently, pointing to the inter-judge reliability of the scoring instructions, they were unable to rate students' progress on the basis of the portfolio contents—bringing into question the validity of the assessment procedures. On the basis of their findings, the authors stated, "Our study provides evidence that portfolios are not an easy panacea for current, widely heralded problems in large-scale assessment" (p. 222). The authors found the same low validity level in a second study in which elementary school teachers attempted to assess student progress in writing content, organization, and mechanics.

According to the researchers, "the study raises questions concerning validity of inferences about student competence based on portfolio work" (p. 1).

The findings of Herman, Gearhart, and Baker (1993) were corroborated with findings reported by Stevens and Clauser (1996). In a longitudinal 4-year study of 2,351 students in a large Southwestern school district, these researchers found low predictive validity of the *Writing Portfolio Assessment* (WPA) across time periods compared to the high predictive validity of the more traditional *Iowa Tests of Basic Skills* (ITBS).

Despite the many challenges faced by the instructor attempting to use POA, some writers see some promise in the approach. In Hambleton's (1996) view,

> The portfolio format has the advantage of enhancing realism for the student, thereby increasing face validity. Moreover, this format opens the possibility for the assessment of a variety of higher order thinking skills involving analysis, synthesis, problem solving, organization, and so on....Current thinking is that portfolio assessments can provide classroom teachers with valuable information about the performance and progress of their students. (p. 908)

This, in Hambleton's view, is true despite the fact that the criteria for portfolio item inclusion, consistent scoring, and performance standards have yet to be worked out in this approach to the assessment of student progress.

The Debate Concerning the General Approach of Authentic Assessment

In a particularly pointed critique of the general approach of authentic assessment, Terwilliger (1997) summarized his reservations concerning AA as follows. First, in his view, the term *authentic* is misleading because it implies that AA approaches are superior in their employment of tasks that are more "genuine" or "real" than traditional assessment forms. According to Terwilliger, the issue is especially sensitive because AA proponents present no validity data, "evidential or consequential" (p. 26), in their writings on AA. In fact, if anything, as noted above, validity data presented on PEA and POA have shown the methodology to be lacking in this respect.

Second, according to Terwilliger, AA proponents denigrate the value of the memorization of facts. For example, in his treatment of AA, Wiggins (1989b)

> Disavows any interest in 'atomized tasks,' corresponding to 'isolated outcomes,' 'mere recall,' and 'plug-in skill.' [But] Such pejorative terms make it clear that Wiggins has little respect for the assessment of knowledge or basic skills. (p.26)

And yet, most situational challenges call for responses involving an extensive knowledge base: "Individuals who lack the knowledge base have little or no chance of performing successfully in the 'real-life' roles that Wiggins describes" (p. 26). In Terwilliger's view, these trends are particularly disturbing because they point to the danger that perfectly useful and appropriate assessment methods will be discarded in a rush to adopt a variety of other techniques of unknown psychometric and educational quality.

Wiggins (1998) responded to Terwilliger's critique of AA by holding it to represent, in effect, a set of Type *i* (dismissive, invalid) reservations. First, in Wiggins' view, Terwilliger confuses situational realism with psychometric quality. But

> "Authentic" refers to the proposed tasks, not to the technical quality of the designer's items—"performance faithful to criterion situations". To call a task "inauthentic" is not to condemn it psychometrically but to describe its lack of fidelity to the ultimate performances and contexts being assessed. (p. 20)

To this objection, Terwilliger (1998) responded that construct theory, which is essentially psychometric in nature and goes beyond mere issues of criterion validity, is central to all educational assessment: "This is especially true when claims are made about the assessment of higher order thinking skills, a favorite topic of school reformers" (p. 23). It may be noted that in fact, a study examining validity issues in a program in Arizona using AA to assess written communication, Howell (1993) found deficiencies in the AA measures used, and concluded that "authentic measures lack meaningful standards. Major flaws were reported in the areas of 'fairness', 'transfer and generability', 'content quality' and 'meaningfulness'" (p. 387).

Second, in Wiggins' (1998) view, Terwilliger misrepresents Wiggins' position on basic knowledge, since Wiggins has been in fact calling for a *balanced* assessment approach to the lower and higher levels of the cognitive domain taxonomy—a balance upset by conventional standardized testing in favor of the lower levels. To this objection, Terwilliger rejoined that

> It is true that Wiggins makes such an argument early in his book. But the tone of later statements suggests that he equates "knowledge" with rote memory of isolated facts that is tantamount to brainwashing students. (p. 23)

In the light of the consistent lack of validity found in authentic assessment methodology and of general reservations voiced by a number of critics of AA, writers have pointed to the need for further inquiry into the approach's potential before educators begin using it in lieu of more traditional assessment forms. Hambleton and Murphy (1991), for example, writing on the relative merits of multiple-choice and authentic assessment tests, stated that

> The evidence against multiple-choice tests is not nearly as strong as has been claimed. It is not clear whether authentic measurements are always better. Substantially more research into the strengths and weaknesses of various item formats for meeting particular measurement needs should be conducted. (p. 1)

Actually, as noted by Hambleton (1996), Bennet and Ward (1993) and Hambleton and Murphy (1991) have presented psychometric evidence in support of multiple-choice tests, even in the testing of higher order thinking skills. Using stronger terms, Cizek (1991) expressed the conviction that AA is not a true substitute for more traditional assessment forms:

> True educational reform will undoubtedly be evidenced by something more substantial than pocket folders bulging with student work. Labeling performance tests "authentic" does not ensure their validity, reliability, or incorruptibility. Such tests are neither replacements nor cure-alls for other assessment shortcomings. (p. 150)

Particularly in the use of authentic assessment for the purpose of teacher evaluation, considerable work remains to be done to show the validity and reliability of the approach. In the view of Dwyer and Stufflebeam (1996),

> Emerging innovative evaluation models employing "authentic" assessment or applied performance examinations, in situ examination of teachers' performances in professional development or "teaching

schools"... duties-based evaluation... and video portfolios... have yet not been tested sufficiently as to purpose, cost, ease of use, validity, and long-range significance (p. 771)

Given the promise of authentic assessment offered by its proponents, it seems understandable that many educators will want to explore its possibilities. At the same time, given the disagreement regarding some of its fundamental assumptions, the logistical problems involved in its implementation, and the consistent lack of validity reported attending AA procedures, it may be difficult to disagree with Hambleton and Murphy (1991) that, despite what some consider AA's promise, more research is needed before traditional forms of assessment are replaced with alternative, "authentic" forms.

PART 3

THE ENGAGEMENT PHASE OF INSTRUCTION

In the engagement phase of instruction, the educator undertakes those activities he or she has designed to involve the student in the teaching-learning effort. First, the instructor appraises the situation in which instruction is about to take place and makes last-minute adjustments as necessary. Then he or she proceeds to engage the student in the teaching-learning effort. Finally, in the engagement phase, the instructor conducts formative assessment, in which he or she monitors the progress of the engagement effort and takes corrective action as necessary to insure the likelihood of the effort's ultimate success. The engagement phase of instruction is discussed in Chapter 4.

Chapter 4

Engagement

INTRODUCTION

Chapter 3 discussed the activities the instructor undertakes to prepare to engage the student in the teaching-learning effort; Chapter 4 discusses the actual engagement of the student in this undertaking. The present chapter considers three aspects of the engagement phase of instruction: appraisal of the situation in which instruction is about to take place, engagement of the student in the learning process, and formative evaluation of the engagement effort.

SITUATIONAL APPRAISAL

Situational appraisal involves a last minute check to insure that conditions in the learning setting are likely to promote the success of the teaching-learning effort about to take place. There are at least five aspects of the learning setting for which the instructor conducts last-minute appraisal activities: *administrative support; school staff support; the physical setting of the engagement effort; availability of instructional materials;* and *student and instructor readiness to embark on the teaching-learning effort.*

Administrative Support

Administrative support involves help lent by school administrators to the instructor as he or she carries out the teaching-learning effort. Areas in which the instructor needs the support of school administrators are: guidance concerning performance expectations; backing in disciplinary cases; backing in dealings with parents, the community, and upper echelons in the school system; ensuring the availability of school supplies; and encouragement and recognition of good performance.

In addition, administrators can support the teaching-learning effort by insuring the quality of security and first aid services, and by insuring the existence of clear fire routes and fire evacuation plans. The degree to which administrators provide this form of support is the degree to which they can be said to contribute to the success of the teaching-learning effort (Smith, Neisworth & Greer, 1978).

School Staff Support

Many schools use a professional support team consisting of security personnel, at least one counselor, a school psychologist, a social worker and a nurse. The instructor must insure that he or she has established lines of communication with these individuals in case the need arises to appeal to them for aid during engagement of the student in the teaching-learning effort. A campus security force, a student advisement center, and a first aid station are typically found at the college level, and the instructor functioning at this level must be familiar with the range of services offered and the persons performing these services in order to access them as the need arises.

Physical Environment

As noted in Chapter 3, the quality of the physical environment of the instructional setting can affect the success of the teaching-learning effort. In terms of environmental health hazards, cosmetic and aesthetic elements of the environment, comfortable seating, and adequate lighting, the instructor must take last-minute steps to insure that the state of the setting's physical plant is conducive to the success of the teaching-learning effort. In addition, a number of elements of the physical environment were cited by Smith, Neisworth and Greer (1978) as targets for situational assessment: designation of special places where students can go for isolation, quiet, self-reward, independent work, and private discipline; movable furniture for grouping purposes; and storage facilities for students to put away personal effects and study materials.

Instructional Materials

The instructor must ensure that visual aids, textbooks, handouts, lesson plan, student writing materials, etc., are on hand before beginning the engagement effort. A checklist developed well in advance of engagement can be of great help in ensuring that the necessary materials are on hand before beginning the engagement process.

Students

A last minute check by the instructor is necessary to ensure that all students are present, alert and motivated to participate in the engagement process. Of particular importance is the students' psychophysiological state at the time of engagement. For example, Rapp (1990) noted that some children suffer from allergies to foods such as dairy products and carbohydrates. Their consumption of such foods before class can induce in them allergic responses in the form of hyperactivity and attention deficit disorder during class. Whenever a student exhibits early signs of such responses before class begins, the instructor may have to take steps to address the condition before beginning the engagement activities.

Instructor

The instructor's mood, alertness, and enthusiasm for the topic at hand will significantly influence his or her performance in class. Tension-reducing deep breathing and relaxation exercises can be useful at this point.

ENGAGEMENT MODULE IMPLEMENTATION

In the module implementation part of engagement, the instructor executes the plan he or she developed in the pre-engagement phase of instruction. There are four key elements of module implementation of interest at this point: implementation of the engagement plan, the instructor's conduct during engagement, formative evaluation of the engagement process, and crisis intervention.

Implementation of the Engagement Plan

At this point, the instructor implements the plan for engagement he or she developed in the previous phase of the instructional process. The reader will recall that, in general terms, this plan involves the following activities:

1. Introduction
2. Exposition
3. Clarification
4. Student enactment
6. Feedback
7. Transfer
8. Deliberate practice

The details of each of these aspects of the plan constitute the activities of the module's implementation.

Instructor's Engagement Behavior

In behavior closely related to the general principles of instructional design described in Chapter 3, in what might be called the tenet that "people, not methods, teach people", the more successful teachers this writer has observed in the classroom have followed what amounts to basic principles of social cognitive learning theory: modeling, encouragement, facilitation and rewarding. These behaviors were briefly introduced in Chapter 2 in the discussion of parental inducement of academic self-regulation.

Modeling. Social cognitive theorists have demonstrated the effect of modeling in the learning setting (Bandura, 1986; Rosenthal & Zimmerman, 1978, Martinez-Pons, 1996). For instruction in the cognitive and psychomotor domains, the form of modeling that ideally occurs during engagement involves not only enactment of working of the cognitive material, but also enactment of affective involvement (enthusiasm, commitment) with the material.

Encouragement. Particularly in the early phases of learning, students need encouragement to persist in their learning effort as they originally fail to meet performance criteria. According to Martinez-Pons (1996),

Under such circumstances, it becomes important for the [teacher] to encourage the child's persistence with statements such as "I know you didn't get it perfectly right, but that's natural the first time you try to do anything. The important thing is that you started doing it. If you keep trying, you will keep getting better until you get it right". (p. 215).

Facilitation. Many times, teacher modeling and encouragement are not enough to enable a student to master new material. Often, it is necessary to take time to facilitate the student's learning effort by offering concentrated guidance through the forms of activities described by Collins et al. (1989) in their method of apprenticeship learning. This method was described in Chapter 3.

Rewarding. It is well known that behavior that is rewarded is likely to recur and that behavior that is punished or not rewarded is unlikely to recur—although there are some theoretical limitations to this observation. According to Peterson, Maier and Seligman (1993), one limitation in the effect of rewards involves the context of performance:

> If Suzie Student receives an A grade in organic chemistry, she does not repeat the course the next term, even though the A grade was the highlight of her academic career. There is good reason for her to expect that a repeat performance would not be reinforced. (p. 145)

The point made by Peterson et al. is that reinforcement does not generalize indiscriminately but according to an estimate on the person's part regarding the likelihood that the behavior will be rewarded in subsequent situations. (This is the point made by Bandura, 1977b, 1986, in differentiating between social cognitive and operant conditioning accounts of reinforcement. While in operant conditioning reinforcement is *followed* by repetition of the behavior; in social cognitive theory the behavior occurs in *anticipation* of the reinforcement: if a person does not perceive that a given behavior will be rewarded, he or she will not enact it, even if it has been rewarded in the past.) Still, although a high grade may not induce the student to repeat the course, it may well induce her to work as diligently in other courses in the hope and expectation of continuing to earn high grades.

An important rule that applies during engagement is that, in order to try to capitalize on the thinking and effort that went into its development, the teaching-learning endeavor must begin with implementation of the module as originally planned. If in the course of engagement the need arises to modify elements of the plan, it is important to know the exact aspect in need of modification. But if the original plan is not at first adhered to, if something goes awry in the engagement process it may be difficult if not impossible to determine with confidence which part of the process is in need of modification—or how such modification may impact on other elements of the process.

This last point leads to the next consideration concerning engagement: although module implementation may seem like a straightforward matter, it typically does not prove to be a cut-and-dry affair. First, rather than delivering the information exactly as planned, in the same way that a wind-up toy enacts the movements called for by its mechanical makeup, the successful instructor continually adjusts the structure, sequence, intensity, and pace of the engagement activities to accommodate unforeseen events. Second, crises during engagement can and typically do arise to which the instructor must attend to ensure the likelihood of the success of the teaching-learning effort. Thus, in this phase of the process of instruction, at the same time that he or she engages the student in the learning activities at hand, the instructor conducts what is termed the *formative evaluation* of the effort in progress.

Formative Evaluation

It is the purpose of formative evaluation to enable the instructor to ascertain whether what is taking place in the teaching-learning setting is likely to lead to the attainment by the students of the objectives of instruction.

Targets of Formative Evaluation

Targets of formative evaluation include student performance, teacher performance, and the quality of support provided by school administrators and staff. In each case, the instructor continually monitors the performance of the different parties involved and, when detecting any problem, takes steps to address it.

Formative Evaluation Methods

There are a number of ways in which the instructor can monitor the progress of the engagement effort. Some of the more widely used are *observations, tests and quizzes,* and *consultations.*

Observations. Observations are notes the instructor makes concerning critical incidents that occur during the process of engagement.

Quizzes. The instructor can use quizzes to ascertain whether students are mastering skills specified in the objectives of instruction. In cases in which mastery has not occurred, the instructor can ascertain the reason and take corrective action.

Consultations. Consultations are conversations the instructor conducts with students and others to ascertain how they feel the engagement effort is progressing. The instructor can evaluate concerns raised by students and others during consultation using the issues analysis framework depicted in Table 2 in Chapter 1. He or she can then address those concerns he or she deems legitimate and relevant to the likelihood of the success of the engagement effort.

Crisis Intervention

Often in the course of formative evaluation, the instructor will note conditions that threaten to impede learning and that require some sort of action to ensure the success of the teaching-learning effort in progress. This type of activity is termed *crisis intervention.* The following paragraphs discuss the topic in terms of the manner in which *crisis* is defined, the use of the scientific method in crisis intervention, types of classroom crises the instructor is likely to encounter, and the crisis intervention process.

Definition of *Crisis*

A crisis is the occurrence of any event in the teaching-learning setting that threatens to interfere with students' reaching of the objectives of instruction.

The Use of the Scientific Method in Crisis Intervention

Use of the *scientific method* can help in the effective resolution of crises in the teaching-learning setting. In this method, the worker takes five steps to address the problem at hand: He or she *describes the problem, analyzes the situation in which the problem occurs to ascertain the reason for the crisis, develops hypotheses for explaining the reason for the crisis, formulates and examines the relative merits of possible courses of action for addressing the crisis, implements the course of action deemed most promising for addressing the crisis,* and *decides whether the crisis has been resolved.*

Types of Crises

Two general types of crises can occur in the teaching-learning setting: *student-originated* and *non-student-originated* crises.

Student-Originated Crises. There are at least three major forms of student-originated crises the instructor is likely to encounter in the classroom. These are: *individual discipline problems, group discipline problems* and *decrement in self-efficacy.* The first crisis type considered in the following pages is that involving individual discipline problems.

Individual Discipline Problems. Individual discipline problems are crises of the teaching-learning setting involving one or two students. The following is an example of an individual discipline problem:

> *Billy, a 10-year old boy of normal intelligence, began the school year disrupting the class by making loud noises, throwing things at other students, and taking things away from them. At one point, feeling annoyed by Billy's behavior, the teacher, Mr. Brown, said to Billy, "Be quiet and do your work!" Billy replied, "Shut up yourself!" As punishment, Mr. Brown kept Billy two hours in detention after school. The next day, Mr. Brown came to the classroom to find paint splashed on his desk. Suspecting Billy, Mr. Brown confronted him and Billy admitted to the misdeed. Mr. Brown reported Billy to the school principal, who suspended Billy for a period of three days and in turn reported the incident to Billy's father. His father severely spanked Billy and "grounded" him for a*

period of two weeks. Now Billy sits in the back of the classroom, seemingly afraid to respond to questions posed by the teacher. He shies away from interaction with other students and seems incapable of functioning at the same level as the other pupils.

There exist a large number of theoretical approaches to the type of individual discipline problem posed by Billy above. Hallahan and Kauffman (1978) classified such approaches in terms of the following underlying theories of human behavior: *psychoanalytic* theory, in which a pathological imbalance among the id, ego and superego is assumed to cause the misbehavior; *psycho-educational* theory, in which an interaction is assumed between underlying psychological disorders and academic expectations set for the student; *humanistic* theory, in which obstacles to self-actualization are seen as the bases of the student's misbehavior; *ecological* theory, in which poor interactions between the student and his or her environment is assumed to underlie the misbehavior; and *behavioral* theory, in which it is assumed that the misbehavior consists of a surfeit of learned inappropriate responses and a dearth of learned appropriate responses.

Wolfgang (1977) developed the *Teacher Behavior Continuum* (*TET*), a frame of reference for ordering the various theoretical approaches to individual discipline problems in terms of the level of power a teacher exerts over the student in addressing the crisis. The ordered categories of the TET are *visually looking on* (e.g., observing the student's behavior to gain information or giving the student a warning look), *non-directive statements* (e.g., "I saw you pull Martha's hair", "You must be trying to get attention by pulling Martha's hair"), *questions* (e.g., "Why did you pull Martha's hair?"), *directive statements* (e.g., "Stop pulling Martha's hair"), *modeling* (taking the child to his seat and concretely showing him what he should be doing), *reinforcement* (e.g., ignoring the undesired behavior and rewarding the desired behavior), and *physical intervention and isolation* (e.g., physically removing the student from the situation in which the problem occurs).

Wolfgang and Glickman (1980) used the TET to contrast the work on discipline problems advanced by nine different theorists. Their classification of the nine approaches in terms of the TET appears in Table 21. In this table, the *Approach* column shows the different theories considered by Wolfgang and Glickman. Each of these theoretical stances is placed in Table 21 within one of three row categories: *non-interventionists, interactionists,* and *interventionists.*

The *Behavior Continuum* column in Table 21 shows the types of teacher behaviors arranged in the TET continuum ranging between the lowest level of power exerted by the teacher (visually looking on) to the highest level of teacher power exerted by the teacher (physical intervention and isolation of the student).

Table 21. Approches to Individual Discipline Problems in Relation to the Teacher Behavior Continuum. Compiled from Wolfgang and Glickman (1980).

Approach	Behavior Continuum						
	Visually Looking on	Non-Directive Statements	Questions	Directive Statements	Modeling	Reinforcement	Physical Inter-vention and Isolation
Non-Interventionists Gordon (1974) Harris (1969) Raths, Harmin and Simon (1966)	X	X	X				
Interactionists Dreikurs (1998) Glasses (1969)		X	X	X	X	X	X
Interventionists Axelrod (1977) Homme (1970) Engleman (1969) Dobson (1970)				X	X	X	X

Non-interventionist theorists such as Gordon (1974) and Raths et al. (1966) advocate the exercise of a low level of teacher power, ranging between visually looking on and questioning the student when the student misbehaves; *interactionist* theorists such as Dreikurs (1998) and Glasser (1969) advocate the exercise of teacher power in a broad spectrum, ranging between non-directive statements to physical intervention and isolation of the student; and *interventionists* such as Axelrod (1977), Homme (1970), Engleman (1969) and Dobson (1970) advocate the exercise of a high level of teacher power, ranging from modeling of the desired behavior to physical intervention and isolation of the student.

Along with the method of Glasser, that of Dreikurs allows for the widest range in the exercise of teacher power; in addition, Dreikurs' is one of the more widely known of the methods cited by Wolfgang and Glickman (1980). For these reasons, the Dreikurs method will be described in detail in the following paragraphs.

The type of individual discipline problem described above involving Billy is addressed by Dreikurs (1998) in his *Social Discipline Theory*. According to the author, there are four reasons children misbehave: a desire for attention (*attention getting*), a desire for social power (*power seeking*), a desire to hurt others in the way they feel they themselves have been hurt (*revenge seeking*), and a sense of powerlessness in coping with the world around them (*display of inadequacy*). The forms of misbehavior postulated by Dreikurs occur in a hierarchy, beginning with attention getting at the least serious level and ending with display of inadequacy at the most serious level. (Display of inadequacy seems to be what Peterson, Maier and Seligman, 1993, referred to as *learned helplessness*, the feeling that one has no control over adverse events in one's life. In their reformulation of their learned helplessness theory, Peterson et al., 1993, postulated a three-component model: *uncontrollable negative events,* leading to *expectation of future uncontrollability regardless of one's actions,* and *difficulties in motivation, cognition and emotion based on this expectation.*)

One of the more important principles of *Social Discipline Theory* is that the higher in the hierarchy, the more serious the form of misbehavior and the more challenging its solution becomes. Another is that any given discipline problem should be dealt with in the appropriate manner at the level at which it occurs: If the problem is treated at a lower level, the attempt will not succeed, although the effort can be refocused at a higher level to increase the likelihood of success; if it is treated inappropriately at a higher level, the attempt will likely escalate the crisis. In the above example, the second principle was violated at four different points: Assuming that Billy had been seeking attention, had Mr. Brown approached the problem at that level, he would have had a good chance of resolving the crisis outright. Instead, Mr. Brown's response induced Billy to enter into a power-seeking struggle in which, in attempting to "save face" in the eyes of his classmates, Billy ordered the teacher to "shut up yourself". When punished for his response, Billy moved on to a higher crisis level: he sought revenge by splashing paint on Mr. Brown's desk; and when punished even more severely for the paint splashing misdeed, Billy began to feel powerless to assert himself in the classroom setting—and ended by displaying inadequacy in dealing with his classroom environment.

The approach proposed by Dreikurs to individual discipline problems is fourfold: *ascertain the level at which the misbehavior occurs, test the diagnosis, elicit student involvement in resolving the problem,* and *intervene to reduce the misbehavior.*

1. Ascertaining the level at which the misbehavior occurs. Dreikurs' method for diagnosing the motive for student misbehavior requires that the teacher ask himself or herself, "How does the behavior make me feel?" According to Dreikurs, the teacher's feelings are the most reliable indicator of the motive for the student's misbehavior. Table 22 shows the diagnostic frame of reference developed by Dreikurs using teacher feelings as indicators. If the teacher feels annoyed, the student is likely to be seeking attention; if the teacher feels threatened, the student is likely to be seeking power; if the teacher feels hurt, the student is likely to be seeking revenge; if the teacher feels helpless in trying to handle the situation, the student is likely to be displaying inadequacy.

Table 22. Dreikurs' Diagnostic Method of Student Misbehavior

How the teacher feels	Likely level of student misbehavior
Annoyed	Attention seeking
Threatened	Power seeking
Hurt	Revenge seeking
Helpless	Display of inadequacy

2. Testing the diagnosis. To test the diagnosis developed in Step 1, the teacher tests his or her hypothesis concerning the student's misbehavior by consulting with the student. Here, Dreikurs warns of the necessity of having previously established a relationship of confidence and trust with the student, since the success of the procedure depends on the student's trust in the teacher. The teacher takes the student aside and says, "I've noticed that you have been [*name the disruptive behavior enacted by the student*]. Is it possible that the reason you are doing this is that you are [*seeking attention, competing for power, seeking revenge, displaying inadequacy*]?" According to Dreikurs, if the teacher is right in his or her diagnosis, the student will corroborate the teacher's conclusion. The way the student will corroborate the diagnosis is through what Dreikurs terms the *recognition reflex* (e.g., the student's smiling sheepishly, laughing, looking up suddenly, shifting on his or her feet). This behavior is indicative of the student's recognition of his or her motive for the misbehavior.

3. Explaining to the student that the behavior is not acceptable, and eliciting from the student a commitment to work with the instructor to resolve the problem.

4. Intervening to reduce the problem behavior. The method described by Dreikurs for reducing disruptive behavior is termed *logical consequences.* As opposed to *natural consequences* (e.g., being scolded by boiling water), logical consequences are socially administered payoffs on the basis of student behavior. Examples of logical consequences are reinforcing positive behavior by providing the student with a sense of being appreciated for the desired behavior, and removing the student from the setting if he or she behaves in a disruptive fashion.

In this writer's view, Dreikurs' social discipline model is one of the more powerful methods of crisis management for individual discipline problems available to the instructor: it uses the teacher's own response to diagnose the form and cause of the discipline problem, it uses a specific form of observable student behavior (the student's reflex response) to corroborate the diagnosis, and it recognizes the need to address any given discipline problem at the level at which it occurs. On the other hand, the present author also sees a need for the expansion of the framework: it seems possible that behavior such as Billy's can be caused by at least two conditions in addition to those stipulated by Dreikurs: physiologically determined states such as hyperactivity due to allergic responses, noted earlier (one teacher reaction to this condition can be *alarm* due to the uncontrolled nature of the behavior); and the possibility that the student is simply not familiar with the proper way to behave in a given situation (one teacher reaction to this condition can be *puzzlement*, particularly if the behavior is not characteristic of the student). Under such conditions, the instructor must take action (e.g., controlling an allergic response or explaining the rules of behavior to the student) differing from that involving the four original levels of intervention stipulated by Dreikurs. With these two additional sources of student behavioral problems, a frame of reference expanding on Dreikurs' original model looks like that appearing in Table 23.

Table 23. Expanded Diagnostic Method of Student Misbehavior

How the Teacher Feels	Likely Level of Student Misbehavior
Alarmed	Physiological (e.g., allergic) conditions
Puzzled	Lack of familiarity with rules
Annoyed	Attention seeking
Threatened	Power seeking
Hurt	Revenge seeking
Helpless	Display of inadequacy

In addition, this writer believes that simply providing a student with logical consequences is not enough to reduce the occurrence of negative behavior and increase the amount of desired behavior. In terms of social cognitive theory, it seems also necessary to carry out the forms of social inductive behavior involving academic and emotional self-regulation described in Chapter 2: modeling, encouragement, facilitation and rewarding of the desired behavior. This is especially true regarding the more serious levels of misbehavior described by Dreikurs: concerning power seeking, revenge seeking and display of inadequacy, it is well to recognize the fact that emotional dysfunction plays at least a contributory role in these forms of behavior problems, and that often it may be necessary to help the student to develop emotional self-regulatory skills to address problems at these different levels.

Group Discipline Problems. Group discipline problems are crises of the teaching-learning setting involving two or more students. The following is an example of a group discipline problem:

> *Miss Johnson, a new teacher, has just taken over a ninth-grade class in the inner city, in the middle of the school year, from the regular teacher who has suddenly taken ill. The regular teacher is not expected to return. On her first day of class, Miss Johnson walks into the classroom to find a*

*situation that is out of control. Half the students are not in
class but roaming around the school grounds. Of those in the
classroom, few are sitting at their desks. Most are running
around the room throwing things and shouting. Physical
violence prevails. At any particular moment, at least one
student is striking another. Miss Johnson's voice cannot be
heard above the din. A few seconds after Miss Johnson walked
into the room, one student punched his fist through a wall.*

A situation such as this was addressed by Orme and Purnell
(1968), in a prime example of work with group discipline problems.
One of the researchers' former students contacted him to tell him of the
out-of-control classroom to which she had been assigned as an assistant
teacher. The regular instructor had been teaching in the school for
eleven years. Reminding him of his teachings concerning classroom
management, she invited the researcher to visit the school and
demonstrate in a real-life situation the power of the method he taught
his student teachers. The researcher accepted the invitation, and he and
some colleagues visited the classroom and found the situation described
above. The research team used the scientific method as follows to
address the problem.

*1. Observe the situation to ascertain the dynamics involved in
the misbehavior.* The workers observed the classroom for a period of
several days to get an idea of what might be causing the lack of control.
The room as they found it is shown in Figure 22. The room's major
features included a restroom built within the classroom, a cage on the
right side in which classroom pet animals had at one time been kept,
and on the left hand side some tall bookcases and an upright piano. The
students' desks were set between the teacher's desk and the room exits
into the hallway.

*2. Formulate hypotheses concerning the causes of the
misbehavior.* After observing the behavior of the students for several
days, the workers developed two hypotheses to explain the students'
misbehavior: a) the students had little motivation to study, and b) the
class was out of control because the classroom was structured in such a
way that the teacher had little or no control over the students' physical
movement.

*3. Formulate and examine the relative merits of possible
courses of action for solving the problem, and implement the course of
action deemed most promising for solving the problem.* The approach
the workers decided to take was designed to address two objectives: a)
to enable the teacher to develop and maintain classroom control and

increase pupil learning; and b) to produce pupil behavior that could be transferred from one classroom to another in which the strategies were not being used.

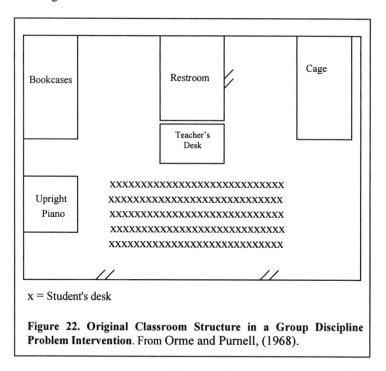

x = Student's desk

Figure 22. Original Classroom Structure in a Group Discipline Problem Intervention. From Orme and Purnell, (1968).

To pursue the first objective, the workers restructured the classroom to enable the teacher to regain physical control of the situation. They used the bookcases and upright piano to divide the classroom into two rooms, A and B. Next they arranged the two rooms so that the teacher's desk stood between the students' desks and the doors. This step enabled the teachers to regain control of classroom traffic to and from the hallway. The layout of the restructured classroom is shown in Figure 23. To pursue the second objective (to induce the students to enact learning behavior), the researchers developed a token system. They converted the cage in what was now Room B into a "store" stocked with toys, candy, comic books and other goods that the researchers deemed students would find desirable. To stock the store, the researchers canvassed merchants in the school's neighborhood for donations (the merchants were forthcoming with goods the researchers used for the store). The workers used a two-stage sequence as follows for the token system: All the students began the day in Room A, which was manned by the assistant teacher. While in this room, they earned points or tokens if they followed three simple rules explained to the students and posted in large banners in front of the room:

**SIT AT YOUR DESK
DON'T' BOTHER YOUR NEIGHBOR
KEEP BUSY ALL THE TIME**

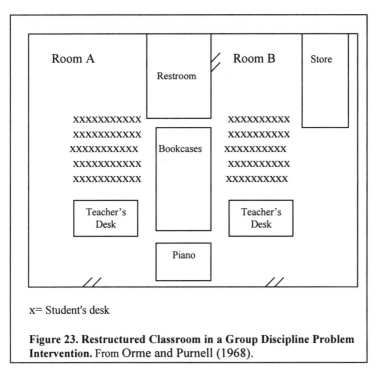

x= Student's desk

Figure 23. Restructured Classroom in a Group Discipline Problem Intervention. From Orme and Purnell (1968).

If a student earned enough points during the day, he or she could "buy" his or her way into room B, staffed by the regular teacher, where the pupil could then proceed to earn tokens he or she could use at the end of the week to "buy" goods at the "store".

4. Test the program. The researchers tested the token system for a period of several weeks.

5. Decide whether the problem has been solved. By the end of the first day, the researchers had succeeded in regaining physical control of the classroom, without one single serious incident of misbehavior taking place. By the end of the sixth week of the program, undesirable student behavior had virtually disappeared, and desirable pupil behavior had increased by approximately 30 percent.

There are a number of important rules that must be observed in order for a token system like the one used by Orme and Purnell, (1968) to work: first, the rules must be made clear to the students. Second, the rewards must be administered consistently: If a student does what the rules stipulate, he or she *must* be rewarded; otherwise, it is likely that the students will lose confidence in the program and cease to participate. Third, at some point, the external rewards (tokens, and ultimately goods bought with the tokens) must be replaced with more intrinsic forms of motivation. One way of doing this is to gradually withdraw the material tokens and replace them with symbolic rewards such as praise and other forms of social recognition.

Some issues have been raised concerning the use of token systems as tools for behavior modification: first, according to Dreikurs and Cassel (1972) adults should not have to pay children to induce them to behave as members of the human community. This seems to be a Type *h* (dismissive, debatable) issue. While Dreikurs dismisses the use of rewards like tokens outright, his own way of dealing with desirable behavior is to reward it through social recognition. But it is difficult to understand why social rewards are permissible while token rewards are not.

Second, it may be difficult to know when to begin replacing external rewards (tokens) with social recognition. This seems to be a Type *i* (cautionary, valid) issue; it calls attention to the need to exert sufficient effort to overcome the difficulty in deciding when to begin replacing one type of reward with another.

Decrement in Self-Efficacy (DSE). Self-efficacy involves one's belief that one can successfully perform some task (Bandura, 1977b, 1986). According to Bandura, self-efficacy serves three important motivational functions in learning: first, it motivates the student to undertake courses of action he or she might not otherwise consider. Second, it motivates the student to persist at some task to the point of mastery. Third, it motivates the student to apply what he or she has learned to novel situations.

A number of factors influence the development of self-efficacy: one's prior success or failure; the success or failure of others with whom one identifies; and of particular importance, attributions made by others regarding one's success or failure (Bandura, 1986). Decrement in self-efficacy (DSE) involves the feeling that one is incapable of performing some task. A key element of DSE is the attribution of lowered efficacy to lack of ability rather than to the use of the wrong strategy or to lack of persistence in attempts to master some task. The following is an example of DSE:

> *Martha, a 12-year old student in Mr. Jones' class, has been experiencing difficulty with her schoolwork in mathematics. She has failed the last two exams and does not seem to be able to follow Mr. Jones' class lectures. She has scored slightly above normal on a standardized mental ability test. When Mr. Jones asked her several days ago why she thought she was experiencing difficulty with mathematics, she responded, "I guess I'm not very smart when it comes to math". Today, Mr. Jones met with Martha's father, Mr. Clark, during the school's parent-teacher conference, and he brought the problem to Mr. Clark's attention. Mr. Clark replied, "I know Martha's having problems with math, but I'm not worried about it. She's a girl, and girls just lack the ability to do math. I've told her so, and told her to concentrate on topics more appropriate for girls, like home economics and poetry."*

Of particular interest regarding DSE is what often proves to be its social origin. As noted earlier, an effective adult serving as teacher is one who models desired behavior for a student, encourages the student's continued attempts at enactment of the behavior, facilitates the student's attempts at mastery of the behavior, and rewards the student's attempts at mastery. A risk for the onset of DSE occurs in the early phases of learning: in general, it is unlikely that a person can completely succeed the first time he or she attempts to enact some complex behavior. An important source of DSE at this point can take the form of someone persuading the learner that the reason he or she has failed to accurately reproduce the behavior is lack of ability, rather than lack of proper strategy usage (the opposite, encouragement, would involve persuading the person that "failure" is natural in the early phases of learning—that if he or she persists in attempts at "fine tuning" of his or her effort, he or she will succeed). Incidentally, some major differences between the DSE concept and Peterson et al's. (1993)

concept of learned helplessness (LH) are that first, while in DSE the condition's possible social origin is taken into account, in LH no such origin is considered (in the latter, only the facts of non-contingency and spontaneous attribution to lack of ability are considered as sufficient for the onset of helplessness); and second, while in LH some form of aversive experience occurring randomly, independently of one's actions, is assumed to generate the feeling of helplessness, in DSE an aversive experience is not required for decrement in self-efficacy to develop—often only a persuasive message by another person is necessary to induce one to attribute failure to lack of ability on one's part.

The instructor can deal with DSE by first, identifying and neutralizing its source; and second, by enabling the student to begin making attributions for failure to personal effort or ineffective strategy usage rather than to lack of ability. In Martha's case, in which the DSE source was her father's behavior, it would be important to help her father a) to realize that early failure in any subject is not necessarily a sign of lack of ability, but a natural part of the learning process, and b) to begin encouraging Martha to persist in her attempts at mastery of the subject at hand. Then, it would be important to help Martha to overcome DSE through training in self-regulatory skills involving self-motivation, goal setting, strategy usage, and self-monitoring. One way can involve assigning Martha a math task that she has not performed before, which is slightly beyond her present capability, and which Martha is unlikely to perform well the first time she attempts it. Following her initial failure, Martha can observe a model using self-regulatory skills to successfully master the task after initially failing to do so. Then she can be persuaded that her own "failure" is natural, and that, as with the model, further attempts on her part to master the material will likely lead to success. Finally, after coaching, Martha can be induced to attribute her eventual success to her proper exercise of self-regulatory skills and her persistence in working at the task.

Thus, student-generated crises involve pupil behavior threatening to interfere with the success of the teaching-learning effort. Three forms of student-generated crises are individual discipline problems, group discipline problems, and decrement in self-efficacy. Each crisis form calls for its own unique form of intervention, and an instructor skilful in addressing them will be in a favorable position to ensure the success of the teaching-learning effort even when such crises arise.

Table 24 displays an instrument the instructor can use for the formative evaluation of student behavior during the engagement phase of instruction. The instructor can use the instrument to keep a record of any specific problem encountered (under the column heading *Critical Incident(s)*), the level of seriousness of the problem (under the column heading *Seriousness*), and the degree to which the problem is resolved during engagement. The instructor can use this record later, during the post-engagement phase of instruction, to decide on any remediation steps to be taken before initiating any subsequent engagement activity.

Table 24. Student Observation Record

Area	Critical Incident(s)	Degree of interference with learning				Degree of resolution of the problem		
		Low *1*	*2*	*3*	High *4*	None *1*	Part *2*	Total *3*
Health issues								
Academic self-regulation *motivation (self-efficacy, outcome expec-tations)*								
goal setting								
strategy usage								
self-monitoring								
Emotional functioning								
Mental acuity *acquisition*								
retention,								
utilization								
Interactions with peers								
Other								

Teacher-Induced Crises. Often, the instructor himself or herself can be instrumental in the incidence of crises during the engagement phase of instruction. Callahan, Clark and Kellough (1998) discussed ways in which the instructor can contribute to crises that arise involving student discipline and learning problems.

Teacher-Induced Crises Involving Student Discipline Problems. Callahan et al. (1998) described a number of ways in which teachers can contribute to the generation of student misbehavior during the engagement phase of instruction. Among them are *premature judgments and actions,* in which the instructor fails to accurately identify a misbehaving student and reprimands the wrong pupil; *group punishment*; *inconsistent enforcement of classroom rules*; and *extra assignments as punishment.* These teacher behaviors can cause students to lose respect for the teacher, leading to his or her loss control of the class. Delaying judgment until sure about the nature of the problem, avoiding group punishment, being consistent in the enforcement of rules and not using class assignments as a form of punishment can significantly reduce instructor-induced classroom crises.

Teacher-Induced Crises Involving Student Learning. Callahan et al. (1998) noted upward of 50 mistakes teachers can make that impede students' learning. Among them are *using sketchy lesson plans* that fail to attend to individual differences; *spending too much time (over 30 seconds) with one student or one group and neglecting the rest of the class; beginning a new activity before gaining students' attention; not learning and using student names, manifesting nervousness and anxiety*; and *ignoring student thinking processes and concentrating only on correct answers when reading student papers.* Callahan et al. recommended that, in order to minimize teacher-induced student learning problems, the instructor avoid these and similar forms of teacher behavior while conducting the student engagement phase of instruction.

Table 25 displays an instrument the instructor can use for the formative evaluation of the instructor's performance during the engagement phase of instruction. The instructor can use the instrument appearing in Table 25 to keep a record of any specific problem encountered (under the column heading *critical incident(s)*), the seriousness of the problem (under the column heading *seriousness*), and the degree to which the problem is resolved during engagement. The instructor can use this record later, during the post-engagement phase of instruction, to decide on any remediation steps to be taken before initiating any subsequent engagement efforts.

Table 25. Instructor-System Observation Record

Area	Critical Incident(s)	Degree of interference with learning				Degree of resolution of the problem		
		Low *1*	*2*	*3*	*High* *4*	*None* *1*	*Part* *2*	*Total* *3*
Administrative support								
Staff support								
Instructor's efficacy *knowledge of subject taught*								
pedagogical skills								
Instructor's commitment to the teaching endeavor								
Other								

A second set of what may be termed teacher-induced crises related to student learning involves the effectiveness of the methods and procedures the instructor uses in the pre-engagement and engagement facets of instruction. The instructor must ask whether the way in which the needs assessment, diagnostic procedures, instructional objectives, task analysis, assessment methodology, engagement plan and situational appraisal were designed and executed served their purpose. Table 26 displays an instrument the instructor can use to keep a record of problems encountered in these areas, their seriousness and the degree of success in attempts at their resolution.

Table 26. Procedural Observation Record

Area	Problem in design or execution	Degree of interference with learning				Degree of resolution of the problem		
		Low 1	2	3	High 4	None 1	Part 2	Total 3
Needs assessment								
Diagnostic procedures								
Instructional objectives								
Task analysis								
Assessment methodology								
Engagement procedure								
Situational appraisal								
Other								

Crises Induced by School Administrators and Events Outside the Classroom. Callahan et al. (1998) described a number of ways in which school administrators and events outside the classroom can contribute to the generation of crises in the classroom, e.g., *interruptions by loudspeaker or messenger announcements from the office, last minute dismissals for pep rallies, loud noises from outside the classroom.* Problems that arise in these areas can probably be best resolved by appealing to the school's administration for intervention:

"Teachers should appeal to their administrators to keep class disruptions, interruptions, and outside distractions to a minimum" (p. 188). The instructor can use the instrument displayed in Table 25 for the formative evaluation of the quality of support provided by administrators' and staff during the engagement phase of instruction as well as the quality of the instructor's performance.

Thus, teacher- and system-induced crises involve teacher behavior and school conditions that threaten to interfere the success of the teaching-learning effort. Two forms of teacher-induced crises are teacher behavior that generates student misconduct and teacher behavior that interferes with student learning. System induced crises are actions taken by administrators or events taking place outside the classroom that may interfere with classroom learning activities.

SUMMARY

In summary, in the engagement phase of instruction the educator makes a last-minute check of the conditions under which instruction is to take place, engages the student in the teaching-learning effort, conducts formative evaluation of the proceedings, and intervenes in cases in which crises arise that may threaten to interfere with the attainment of the objectives of instruction. In the next phase of the instructional process, the instructor assesses the success of the instructional activities and takes steps to resolve whatever issues emerge in the evaluation.

PART 4

THE POST-ENGAGEMENT PHASE OF INSTRUCTION

In the post-engagement phase of instruction, the educator examines the success of the pre-engagement and engagement phases of the teaching-learning effort. He or she also takes steps to make corrections as necessary in the procedures of the pre-engagement and engagement phases with a view to insure the likelihood of success of subsequent instructional efforts. Chapter 5 discusses the summative evaluation and corrective activities the instructor undertakes in the post-engagement phase of instruction.

Chapter 5

Summative Evaluation and Remediation

INTRODUCTION

Following the engagement phase of instruction, the educator assesses the success so far of the teaching endeavor and addresses whatever deficiencies in the process he or she identifies through the evaluation effort. The instructional appraisal that comes following engagement is termed *summative evaluation*; and the action the instructor takes to address deficiencies he or she identifies through summative evaluation is termed *post-engagement remediation*, or more simply, *remediation*. Chapter 5 describes these two facets of the post-engagement phase of instruction. The chapter begins with a discussion of summative evaluation.

SUMMATIVE EVALUATION

Five aspects of summative evaluation will be addressed in the following pages: targets of summative evaluation, sources of summative evaluation, evaluation methodology, the process of summative evaluation, and decision-making on the basis of evaluation findings.

Targets of Summative Evaluation

The major targets of summative evaluation are the students' academic performance, the instructor's own performance during the various facets of the instructional process, the level of support provided by the school administration and support staff, and the procedures used in the three phases of instruction. The way in which each of these targets is addressed will be examined following a discussion of the sources of summative evaluation and the methodology involved in the evaluation effort.

Sources of Summative evaluation

As noted in Chapter 3, Dwyer and Stufflebeam (1996) cited several sources of evaluation in education: The instructor himself or herself, other instructors, school administrators, university researchers, trained evaluators, and independent observers. Students, parents and community members can also serve as sources of summative evaluation. Although evaluation by administrators, parents, and students will be touched upon in the following pages, the major source of summative evaluation discussed will be the instructor. The usefulness of administrators, parents, and students as evaluation sources will be briefly considered.

The Administrator as Source of Summative Evaluation

According to Dwyer and Stufflebeam (1996), the assessment methodology available to administrators for teacher evaluation has for the most part been appraised on the basis of the intuitive appeal of the method rather than on technical grounds. For this reason, there has been some controversy concerning administrators as sources of summative evaluation of instruction. The substance of such methodology, easily agreed upon, has included the teacher's knowledge of the subject and the ability to impart it, ability to establish and maintain a learning climate in a well-disciplined classroom, and ability to establish rapport with students and parents. Where the disagreement has occurred is in the method used to generate and record the information. First, the research offered in support of the methodology has been narrow, concentrating on mathematics teaching in Grades 1 through 3. Second, the studies presented are typically *meta-analytical* in nature, aggregating the results of investigations that differ fundamentally in conceptualization and research design. Third, the prescribed teaching method on which the evaluation is gauged often penalizes the creative teacher who uses an innovative approach to meet situational demands.

The Parent as Source of Summative Evaluation

Dwyer and Stufflebeam (1996) noted that parental complaints are often used as additional sources of evaluation of teacher performance, but that, as with administrative sources of teacher assessment, the validity and reliability of such information for the purpose of summative evaluation is open to question.

The Student as Source of Summative Evaluation

Concerning the validity and usefulness of student ratings of instructon, the literature during the past several decades has shown inconsistent findings. For example, Aubrecht (1979) reported that her review of the literature up to the 1970's suggested that adequately reliable and relevant student ratings of teacher efficacy are possible, and that students can make fine distinctions among different dimensions of teacher performance. She reported that when accompanied by other evaluation information, student ratings of teacher performance can be helpful to teachers seeking to improve instruction. On the other hand, on the basis of their reviews of the literature up to that time, Owen (1976), Morrow (1977), and Charles (1978) expressed concern with the objectivity, validity, reliability and utility of instruments used for student ratings of teacher performance. Based on his review, Morrow (1977) held their use in decision making to be ill advised.

More recently, Cashin (1995) argued that student ratings can be both reliable and valid, and that when employed in conjunction with other evaluation information they can be useful in the improvement of instruction. On the other hand, d'Apollonia and Abrami (1997) reported meta-analytic findings showing that while many forms of student ratings can exhibit small degrees of validity, they are subject to enough administrative and instructor effects to make their use questionable.

In this author's view, the inconsistent findings and positions concerning student ratings of the quality of instruction may have more to do with the way the evaluations are designed, executed, and interpreted than with any inherent property of student evaluation of teacher performance. The following are some factors that, in the view of this writer, may engender student differences in teacher ratings independently of instructional quality. Each factor is accompanied by a way in which its confounding effect may be reduced:

1. Student differences may influence their responses to evaluation questions and thus confound the findings. Consider for example the following question:

How would you rate the difficulty of the reading material regarding solution of quadratic equations used in this course?

Too easy			*Appropriate*			*Too difficult*
-3	*-2*	*-1*	*0*	*1*	*2*	*3*

It is possible that students with a very high level of learning readiness will have found the material easy, and that students with a very low level of learning readiness will have found it difficult. Averaging their ratings would produce a false indication that the students found the material's level of difficulty appropriate—diluting the rating's value in helping to determine the reading material's difficulty level. One way to control for this artifact is to take into account the learning readiness of the students before engagement, and to then separately examine and utilize the responses according to learning readiness groupings.

2. Some students may lack objectivity in responding to a given query. For example, it is possible that, through what is termed a *halo effect*, a student who disapproves of an instructor's classroom discipline policies may unfavorably rate the teacher's ability to communicate effectively, although by all other accounts the instructor's ability in this area may be high. One way to control for this effect in decision making for remediation is to correlate responses regarding such conceptually mutually independent properties. After controlling for possible confounding effects, the instructor can consider a high correlation between such mutually independent elements indicative of a halo effect.

3. Lack of specificity in the questions may negatively impact on the usefulness of responses. It is well known that when eliciting student self-ratings of academic efficacy, general statements such as "I can do well in school" are not as predictive of academic achievement as specific statements such as "I can earn an A in this social studies course" (Bandura, 1998)—and the same may hold true for student ratings of instruction when queries are posed at a general level. One

way to avert this possibility is to pose queries that refer to specific features of the behavior enacted by the instructor or of the materials and procedures utilized in the engagement effort—and then to specifically inquire of the student how instrumental he or she believes the item was in helping him or her to master the material. Table 27 shows a general framework for the development of student queries for the summative evaluation of instruction. In this table, the *Item* column contains major groups of elements for evaluation, and the *Reponse Format* column shows a response format the student can use to gauge the degree to which each item in a questionnaire served to enable him or her to master the material covered during engagement.

Table 27. Framework for Development of Student Queries for Summative Evalatuion of Instruction

Item	Response Format		
	Interfered with my mastering of the material *1*	*Had nothing to do with my mastering of the material* *2*	*Greatly facilitated my mastering of the material* *3*
List of specific instructor behaviors			
List of specific procedural features			
List of specific materials used			

The Instructor as Source of Summative Evaluation

The instructor becomes a source of summative evaluation when he or she uses his or her own perceptions or judgments as bases for decision-making in remediation. Although it may be possible for the instructor to use information provided by administrators, parents and students for decision making, ultimately it will be his or her own judgment, based on the information available, which will serve as the basis for remediation in the post-engagement phase of instruction. The quality of his or her decision will be a function of the degree to which he or she adheres to the principles of summative evaluation methodology described next.

Summative Evaluation Methodology

The methodology the instructor uses in summative evaluation is that used in research in general in the social sciences and education. It involves instrumentation for the collection and recording of evaluative data, research design for the control of internal validity, data generation procedures that insure the external validity of findings, data analysis methodology appropriate to the evaluation task at hand, and frameworks for decision-making on the basis of data analysis outcomes.

Instrumentation in Summative Evaluation

The types of instruments available to the instructor for the purpose of evaluation were discussed in Chapter 3. To summarize, they are *questioning instruments,* involving interviews, questionnaires, checklists and critical incident reports; *measurement instruments,* involving tests, projectives, inventories, sociograms and scaling techniques; and *observation instruments.*

Tests and critical incident records play central roles in summative evaluation, and they will be highlighted in the discussion that follows. The former are assessment instruments used to evaluate performance by reference to some set of criteria, and the latter are written records of crises encountered in the course of some activity. The *Student Observation Record (SOR),* the *Instructor-System Observation Record (ISOR),* and the *Procedural Observation Record (POR)* shown in tables 24, 25 and 26, respectively, are three critical incident reports the instructor can use retrospectively for the purpose of summative evaluation.

Methods of Data Generation in Summative Evaluation

The major methods of data generation available to the instructor for the purpose of summative evaluation are surveys, interviews, observations, and archival search. The manner in which the investigator uses these methods can differ in terms of the control he or she exerts over the processes examined. One way is termed *manipulative*; and involves some action (e.g., delivering a lecture) assumed to bring about some outcome (e.g., student learning). The other way is termed *non-manipulative*; it involves the instructor's allowing whatever brings about the result of interest to take place outside of his or her control and simply recording the levels at which the events of interest occur. An example of non-manipulative data generation in summative evaluation is that of an investigator who collects information regarding student self-regulated learning and emotional functioning during instruction and then examines their impact on the students' mastery of the material. Assuming the instructor does nothing to influence the two former student attributes, the data generation method involving them would be considered non-manipulative.

The manipulative and non-manipulative approaches to data generation can be combined in one evaluative effort. For example, the instructor can implement an engagement module (manipulation) and at the same time unobtrusively collect student self-regulation and emotional functioning information during engagement—following which he or she can examine the way in which these student processes have impacted on the pupils' mastery of the material hand covered in instruction.

Research Design in Summative Evaluation

As noted in Chapter 3, whenever he or she conducts research, it is important for the investigator to control for possible confounding effects that may mislead him or her into concluding that something is causing something else to happen when that is in fact not true. The concern, involving the matter of the internal validity of findings, is as true of summative evaluation research as it is of any other research form.

Relevant to research design, there are two levels at which student summative evaluation can take place: at the individual level, in which the interest lies in whether a given student has met the performance criteria stipulated in some set of instructional objectives; and at the group level, in which the emphasis is on the use of inferential statistics to examine trends in the effectiveness of instruction. Research design at each of these two evaluation levels will be examined in turn in the following paragraphs.

Research Design in Individual Student Summative Evaluation. The essential element of research design in individual summative evaluation is the use of pre- and post-tests. An individual student's post-test performance is compared with his or her pre-test performance to determine his or her success in mastering the material covered during the engagement phase of instruction.

Often, a student's success in meeting instructional objectives is due to factors extraneous to the engagement effort. For example, parental tutoring rather the teacher's efforts can be responsible for a student's meeting the instructional objectives of a module on the addition of fractions. In that case, it would be erroneous to conclude that the engagement effort has been successful—and, while the student's meeting of the objectives would be cause for celebration, the same could not be said in this case for the effectiveness of instruction. In other cases, student success can be due to a combination of engagement and extraneous factors, and it may become impossible to ascertain how much was due to the instructional activities. Since it is seldom that an instructor can know or control for all the extraneous factors involved in an individual student's academic success, these observations highlight key concerns regarding evaluation of the effectiveness of instruction in the case of an individual student. These issues of internal validity (i.e., the degree to which an intervention and not extraneous factors is responsible for the outcomes) are easier to address through the research design of the summative evaluation of groups of students.

Research Design in Group Summative Evaluation. In addition to the pre- and post-tests of individual summative evaluation, research design in group summative evaluation requires the use of *control* as well as *instructional*, groups. When the instructor randomly assigns students to the groups in use, the research design is termed *experimental*, and when he or she does not assign the students at random the design is termed *quasi-experimental*.

As noted in Chapter 3, the most sophisticated of the research designs available for the control of internal validity in group research is termed the Solomon Pretest, Posttest Multiple Group Design (SPPMGD; Campbell & Stanley, 1963). This design, shown in Table 16 on page 123, enables the evaluator to control for a variety of factors, including test-retest and historical processes that may distort the relation between instruction and achievement.

As already noted, because the SPPMGD requires the employment of two separate experimental groups and two separate control groups, its use may not be feasible in many, if not most, instructional evaluation efforts. Nevertheless, it is important to emphasize that, particularly in the case of quasi-experimental studies, the degree to which the design for a given evaluation task approximates that of the SPPMGD is the degree to which the evaluation findings can be considered credible. When randomization is limited, as it is in the typical instructional effort, the most restricted version of this design retaining any degree of credibility is one, shown in Table 28, using single experimental and control groups. The use of this restricted research design will be assumed for the remainder of this discussion of summative evaluation of academic achievement.

Table 28. Pretest, Posttest Control Group Research Design

	Pre-Test	Instruction	Post-Test
Experimental Group:	O	X	O
Control Group:	O		O

Method of Data Analysis in Summative Evaluation

The literature often distinguishes between two major methods of data analysis: *Qualitative* and *quantitative*. In fact, as noted in Chapter 1, the difference between the two approaches is not clear-cut, since the basis of all truly scientific quantitative analysis is qualitative, and a properly conducted qualitative analysis culminates with the quantitative processing of information. In fact, the best way to think about these two "forms" of analysis is in terms of a continuum ranging between qualitative and quantitative poles, and the question facing the researcher for any evaluation effort is, "Where in the continuum is the evaluation task facing him or her?" If the information at hand is purely qualitative in form, the researcher has to begin at the extreme qualitative end of the continuum and work toward the quantitative end using the approach described next.

Qualitative Analysis in Summative Evaluation. For either individual or group evaluation, if the information he or she collects is purely qualitative in nature (e.g., written reports of student performance or completed written assignments such as those found in portfolios and performance test records), lacking any previously formulated methodology for content quantification and interpretation, then the instructor will have to devise some set of criteria for the interpretation and evaluation of the material. Knudson (1998) described the following method for the purpose in a study that author conducted to evaluate the essays of college-bound high school students:

1. Determine the criteria to be used for interpretation or evaluation of the work.

2. Test for expert consensus regarding the educational relevance of the criteria.

3. Develop a decision-making system for assigning a numerical value indicative of the degree to which the criteria are met.

4. Develop instructions for the use of the decision-making system.

5. Test the inter-judge reliability of the decision-making system.

6. Test the criterion validity of the evaluation scheme by correlating evaluation results with other, previously validated measures of the same type of work.

7. Employ the criteria to assign a numerical value indicative of the judgment made concerning the quality or significance of the material at hand.

8. Process the quantitative information in the way described below.

The important point the instructor must keep in mind regarding this process of criteria development, quantification and validation is that he or she must follow it before undertaking the evaluation of qualitative information when no previously developed methodology exists. Failure to do so is likely to yield evaluative conclusions that are unreliable, invalid, or both.

Quantitative Analysis in Summative Evaluation. If the information at hand is in the form of numerical values such as test scores, scaled questionnaire responses, or ratings, the evaluator can begin at Step 8 above and use numerical analysis to process and interpret the information.

Quantitative Analysis in Individual Summative Evaluation.
When evaluating the performance of an individual student, the
instructor typically follows comparison of pre- and post–test scores
with a determination of whether whatever difference emerges is large
enough to be considered satisfactory. The criteria the instructor uses to
make this determination are discussed below.

Quantitative Analysis in Group Summative Evaluation. It
was earlier noted that research design is intended to control for the
internal validity of research findings. Now, there is also a need to
control for the *external validity* of research outcomes. This second
concern with validity revolves around the question of whether the
outcomes of instruction are due to the activities of the engagement
effort or due to chance. Inferential quantitative methods of data analysis
exist to enable the investigator to address this question (the topic of
inferential statistics was introduced in Frame 1 in Chapter 1).

The more widely used inferential quantitative procedures
available for group summary evaluation fall into three major categories:
Procedures for *the comparison of means*, procedures for *the test of
correlations*, and procedures for *the comparison of proportions*.

Statistical Analysis for the Comparison of Means. The
Analysis of Variance (ANOVA) is the principal inferential statistical
procedure used to examine differences between means in group
summative evaluation[3]. A variety of ANOVA models exist (see Hays,
1997, for an in-depth account of the different ANOVA models), of
which one, termed the *mixed model,* is especially applicable for use in
summative evaluation in instruction. This model is considered "mixed"
because it enables the investigator to simultaneously examine
differences *between groups* as well as differences across time for
individuals *within the same group*. In this way, the procedure enables
the investigator to analyze data in accordance with the research design
appearing in Table 28. For example, to ascertain instructional effects, a
teacher may have administered a math test to a control group and to an

---

[3]A family of *t*-tests for means is often cited for possible application in
summative evaluation in instruction. While the procedures involved have
serious limitations for use in this capacity, their prevalence in educational
research merits their discussion. The *postscript* at the end of this chapter
discusses *t*-tests for means and their limitations when used in instructional
summative evaluation.

instructional group before and after engagement. To determine whether the interventions have had their desired effect, the instructor can then perform a mixed model ANOVA on the pre- and post-test data.

ANOVA yields two items of information: First, in what is termed an *omnibus* test, it shows whether an overall statistically significant difference exists between any two of the means involved, without specifying which means they are. Then, assuming a statistically significant omnibus outcome, through what are termed *post-hoc* pair-wise comparisons, the investigator contrasts the means two at a time to determine which pairs differ statistically significantly. In the above example, if, following a statistically significant omnibus outcome, *post-hoc* comparisons disclose a statistically significant gain for the instructional group but not for the control group, the teacher can probably conclude that the engagement activities have had their desired effect. When the researcher specifies in advance how he or she expects the means to differ, the pair-wise contrasts are termed *a priori* comparisons.

In order for ANOVA to yield credible findings, the pre- and post-test data must be normally distributed; their variances must be equal; and the sample must be large, involving upward of 30 cases per group. When the data do not meet these requirements, the instructor may be able to use a less powerful (*power* in this case refers to the procedure's ability to detect statistical significance) but also less restrictive approach by ranking the data and then performing the ANOVA procedure with the rank values rather than with the original, raw data.

Statistical Analysis for the Test of Correlations. Regression analysis (RA – see Martinez-Pons, 1999b) is the principal statistical procedure available to the educator for the test of correlations in group summative evaluation. RA can be used to test for instructional effects while controlling for pre-test influences on post-test performance. In its simplest form, to address the analysis requirements of the research design of Table 28, the model, termed a *multiple regression* model, can appear as in Figure 24. In this figure, the instructor has administered a test to control and experimental, or instructional, groups before instruction (pre-test) and following instruction (post-test). He or she begins the analysis with the calculation of Pearson correlations (introduced in Frame 1 in Chapter 1) and ends with the calculation of *regression weights* indicative of the real effect of instruction after controlling for pre-test effects.

If the instructor suspects that three or more student variables are interconnected in a relational network, he or she may be able to use path analysis (Martinez-Pons, 1999b) in a more complex regression model than that shown in Figure 24. Introduced in Frame 2 in Chapter 2, path analysis can be used to test hypotheses involving intervening variables. For example, the instructor may ask whether in addition to the activities of the engagement effort, students' self-regulatory behavior and emotional functioning come together in some way to influence their mastery of instructional material. To address these questions, he or she can draw a path diagram such as that appearing in Figure 25. As before, in this figure, the dashed linkage represents the statistical control of pre-test effects. Note that in this design, both manipulative and non-manipulative data generation procedures are used: while the post-test data are generated manipulatively through the instructional interventions, the data regarding academic self-regulation and emotional functioning are generated non-manipulatively through the use of simple survey, interview or observation methodology.

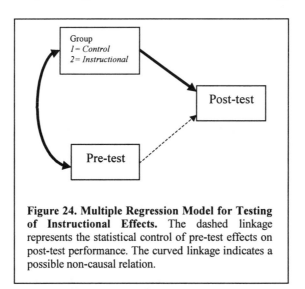

Figure 24. Multiple Regression Model for Testing of Instructional Effects. The dashed linkage represents the statistical control of pre-test effects on post-test performance. The curved linkage indicates a possible non-causal relation.

Statistical Analysis for the Comparison of Proportions. A *z*-test exists that enables the instructor to determine the statistical significance of the difference between the proportions of students in a control and an experimental group meeting the performance criteria stipulated in a set of instructional objectives (Martinez-Pons, 1999b).

The preceding paragraphs discussed the methodology used in summative evaluation, including the types of instruments, the methods of data generation, and the methods of data analysis available to the investigator in this phase of the process of instruction. The following paragraphs describe how this methodology is employed in summative evaluation.

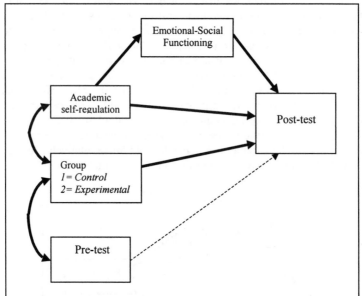

Figure 25. Hypothetical Path Model of Instructional Effect Controlling for SES, Self-Regulation and Pre-Test Effects. The dashed linkage depicts the statistical control of pre-test effects. The curved linkages indicate possible non-causal relations.

The Process of Summative Evaluation

The process of summative evaluation will be addressed separately in the following pages for student performance, for the performance of the instructor and of the school's administration and support staff, and for the effectiveness of the instructional procedures the instructor employs in the teaching-learning effort.

The Process of Summative Evaluation of Student Academic Performance

There are two aspects of student academic performance the instructor evaluates in the post-engagement phase of instruction: student academic achievement and student learning behavior.

Academic Achievement. Academic achievement involves the degree to which a student demonstrates mastery of material covered during the engagement phase of instruction. As already noted, the instructor will be interested in evaluating the academic achievement of *individual students* as well as of *groups of students*; in the following pages, this feature of the post-engagement phase will be termed the *level* dimension of achievement evaluation. In addition, the instructor can take one of two approaches to evaluate student academic achievement: *criterion-referenced* testing and *norm-referenced* testing; in the following pages, this feature of the post-engagement phase of instruction will be termed the *reference* dimension of achievement evaluation. While criterion-referenced testing involves the gauging of student test performance against instructional objectives, norm-referenced testing involves the gauging of student test performance against test performance by other students. As shown in Table 29, the level and reference dimensions produce four testing contingencies possible in academic achievement evaluation. Each of these contingencies will be considered in turn in the following paragraphs.

Table 29. Testing Contingencies by Level and Reference in Summary Evaluation

Level	Reference	
	Criterion	Norm
Individual		
Group		

Summative Evaluation of Individual Academic Achievement. As already noted, there are two forms of summary evaluation of individual academic achievement: criterion-referenced and norm-referenced.

Individual Criterion-Referenced Summative Evaluation. In individual criterion-referenced summative evaluation, the difference between a student's pre- and post-test scores is compared against a criterion to determine the success of the teaching-learning effort. For example, assume that that Martha, a fifth grade student, obtains a score of 70 on a post-test in mathematics. Also assume that the instructional objectives for the engagement module stipulate a passing score of 65.

Assuming that Martha scored substantially lower on a pre-test (say, 20), and that nothing else occurred that may have influenced Martha's post-test performance, the instructor may be justified in concluding that the teaching-learning effort was successful in enabling Martha to meet the lesson's objectives.

Individual Norm-Referenced Summative Evaluation. In this form of evaluation, a student's test performance is typically interpreted as a percentile score derived from a table showing the proportion of students in a norm group (that group made up of the students against whom the performance is measured in norm-referenced testing) falling below his or her test score. For example, assume that Martha, the above fifth grade pupil, obtains a score of 30 on a mathematics test nationally normed with fifth grade students. A norm table may disclose that 84 percent of the students in the norm group scored below 30 on this test. In this case, Martha's percentile score is 84.

If no norm table exists for comparison but the mean and standard deviation of the norm group are available, the instructor can calculate a z-score (introduced in Frame 3 in Chapter 2) to determine the number of standard deviations above or below the norm group mean that Martha's score lies. For example, if the norm group mean is 28 and its standard deviation is 2, Martha's z-score, calculated as

$$z = (30\text{-}28)/2,$$

is 1. Martha's score thus lies 1 standard deviation above the norm group's mean. This value is the rough equivalent of the 84th percentile.

Some workers consider the findings of nationally norm-referenced evaluation useful for placement in competitive programs such as select schools or colleges, or for the awarding of honors and scholarships.

Norm-referenced testing can be used to interpret a student's test performance relative to students in his or her own class as well as to students in an external group. A student's z-score calculated on the basis of the class' mean and standard deviation is typically used for the purpose.

Summative Evaluation of Group Academic Achievement. As with individual student evaluation, summative evaluation of group academic achievement can take criterion- and norm-referenced forms. It was earlier stated that regardless of the form it takes, group summative evaluation requires the use of inferential statistics for its implementation.   Through the use of inferential statistics, the investigator can determine whether evaluative findings are due to instruction or due to chance.

Group Criterion-Referenced Testing. Group criterion-referenced testing involves a determination of whether on the average, a group of students has reached the instructional objectives stipulated for a given engagement effort. In this case, two questions become the focus of the investigation: First, what is the criterion for satisfactory work for any individual student in the group? Second, what will constitute a satisfactory proportion of the students meeting this criterion? The following is the process of criterion-referenced group summative evaluation:

1. Access of pre-test data for the experimental group(s), and if used, for the control group(s). (This data should have been generated during the pre-engagement phase of instruction.)

2. Administration of the post-tests to the experimental group, and if used, to the control group(s).

3. Reference to the research design in use to insure the appropriate choice of data analysis procedure. As already noted, while the most sophisticated of the research designs available is termed the Solomon Pre-Test, Post-Test Multiple Group Design, it is seldom that conditions in the instructional setting allow for this complex plan, and a compromise in the design such as that shown in Table 16 in page 123 is usually necessary.

4. Analysis of the pre- and post-test data for the control and experimental groups according to the specifications of the research design. Table 30 shows an example of research outcomes comparing experimental and control group pre- and post-test means. Assume that the data relate to instructional objectives stipulating passing an end-of-course 40-point test with at least 65 percent accuracy.

Table 30. Evaluation Findings Using a Pre-Test, Post-Test, Control Group Research Design

	Pre-Test	*Instruction*	*Post-Test*
Experimental Group:	**10**	**X**	**30**
Control Group:	**10**		**14**

In table 30, while students in the experimental and control groups started with the same mean of 10 (25 percent accuracy for a test with a highest possible score of 40) in the pre-test, the experimental students scored with a mean of 30 (70 percent accuracy) on the post-test—in contrast to the students in the control group, who scored with a mean of 14 (35 percent accuracy). Assume that in this fictitious example repeated measures ANOVA outcomes show that while the pre-test-post-test difference for the experimental group is statistically significant, that for the control group is not. Also assume that while the two groups did not differ statistically significantly on their pre-test scores, they do so on their post-test scores. Such outcomes would suggest that criterion-referenced gains for the experimental group are likely not due to such extraneous factors as test-retest effects, history, or chance, but to the activities carried out during engagement.

5. Determination of the difference in the proportions of students in the control and experimental groups who met the passing criteria. Assume that 90 percent of the students in the instruction group obtained a score of 30 or higher and that 2 percent of those in the control group did so—and that the two proportions differ statistically significantly.

Given the above findings, the instructor has all the information he or she needs to decide a) whether the experimental group students have met the objectives of instruction, and b) whether or not their success is due to the activities of the engagement effort. He or she can conclude that the students in the instruction group have met the instructional objectives, and that the engagement interventions are responsible for their doing so.

Group Norm-Referenced Testing. Group norm-referenced testing is often used to determine school and instructor effectiveness by comparing student group performance within a classroom or school with that of some other, usually larger, norm, group.

The instructor can use the same research design appearing in Table 30 with normed data in one of two ways: first, he or she can form the control group himself or herself and then use pre- and post-test norm-based percentile or z-scores to carry out the control-experimental group comparisons. In the second approach, the investigator can forego his or her formation of a control group and use the norm group as a kind of control against which to gauge the success of his or her students in mastering instructional material. It is the second alternative that is typically involved when the term *norm-referenced testing* is used—and it is the process of norm-referenced testing in this sense of the term that will be described next.

The following is the procedure the instructor follows for norm-referenced summative evaluation of group academic achievement. He or she:

1. Compares the instruction groups' pre-test performance with that of the norm group through the use of percentile scores or z-scores.

2. Administers the post-test to the instruction group.

3. Determines the post-test percentile scores or z-scores of the members of the instruction group.

4. Determines the difference between the pre- and post-test percentile or z-test scores.

As noted by Gabriel, Anderson, Benson, Gordon, Hill, Pfannnestiel and Stonehill (1985), one potential limitation of norm-referenced testing in group summative evaluation has to do with such threats to internal validity as history and test-retest effects. First, in the typical case, the instructor does not randomly assign students to either the instruction or norm groups, rendering the design, at best, quasi-experimental in nature. Second, the instructor typically does not have access to norm group pre- and post-test data collected concurrently with that of the experimental group—information in the absence of which he or she cannot control for such threats to internal validity as those noted above. These conditions can render norm-referenced evaluation findings uninterpretable or misleading. In fact, because the typical norm-referenced evaluation effort lacks this key information, the US Department of Education has discontinued the use of norm-referenced testing in the evaluation of any of a number of federally funded educational programs (Slavin, 1999).

It should be emphasized that the above reservations concerning norm-referenced testing do not hold when concurrently generated pre- and post-test information is available for both the norm and experimental groups.

Thus, the process of summative evaluation of student academic achievement involves the use of criterion-referenced as well as norm-referenced testing, and it can involve the individual student as well as groups of students. When groups of students are the targets of evaluation, inferential statistics are used to control for chance effects, and comparisons between control and experimental groups are used to control for threats to the internal validity of findings.

Often, a student fails to meet performance criteria stipulated in the instructional objectives at hand. When this occurs, the educator may want to ascertain the reason or reasons for the failure. To do so, he or she can examine deficits in student learning behavior during engagement that may have contributed to the problem. The matter of student learning behavior relative to academic achievement is considered next.

Student Learning Behavior. The major aspects of learning behavior relative to academic achievement considered in the following paragraphs are the academic self-regulation, mental acuity and emotional functioning that students bring to bear on their attempts to master material presented in the engagement phase of instruction.

Academic Self-Regulation. As noted in Chapter 2, academic self-regulation consists of motivation to do well in school, the realistic setting of academic goals, the use of effective strategies in pursuit of these goals, self-monitoring to gauge the effectiveness of the strategies used, and strategy adjustment as necessary. Lowered motivation and off-task behavior are opposite to academic self-regulation and are interpretable as deficits in this area.

The instructor can conduct a retrospective evaluation of student self-regulated learning behavior by reference to entries in the *Student Observation Record (SOR,* shown in Table 24) related to self-regulation. The information the instructor seeks in this regard is whether the student manifested any difficulty in self-regulation during engagement; and if so, the seriousness of the problem and the degree of success the instructor experienced in addressing it. An entry in the *SOR* showing that in the instructor's estimate a problem in this area was serious enough to interfere with learning but that it was not fully resolved during engagement points to it as a possible contributor to student failure to reach the instructional objectives; it also suggests that the student will likely continue to experience the problem—and that in his or her case, remediation of academic self-regulation may be necessary before he or she can master the material in any additional engagement activity involving the objectives at hand.

Mental Acuity. Mental acuity, or ability, involves the speed with which a student has been able to acquire the information or skill conveyed during engagement, the effectiveness with which he or she has been able to retain and recall the information, and the extensiveness with which he or she can utilize it. As with academic self-regulation, the instructor can conduct a retrospective assessment of student mental acuity by reviewing the entries in the *SOR* related to this student attribute. The information the instructor seeks in this respect is whether the student manifested any problem in mental acuity during engagement; and if so, the seriousness of the problem and the degree of success the instructor experienced in addressing it. As before, an entry in the *SOR* showing that in the instructor's estimate the problem was serious enough to interfere with learning but that it was not fully resolved during engagement points to it as a possible contributor to failure to reach the instructional objectives; it also suggests that the student will likely continue to experience the problem—and that remediation of mental acuity may be necessary before the student can benefit from any additional engagement activity involving the objectives at hand.

     Emotional Functioning. As with academic self-regulation and mental acuity, the instructor can review entries in the *SOR* for indications of emotional dysfunction manifested by the student during engagement. As before, an entry indicative of a serious, not fully resolved problem in this area during engagement is indicative that remediation of emotional functioning will likely be necessary before the student can benefit from similar instruction in any additional engagement activity.

     In the case of group summative evaluation, if he or she hypothesizes that factors such as self-regulation and emotional functioning are interrelated in their effect on the academic achievement of his or her students, the instructor may decide to use path analysis to test for these possible influences. A hypothetical outcome of such an analysis might be as that shown in Figure 26.

     The fictitious outcomes appearing in Figure 26 show an effect of engagement activities on academic achievement for the instructional group—even after academic self-regulation, emotional functioning and academic achievement pre-test performance have been statistically controlled. Of additional interest, the outcomes show that the effect of self-regulation on post-test scores has been partly through mediation of emotional functioning.

     Thus, summative evaluation of student academic performance involves a determination of the degree to which students have benefited from instruction. In this respect, the interest lies in whether or not they have reached the instructional objectives (criterion-referenced summative evaluation), or in how their performance compares with that of other students (norm-referenced summative evaluation). In the case in which a student has failed to benefit from instruction, summative evaluation addresses the manner in which such student processes as self-regulatory, mental, and emotional functioning may have contributed to the problem.

Summative evaluation also examines the degree to which factors besides the student's learning behavior have contributed to the students' academic achievement. When a student fails to attain the instructional objectives at hand, this part of the post-engagement phase addresses the manner in which the instructor's performance, the quality of support provided by administrators and staff, or the effectiveness of the procedures used in the instructional process have contributed to the failure.

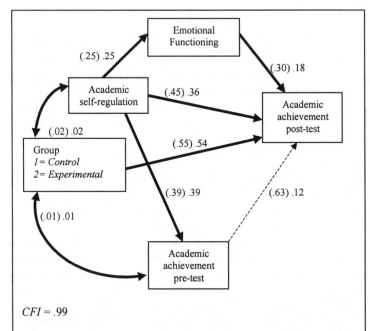

CFI = .99

Figure 26. Hypothetical Path Analysis Outcomes of the Effects of Instruction, Controlling for SES, Self-Regulation, Academic Achievement, and Pre-Test Scores. The dashed linkage depicts the statistical control of pre-test effects. The curved linkages indicate possible non-causal relations.

The Process of Summative Evaluation of Instructor and School Support Performance

To evaluate his or her own performance as well as the support offered by the school's administration and staff during the recently completed engagement effort, the instructor can examine the *Instructor-System Observation Record (ISOR)*, shown in Table 25, to review any problem encountered in these areas during engagement, the level of seriousness of the problem, and the degree to which the problem was resolved during the engagement phase. The *ISOR* makes provisions for recording critical incidents involving the instructor's own pedagogical skill and subject matter expertise as well as the level of commitment he or she experienced during the engagement phase. The form also makes provisions for recording information regarding the quality of the support provided by the administration and school support staff during engagement.

An entry in the *ISOR* to the effect that in the instructor's judgment a problem encountered was serious enough to interfere with the success of the engagement effort but that its was not successfully addressed is indicative that the problem was not fully resolved—and that some sort of action will likely be necessary to improve the instructor's performance or the quality of school support before much more than before can be easily accomplished in any further engagement activity.

The Process of Summative Evaluation of the Procedures Used in Instruction

To evaluate the procedures used in the instructional endeavor, the instructor can examine the *Procedural Observation Record (POR)*, shown in Table 26, to review any problem encountered with the design or execution of the needs assessment, diagnostic procedures, instructional objectives, task analysis, assessment methodology or engagement plan employed. The instructor can also review the *POR* to examine the seriousness of any problem encountered, and the degree to which the problem was resolved during instructional process.

An entry in the *POR* to the effect that in the instructor's judgment the problem was serious enough to interfere with the success of the instructional process but that its was not successfully addressed is indicative that the problem was not fully resolved—and that some sort of action will likely be necessary to insure the likelihood of success in future implementation of the instructional effort.

Decision-Making on the Basis of Data Analysis Outcomes in Summative evaluation

As noted in Chapter 3, there are at least six major uses to which evaluation in instruction can be put: *instructional improvement, professional accountability and development, administrative supervision, examination of relations of student performance with classroom processes, protection of student interests,* and *awarding of merit pay.* As the term is used here, decision-making on the basis of summative evaluation outcomes refers to a determination of action to be taken to insure the success of subsequent instructional efforts.

REMEDIATION

Remediation becomes necessary when problems identified through summative evaluation are judged serious enough to have interfered with learning—and to be likely to continue to do so unless resolved before undertaking any further teaching-learning activity of the same type as that enacted in the just completed engagement phase of instruction.

The Process of Remediation

The process of remediation in instruction is similar in key respects to that of the teaching–learning effort described throughout this text; it involves, as a minimum, the following activities:

1. Formulation of the objectives to be sought through the remedial effort.

2. Allocation of time and resources for the remedial effort.

3. Development of formative and summative evaluation criteria and methodology for the assessment of the success of the remedial effort.

4. Development of remedial interventions.

5. Execution and formative evaluation of the remedial interventions.

6. Summative evaluation of the remedial effort.

Remediation Targets

As already noted, there are four specific targets of remediation the instructor can identify in the post-engagement phase of instruction: the student's academic performance, the instructor' own performance, the support provided by school administrators and support staff, and any of the procedures or activities of the three phases of instruction. Regardless of the target, the remediation process always involves the six steps noted above.

Student Remediation

In extreme cases involving student remediation, trained specialists such as school psychologists and speech therapists may have to play leading roles in the planning and execution of the remedial activities. Also involving student remediation, if in the judgment of those in the best position to decide, a student can be helped to overcome problems identified through summative evaluation before the next juncture (next lesson, next course, next grade level) in his or her educational program, then the necessary time and resources can be allocated to engage the student in the remedial process before coming to the next educational juncture.

Assuming successful completion of the remedial effort, the student can join his or her peers without delay in the next stage in his or her educational sequence. Otherwise, it may be necessary for the student to be held back for further remedial work, following successful completion of which he or she can join the next cohort in his or her educational program. This last disposition differs from the practice of *retention*, in which a low-performing student is required to repeat a course or school year. The literature generally seems to argue against retention, consistently showing that even when the practice yields any degree of improvement, the academic advantage disappears within a short period of time (Bell, 1972; Gredler, 1984; Holmes and Matthews, 1984). In this writer's view, the problem may be that retention too often takes place without any attempt at remediation, involving simply the repetition of a previously ineffective set of instructional activities in a stated effort to bring the student to the desired level of performance. By contrast, the remedial approach alluded to above involves the active correction of deficit in such areas of student learning behavior as self-regulation, mental acuity and emotional functioning—and the identification of instructional methodology better suited to a particular student before attempting to bring him or her to the desired performance level in subsequent engagement activity.

Instructor Remediation

In the case in which the instructor perceives a need to improve his or her performance in instruction, he or she can seek to address the matter through one or more avenues available for the purpose. Callahan, Clark and Kellough (1998) listed a number of ways in which the instructor can seek to improve his or her teaching performance. One way is through *mentoring* or *peer coaching*, in which a) the teacher and mentor meet in a pre-observation conference and discuss the behavior to be observed b) the mentor observes and coaches the instructor to help him or her to improve in whatever area is being addressed and c) the mentor observes the teacher once more and in a post-observation conference discusses the progress made and whatever work remains to be done. A second avenue the instructor can follow for self-improvement involves *in-service workshops*, in which training and remedial work in specific areas are offered at the school or district level. A third avenue for instructor self-improvement involves *workshops and clinics* offered by professional organizations. Finally, the instructor can seek assistance in his or her self-remediation effort through *graduate study* through which the instructor can become familiar with the latest theory and research findings concerning the issues at hand.

School Support Remediation

When the instructor seeks to address deficiencies in the quality of support provided by school administrators or support staff, the likelihood of his or her success increases if he or she approaches the problem *constructively*—that is, if he or she refrains from personalizing the problem ("What happened is your fault"), simply presenting the administrator or staff member with a complaint ("Things can't go on like this") or presenting him or her with an ultimatum ("Unless you change the way you do things, I'll complain to your supervisor")—and instead a) presents the problem objectively by referring to a common goal shared by the instructor and the administrator or staff member, and points to the problem as an obstacle to the common goal; b) shows the administrator or staff member how addressing the problem will benefit the school as well as the student; c) proposes a number of attractive alternatives for the solution of the problem; and d) shows a willingness to work with the administrator or staff member to address the difficulty. It may be noted that the instructor can apply many of these same principles when he or she approaches a pupil with the task of embarking on remedial work to address any set of student academic deficiencies.

Methodological Adjustments

Methodological adjustments involve modifications made in the procedures of the pre-engagement, engagement and post-engagement phases of instruction. There are three reasons for making such modifications. First, it is possible that, by reference to the *Procedural Observation Record* shown in Table 26, difficulty in student academic achievement can be traced back to some procedure forming part of one of the three phases of instruction.

A second reason for such modifications is that theoretical and technological advances are constantly being made in virtually every aspect of the three phases of the instructional process, and procedural modifications are often necessary to keep up with of such advances. Finally, even in the absence of externally originated advances, the instructor's own thinking is likely to evolve concerning different aspects of the instructional process, and he or she may deem it appropriate to undertake their "fine tuning" as his or her experience and thinking suggest.

The preceding pages discussed the matter of student, instructor, school support and methodological remediation in the face of student failure to reach some set of instructional objectives. In the this respect, it is interesting to note that remediation may be necessary even though students successfully meet the objectives of instruction. Often, to achieve some set of educational goals, extraordinary efforts are necessary to overcome obstacles encountered in the course of engagement. But such efforts may not be possible in all future cases in which the same obstacles arise, and hence, prior to subsequent engagement activity, it may be necessary to take steps to prevent their recurrence. Thus, following engagement, remediation of some aspect of the instructional process may be required despite the fact that students have successfully met a lesson's instructional objectives.

SUMMARY

To recapitulate, the post-engagement phase of instruction involves a summative evaluation of the success of the activities of the process of instruction. The post-engagement phase also involves a) an examination of the manner in which the behaviors of students, instructor, and school support staff have contributed to or impeded the success of the teaching-learning effort; and b) steps taken to address deficiencies in student performance. In addition, problems identified through summative evaluation can often be traced to some procedure involved in any of the three phases of instruction, and thus, these procedures can themselves become targets for remediation or adjustment.

Summative evaluation has requirements that must be met if the information it generates is to serve any useful purpose. To generate useful evaluative information, the instructor must insure that the instruments he or she uses for the collection and recording of information are valid and reliable, that the research design and data generation method he or she uses promote the internal validity of the findings; and, in the case of group evaluation, that the method of data analysis he or she uses address the external validity of evaluation outcomes. The success of remedial initiatives conducted in the post-engagement phase of instruction depends on the degree to which the evaluation effort meets these demands.

Finally, summative evaluation and remediation are integral parts of the teaching-learning effort because only through the feedback and self-correction afforded by these two components of the post-engagement phase of instruction can the teacher continually improve the quality of his or her educational efforts—and thus continually raise the likelihood that his or her efforts will significantly contribute to the academic success of his or her students.

POSTSCRIPT: THE *t*-TEST FOR MEANS

The *t*-test is a statistical procedure used for the comparison of two means. When the means belong to two different groups, the researcher uses the *t-test for unrelated samples (TTUS)* to determine whether the groups differ statistically significantly. For example, an instructor can use the TTUS to determine whether a statistically significant difference exists in mathematics achievement between male and female students. The instructor can also use the TTUS when a) using one instructional and one control group and administering a post-test following instruction but no pre-test, as shown in Table 18; and b) assigning the students at random to the two groups. When the data do not meet the statistical assumptions of the TTUS (as with ANOVA, normal distribution; equal variances; and large sample, usually consisting of 30 or more cases) the investigator can use the Mann-Whitney *U*-test in its place. Although less powerful than the TTUS, the *U*-test is not subject to the relatively more restrictive assumptions of the TTUS.

When only one group is involved in the analysis and the investigator wants to test whether it differs across two time points on the same variable, he or she can use the *t-test for related samples (TTRS)* to perform the pre- post-test comparison. For example, he or she can use the TTRS to determine whether a statistically significant difference exists in a group of students in writing skills at the beginning and the end of the school year. The TTRS controls for possible confounding pre-test effects, thus enabling the instructor to more reliably gauge the effects of instruction on post-test outcomes than would be possible examining only post-test performance. When the data do not meet the assumptions of the TTRS (as with the TTUS, normal distribution; equal variances; and large sample, usually consisting of 30 or more cases), the investigator can use the *Wilcoxen z-test for two matched samples* to make the comparison.

The reader will note some important limitations in the *t*-tests for means for use in summative evaluation. On the one hand, the TTUS and its *U*-test counterpart do not control for test-retest effects; on the other, the TTRS and its *z*-test counterpart do not afford control-experimental group comparisons. But as already noted, particularly in the case of quasi-experimental designs, the essential elements of research design in summative evaluation are the comparison of experimental and control groups and the control for pre-test effects. These are requirements of summative evaluation that only the Analysis of Variance, described earlier in this chapter, can meet.

APPENDIX A

Parental Inducement of Academic Self-Regulation (PIASR) Scale and Multidimensional Scales of Self-Regulation

Parental Inducement of Academic Self-Regulation (PIASR) Scale
(From Martinez-Pons, 1996)

This questionnaire is designed to help us to study how students learn and how they see the world around them. There are no right or wrong answers in this questionnaire. The value of your answers depends on how closely they reflect your feelings, so be as candid as you can in your responses.

How true of your *MOTHER* are the following things? (If you live with a female guardian, answer the questions with her in mind in place of "mother".) Use this scale to show your responses:

not at all true of my mother	*a little true of my mother*	*moderately true of my mother*	*very true of my mother*	*completely true of my mother*
1	*2*	*3*	*4*	*5*

1. Shows an interest in learning new things (for example, reading books, magazines or newspapers; or listening to the news or to discussion programs on radio or TV)
2. Sets clear goals before she starts doing something new (carefully plans what she is going to do)

3. Uses effective methods for doing what she wants to do
4. Evaluates herself to see how effective she is when trying to do something
5. Switches to a different method of doing something when the one she is using is not working well

How true of your *FATHER* are the following things? (If you live with a male guardian, answer the questions with him in mind in place of "father".) Use this scale to show your responses:

not at all true of my father	*a little true of my father*	*moderately true of my father*	*very true of my father*	*completely of my father*
1	*2*	*3*	*4*	*5*

6. Shows an interest in learning new things (for example, reading books, magazines or newspapers; or listening to the news or to discussion programs on radio or TV)
7. Sets clear goals before he starts doing something new (carefully plans what he/she is going to do)
8. Uses effective methods for doing what he wants to do
9. Evaluates himself to see how effective he is when trying to do something
10. Switches to a different method of doing something when the one he is using is not working well

Sometimes students have trouble doing any of the following things when the task seems too hard or unfamiliar. Whenever this happens to you, how much do your parents reassure you, or "cheer you on", to encourage you to not give up trying? (If you live with a female or male guardian, answer the questions with her or him in mind in place of "mother" or "father".) Use this scale to show your responses:

not at all	*a little*	*a moderate amount*	*a lot*	*a great deal*
1	*2*	*3*	*4*	*5*

Whenever you have difficulty in *motivating* yourself to do your schoolwork,
11. how much does your mother encourage you to not give up trying?
12. how much does your father encourage you to not give up trying?

Whenever you have difficulty in *setting realistic goals* to help you in doing your schoolwork,
13. how much does your mother encourage you to not give up trying?
14. how much does your father encourage you to not give up trying?

Whenever you have difficulty in *mastering new academic material,*
15. how much does your mother encourage you to not give up trying?
16. how much does your father encourage you to not give up trying?

Whenever you have difficulty in *evaluating* the quality of your schoolwork,
17. how much does your mother encourage you to not give up trying?
18. how much does your father encourage you to not give up trying?

Whenever you have difficulty in *finding a better way* of mastering new academic material,
19. how much does your mother encourage you to not give up trying?
20. how much does your father encourage you to not give up trying?

How involved are your parents in doing the following things? (If you live with a female or male guardian, answer the questions with her or him in mind in place of "mother" or "father".) Use this scale to show your responses:

not at all involved	*a little involved*	*moderately involved*	*much involved*	*greatly involved*
1	*2*	*3*	*4*	*5*

Teaching you ways you can use to motivate yourself to do your schoolwork when there are other interesting things to do
38. mother
39. father

Teaching you how to set realistic goals when doing your schoolwork
40. mother
41. father

Teaching you effective methods you can use to master new academic material
41. mother
42. father

Teaching you ways you can use to evaluate the quality of your schoolwork
43. mother
44. father

Teaching you ways of switching strategies when the one you are using to master new academic material is not working well
45. mother
46. father

Rewarding you when you show interest in doing or learning something new in school
47. mother
48. father

Rewarding you when you set realistic goals to help you in doing your schoolwork
49. mother
50. father

Rewarding you when you use effective methods of mastering new academic material
51. mother
52. father

Rewarding you when you evaluate the quality of your schoolwork
53. mother
54. father

Rewarding you when you find a more effective method of mastering new academic material
55. mother
56. father

Multidimensional Scale of Self-Regulation
(From Martinez-Pons, 1996)

For each item below, indicate how often you do the thing indicated when the condition shown comes up. Use this scale to show your responses.

I never do this	*I sometimes do this*	*I often do this*	*I almost always do this*	*I always do this*
1	*2*	*3*	*4*	*5*

How often do you...

1. stop yourself from skipping school when you feel bored or upset?
2. get teachers to help you when you get stuck on schoolwork?
3. get another student to help you when you get stuck on schoolwork?
4. get adults to help you when you have social problems?
6. get a friend to help you when you have social problems?
7. finish school assignments by deadlines?
8. study when there are other interesting things to do?
9. concentrate on school subjects?
10. take class notes of class instruction?
11. use the library to get information for class assignments?
12. plan your school work?
13. organize your school work?
14. rehearse to remember information presented in class and textbooks?
15. arrange a place to study without distractions?
16. motivate yourself to do school work when there are other interesting things to do?
17. participate in class discussions?

APPENDIX B

Self-Regulation Scale of Emotional Intelligence (SRSEI)

(From Martinez-Pons, 2000)

Use this scale show how much you agree with each of the following statements:
completely disagree   *completely agree*
      1   *2*   *3*   *4*   *5*   *6*   *7*

1. I can maintain better control of my life if I keep in touch with my moods and emotions.
2. I am able to overcome any distractions that arise as I try to keep in touch with my moods and emotions.
3. I find it worthwhile to spend the time and effort necessary to keep in touch with my moods and emotions
4. I am able maintain better control of my life if I am able to sort out my moods and emotions.
5. I am able overcome any obstacles that arise as I try sort out my moods and emotions
6. I find it worthwhile to spend the time and effort necessary to sort out my moods and emotions
7. I can maintain better control of my life if I can effectively manage my moods and emotions
8. I am able overcome any obstacles that arise as I try to manage my moods and emotions.
9. I find it worthwhile to spend the time and effort necessary to manage my moods and emotions

How often do you try to reach or maintain the following goals relative to being in touch with your moods and emotions? Use this scale to show your responses:

I never try to reach						*I'm always trying to reach*
or maintain this goal						*or maintain this goal*
1	*2*	*3*	*4*	*5*	*6*	*7*

10. in general, to be in touch with your moods and emotions
11. to know how you are feeling at any point in time
12. to be aware when you are switching between one emotion and another
13. to be able to tell how your behavior is being affected by your emotions
14. to be able to tell *how strongly* you feel about something
15. to keep a daily record of your moods and emotions

How often do you take the following steps in trying to keep in touch with your moods and emotions? Use this scale to show your responses:

						I'm always doing this
						(this is part of
I never do this at all						*my daily routine)*
1	*2*	*3*	*4*	*5*	*6*	*7*

16. taking "time out" to reflect about how you are feeling
17. asking yourself, "how am I feeling now?"
18. ascertaining your feelings by noting your heartbeat, breathing and other bodily processes
19. avoiding the suppression or "squelching" of your moods and emotions
20. being on the alert for early signs of emotional distress
21. ascertaining your feelings by noting how you are behaving
22. observing others' reactions to your behavior to determine how your moods and emotions are affecting you
23. keeping a written record of daily changes in your moods and emotions

How often do you try to reach or maintain the following goals in sorting out your moods and emotions? Use this scale to show your responses:

						I'm always doing this
						(this is part of
I never do this at all						*my daily routine)*
1	*2*	*3*	*4*	*5*	*6*	*7*

24. in general, to sort out the various moods and emotions you are experiencing at any given time
25. to be able to tell the number of moods and emotions you are experiencing
26. to tell how the moods and emotions you are experiencing differ from each other
27. to determine the strength of each mood or emotion you are experiencing
28. to determine how your different moods and emotions interact to affect your general state of mind

How often do you take the following steps in trying to sort out your moods and emotions? Use this scale to show your responses:

						I'm always doing this (this is part of
I never do this at all						*my daily routine)*
1	*2*	*3*	*4*	*5*	*6*	*7*

29. developing a clear idea of the range of moods and emotions you are capable of experiencing
30. naming the different moods and emotions you are experiencing at any given time
31. noting what action the different moods or emotions seemes to elicit on your part
32. noting what happens just before you begin experiencing each mood or emotion
33. noting what is happening during the time that you are experiencing each mood or emotion
34. noting how each mood or emotion is affecting your ability to think clearly
35. noting how each mood or emotion is affecting your ability to complete a task

How often do you try to reach or maintain the following goals relative to your moods or emotions? Use this scale to show your responses:

						I'm always doing this (this is part of
I never do this at all						*my daily routine)*
1	*2*	*3*	*4*	*5*	*6*	*7*

36. in general, to effectively manage your moods and emotions
37. to increase or decrease the strength of a mood or emotion to enable you to regain or maintain your "peace of mind"
38. to increase or decrease the strength of the mood or emotion to enable you to more efficiently perform a task
39. to stop a negative mood or emotion from worsening to enable you to maintain or regain "peace of mind"
40. to stop a negative mood or emotion from worsening in order to arrest deterioration of your performance on some task
41. to compensate for the negative effect of some mood or emotion to enable you to regain your "peace of mind"
42. to compensate for the negative effect of some mood or emotion in order to enable you to perform some task
43. to use information from a daily record of your moods and emotions to plan future activities.

How often do you use the following strategies in trying to manage your moods and emotions? Use this scale to show your responses:

						I'm always doing this (this is part of
I never do this at all						*my daily routine)*
1	*2*	*3*	*4*	*5*	*6*	*7*

44. challenging the thought precipitaing a negative mood or emotion (e.g., reinterpreting a negative situation "to see its bright side")
45. modifying a situation eliciting a bad mood or emotion (e.g., turning down a loud radio or TV)
46. talking about your feelings with someone
47. imagining a pleasant experience to offset a negative feeling

48. working on a hobby
49. thinking of good things you have done
50. actively avoiding situations that depress you
51. taking action to prevent things that depress you from taking place
52. doing things at which you are good in order to help you feel better about yourself
53. helping others in need of help to help you overcome a feeling of depression

In using some strategy to keep in touch with, sort out or regulate your moods or emotions, how often do you do the following things? Use this scale to show your responses:

I never do this   *I always do this*
                    1   2   3   4   5   6   7

54. checking to make sure that you are properly using the strategy
55. checking to ensure that the strategy you are using is having its desired effect
56. adjusting your behavior to better use the strategy
57. switching to a more effective strategy if you notice that the one you are using is not working well

APPENDIX C

Five-Component Scale of Self-Regulation (FCSSR) and Self-Regulated Transfer Scale (SRTS)

Five-Component Scale of Self-Regulation (FCSSR)
(From Martinez-Pons, 2000)

Use this scale to show HOW MANY OF YOUR FAVORITE PASTIMES (hobbies, games, being with friends, watching TV, movies etc.) you are willing to give up to accomplish the following when doing your academic work:

				as many of my
none of my	*some of my*	*a few of my favorite*	*many of my*	*favorite pastimes*
favorite pastimes	*favorite pastimes*	*my favorite pastimes*	*favorite pastimes*	*as necessary*
1	*2*	*3*	*4*	*5*

1. getting some idea of what the material is about
2. meeting the school's passing requirements
3. mastering the material so you can get high grades in school
4. mastering the material so you can apply it to other areas of your life and your academic work

5. Use this scale to show the amount of effort you typically put into your academic work:

1 = not enough effort to accomplish much of anything

2 = just enough effort to say I tried

3 = just enough effort to get some idea of what the material is about

4 = just enough effort to meet the school's passing requirements

5 = enough effort to get high grades in school

6 = all the effort necessary to master the material so I can apply it to other academic work

7 = all the effort necessary to master the material so I can apply it to my life even out of school

Use this scale to show the extent to which you agree with the following statements:

completely disagree						*completely agree*
1	*2*	*3*	*4*	*5*	*6*	*7*

6. When doing my academic work, I always set goals to guide in my efforts

Whenever I set goals for doing my academic work, I...

7. make sure that the goals I set for myself involve objectives I have not yet attained, rather than things I have already achieved

8. check with others (parents, teachers) to make sure that the goals I set for myself are realistic

9. set goals that are so clear that I can describe them to someone else without difficulty

10. set goals for myself that go beyond what I have already achieved.

11. set goals that present me with a challenge

12. check with others (parents, teachers) to make sure that the goals I set for myself are clear

13. give myself plenty of time to achieve the goals I set for myself

14. set goals that I think I have a good chance of achieving

15. check with others (parents, teachers) to make sure that I give myself enough time to work on the goals I set for myself

16. am able to clearly distinguish my academic goals from one-another

17. check with others (parents, teachers) to make sure that my goals involve objectives that I have not yet attained

18. make sure that the number of goals I set for myself is manageable

19. try to organize the goals I set for myself so that attaining one makes it easy to attain another

20. set a definite deadline (date, time) for reaching each goal I set for myself

21. can't make sense from one day to the next of the goals I set for myself

Some students use the following strategies to perform their academic work, while others prefer not to use strategies such as these. How often do *you* use the strategies listed to perform your academic work? Use this scale to show your responses:

never the time	almost never	sometimes	frequently	much of the time	almost all the time	all
1	2	3	4	5	6	7

22. getting your teachers to help you when you get stuck on academic work

23. getting other students to help you when you get stuck on academic work

24. getting adults to help you when you get stuck on academic work

25. getting a friend to help you when you get stuck on academic work

26. motivating yourself to do your academic work when you find the material difficult

27. motivating yourself to do your academic work when you find the material boring

28. motivating yourself to do your academic work when you are tired or fatigued

29. motivating yourself to do your academic work when there are other interesting things to do

30. taking notes of class instruction

31. using the library to get information for class assignments

32. planning your academic work

33. organizing your academic work

34. rehearsing to remember information presented in class or textbooks

35. arranging a place to study without distractions

36. taking steps to be able to continue with your academic work when you find the material very hard

37. taking steps to be able to continue with your academic work when you find the material very boring

38. taking steps to be able to continue with your academic work when you are tired or fatigued

39. taking steps to continue with your academic work when there are other interesting things to do

When using a strategy such as note taking or underlining to do your academic work, how often do you do the following things? Use this scale to show your responses:

almost never	*never*	*sometimes*	*frequently*	*much of the time*	*almost all the time*	*all the time*
1	*2*	*3*	*4*	*5*	*6*	*7*

40. checking to see if you are performing the strategy in the way it's supposed to be carried out

41. having alternative strategies available in case the one you use does not work

42. comparing your performance with that of others to check to see if you are performing the strategy in the way it's supposed to be carried out

43. checking your work to see if the strategy is having its desired effect

44. comparing the strategy to other methods to see which is more effective

45. keeeping records of your performance so you can see how much progress you are making

46. trying out chapter-end problems in textbooks to see how well you have mastered the material

47. taking old tests to see how well you know the material

48. adjusting your behavior as necessary to better use the strategy

49. switching to a more effective strategy when the one you are using is not working

50. reviewing your answers on a test to see what mistakes you have made, if any

51. determining what you did wrong when you find you have not suceeded in mastering the material

52. taking action to rectify the reason for whatever mistakes you have identified

53. checking to make sure you have rectified the mistake

54. rewarding yourself for correcting the mistake

Self-Regulated Transfer Scale (SRTS)
(From Martinez-Pons, 2000)

How true of you are the following things? Use this scale to show your responses:

not at all true of me		*partly true of me*		*completely true of me*
1	*2*	*3*	*4*	*5*

1. Seeking out challenging, novel learning experiences.

Whenever you find yourself in a challenging, novel learning situation:

2. analyzing the situation to see how much of what you already know you can use to help to master new material
3. analyzing the situation to see how much of it requires new learning on your part in order for you to master new material
4. combining and using previously learned material to help you to master new material
5. acquiring some skills as necessary to help you learn further material
6. combining and using newly acquired skills to help you to master new material
7. testing yourself to see if what you are doing is helping you to learn new material

APPENDIX D

NELS:88 Items Extracted for the Teacher Job Satisfaction Study, and Items Extracted for the Family and Student Outcome Study

Items Extracted for the Teacher Job Satisfaction Study

Principal's Behavior

F1T4_1F 'Principal poor at getting resources'
F1T4_1G 'Principal deals with outside pressures'
F1T4_1H 'Principal makes plans & carries them out'
F1T4_1O 'Principal knows what kind of school he wants'
F1T4_2I 'Principal lets staff know what's expected'
F1T4_2M 'Principal consult staff before decisions'
F1T4_1J 'Goals/priorities for the school are clear'
F1T4_1L 'Staff members recognized for job well done'

Help By Others in Developing Teaching Skills

F1T4_8A 'Extent principal helped improve teaching'
F1T4_8B 'Extent department chair improved teaching'
F1T4_8C 'Extent other administratrs improved teachng'

F1T4_8D 'Extent department colleagues improved teaching'
F1T4_8E 'Extent colleagues outside improved teaching'
F1T4_8F 'Extent personnel group improved teaching'

Student Behavior
F1T4_1E 'Student misbehavior interferes with teaching'
F1T4_1M 'Tardiness/cutting interfere with teachng'
F1T4_1I 'Students incapable of learning material'
F1T4_2N 'Students attitudes reduce academic success'
F1T4_2O 'Drug/alcohol use interferes with teaching'
F1T4_3A 'Degree tardiness a problem with students'
F1T4_3B 'Degree absenteeism a problem with studnts'
F1T4_3C 'Degree class cutting a problem'
F1T4_3D 'Degree physical conflicts a problem'
F1T4_3E 'Degree gang activities a problem'
F1T4_3F 'Degree robbery or theft a problem'
F1T4_3G 'Degree vandalism a problem with students'
F1T4_3H 'Degree use of alcohol a problem'
F1T4_3I 'Degree use of illegal drugs a problem'
F1T4_3J 'Degree possession of weapons a problem'
F1T4_3K 'Degree physical abuse of teachers a problem'
F1T4_3L 'Degree verbal abuse of teachers a problem'

Self-Efficacy
F1T4_5D 'Different methods can affect achievement'
F1T4_5A 'Can get through to most difficult student'
F1T4_5C 'Change approach if students not doing well'
F1T4_5E 'Little I can do to ensure high achievement'
F1T4_5F 'Teacher making difference in students lives'
F1T4_1D 'Success/failure due to factors beyond me'
F1T4_11D 'Ensure students perform well on tests'
F1T4_11F 'Create lessons students will enjoy learng'

Job Satisfaction
F1T3_15 'How often feels satisfied with job'
F1T4_2G 'Usually look forward to each working day'
F1T4_2J 'Feel waste of time to do best at teachng'

Items Extracted for the Family and Student Outcome Study

Family SES: F1SES
Student Self-Concept: F1CNCPT1
Student Academic Achivement (Reading and Math composite)
     F12XCOMP

References

Adler, M. (1982). *The paidea proposal.* New York: McMillan.

Ammons, R. B. & Ammons, C. H. (1962). The quick test (QT): provisional manual. *Psychological Reports Monograph Supplement 1-V11.*

Anastasi, A. (1982). *Psychological testing (5th ed.).* New York: McMillan.

Anderson, J. R., Reder, L. M. & Simon, H. A. (1996). Situated learning and education. *Educational Researcher, 25,* 5-11.

Anderson, L. et al. (1979). *Dimensions in classroom management derived from recent research.* R&D Report No. 6006. ERIK document number ED175860.

Anderson, R. C. & Faust, G. W. (1973). *Educational psychology: The science of instruction and learning.* New York: Dodd, Mead & Company.

Andrews, J. B. & Neuroth, R. (1988, October). *Environmentally related health hazards in the schools.* Paper presented at the Annual Meeting of the Association of School Business Officials International. Detroit, MI.

236 The Psychology of Teaching and Learning

Appea, S. (1999). *Teacher management of asthmatic children: The contributions of knowledge and self-efficacy.* Unpublished dissertation, Graduate School and University Center, City University of New York.

Archbald, D. A. & Newmann, F. M. (1988). *Beyond standardized testing: Authentic academic achievement in the secondary school.* Reston, VA: National Association of Secondary School Principals.

Asetoyer, C. (1990). *Fetal alcohol syndrome "chemical genocide"* Copenhagen, Denmark: International Secretariat of IWGIA.

Atkinson, R. C. & Shiffrin, R. M. (1968). Human memory: A proposed system and its control processes. In K. W. Spence & J. T. Spence (Eds.), *The psychology of learning and motivation: Advances in research and theory* (vol. 2, pp. 89-195).

Aubrecht, J. D. (1979). *Are student ratings of teacher effectiveness valid? Idea paper no. 2.* Manhattan, KS. Kansas State University, Center for Faculty Evaluation and Development.

Axelrod, S. (1977). *Behavior modification for the classroom teacher.* New York: McGraw-Hill.

Axelrod, S., Hall, R. V. Tooms, A. (1979). Comparison of two common classroom seating arrangements. *Academic Therapy, 15,* 29-36.

Bandura, A. (1977a). *Social learning theory.* Englewood Cliffs, New Jersey: Prentice-Hall.

Bandura, A. (1977b). Self-efficacy: Toward a unifying theory of behavioral change. *Psychological Review, 84,* 191-215.

Bandura, A. (1986). *Social foundations of thought and action.* Englewood Cliffs, N. J.: Prentice-Hall.

Bandura, A. (1989). *Multidimensional scales of perceived self-efficacy (MSPS).* Unpublished manuscript.

Barber, B. R. (1992). *An aristocracy for everyone: The politics of education and the future of America.* New York: Oxford University Press.

Barber, L. W. (1990). Self-assessment. In J. Millman & L. Darling-Hammond (Eds.), *The new handbook of teacher evaluation* (pp. 216-228). Newbury Park, CA: Sage.

Beatrice, J. A. (1999). *Learning to study through critical thinking.* Document retrieved in June, 1999 from World Wide Web site: http://alaike.lcc.hawaii.edu/lrc/lstest.html.

Bell, M. (1972). *A study of the readiness room in a small school district in suburban Detroit, Michigan.* Unpublished doctoral dissertation, Wayne State University.

Bennett, R. E. & Ward, W. C. (Eds.). (1993). *Construction versus choice in cognitive measurement: Issues in constructed response, performance testing, and portfolio assessment.* Hillsdale, NJ: Lawrence Erlbaum Associates.

Bensman, D. (1994). *Lives of the graduates of CentralPark East elementary school. Where have they gone? What did they really learn?* New York: Center for Collaborative Education and the National Center for Restructuring Education, Schools, and Teaching (NCREST) at Columbia University.

Bentler, P.M. & Bonnett, D.G. (1980). Significance tests and goodness of fit in the analysis of covariance matrices. *Psychological Bulletin, 88,* 588-606.

Berliner, D. C. & Biddle, B. J. (1995). *The manufactured crisis.* Reading, Massachusetts: Perseus Books.

Berliner, D. C. & Calfee, R. C. (1998). *Handbook of educational psychology.* New York: Macmillan Library reference USA.

Berndt, T. J. (1999). Friends' influence on students' adjustment to school. *Educational Psychologist, 34,* 15-28.

Bess, J. (1979). *The social psychology of commitment to college teaching.* A paper presented at the Annual Meeting of the American Association for Higher Education, Washington, DC (March).

Biehler, R. F. & Snowman, J. (1986). *Psychology applied to teaching.* Boston: Houghton Mifflin Company.

Bielaczyc, K. (1995). Training in self-explanation and self-regulation strategies: Investigating the effects of knowledge acquisition activities on problem solving. *Cognition and Instruction, 13,* 221-252.

Blake, H. W. (1954). *Class size: A summary of selected studies in elementary and secondary schools.* Unpublished doctoral dissertation. Teachers College, Columbia University. New York.

Bloom, B. S. (1968). Mastery learning. In *Evaluation comment* (Vol.1, No 2). Los Angeles: UCLA, Center for Evaluation of Instructional Programs.

Bloom, B. S., Englehart, M. D., Furst, E. J., Hill, W. H. & Krathwohl, D. R. (1956). *Taxonomy of educational objectives, handbook I: Cognitive domain.* New York: Longmans Green.

Bolig, E. E. & Day, J. D. (1993). Dynamic assessment and giftedness: The promise of assessing training responsiveness. *Roeper Review, 16,* 110-113.

Bracey, G. W. (1993). Assessing the new assessments. *Principal, 72,* 34-36.

Bradley, R.H. Caldwell, B.M. & Rock, S.L. (1988). Home environment and school performance: A ten-year follow-up and examination of three models of environmental action. *Child Development, 59,* 852-867.

Brown, A. L. & Palincsar, A. S. (1989). Guided cooeprative learning and individual knowledge acquisition. In B. Resnick (Ed.), *Knowing, learning, and instruction: Essays in honor of Robert Glaser.* Hillside, NJ: Erlbaum.

Brown, J. S., Collins, A. & Duguld, F. (1989). Situated cognition and the culture of learning: A systems approach to educational testing. *Educational Researcher, 18,* 32-42.

Burke, K. (1999). *How to assess authentic learning.* Columbus, OH: Merrill/Prentice Hall.

Callahan, J. F., Clark, L. H. & Kellough, R. D. (1998). *Teaching in the middle and secondary schools.* Upper Saddle River, NJ: Merrill/Prentice Hall.

Campbell, D. T. & Stanley, J. C. (1963) Experimental and quasi-experimental designs for research on teaching. In N. L. Gage (Ed.), *Handbook of research on Teaching (*pp. 171-246). Chicago: Rand McNally.

Cashin, W. E. (1995). *Student ratings of teaching: the research revisited. IDEA Paper No. 32.*

Ceci, S.. J. & Roazzi, A. (1994). The effects of context on cognition: Postcards from Brazil. In R. J. Sternberg & R. K. Wagner (Eds.), *Mind in context.* New York: Cambridge University Press.

Charles, B. (1978). Some limits to the validity and usefulness of student ratings of teachers: an argument for caution. *Educational Research Quarterly, 3,* 12-27.

Childs, R. A. (1989*). Constructing classroom achievement tests.* ERIC Digest. ED315426.

Cizek, G. J. (1991). Confusion or effusion: A rejoinder to Wiggins. *Phi Delta Kappan, 73,* 150-53.

Cohen, J. (1992). A power primer. *Psychological Bulletin, 112,* 155-159.

Coladarci, T. (1992). Teachers' sense of efficacy and commitment to teaching. *Journal of Experimental Education, 60,* 323-337.

Collins, A., Brown, J. S. & Newman, S. E. (1989). Cognitive apprenticeship: Teaching the crafts of reading, writing, and mathematics. In L. B. Resnick (Ed.), *Knowing, learning, and instruction: Essays in honor of Robert Glaser* (pp. 453-494). Hillsdale, NJ: Erlbaum.

Cook, P. S. (1990). *Alcohol, tobacco, and other drugs my harm the unborn.* Washington, DC: United States Government Printing Office. ISBN: 016026698X.

Corn, B., Hamrung, G., Ellis, A. Kalb, T. & Sperber, K. (1995). Patterns of asthma death and near-death in an inner-city tertiary care teaching hospital. *Journal of Asthma, 31,* 405-412.

Copple, C. (1993). *Learning readiness: Promising strategies.* Washington, DC: Learning Readiness Sourcebook.

Cornwell, J. M. and Manfredo, P. A. (1994). Kolb's learning style theory revisited. *Educational and Psychological Measurement, 54,* 317-327.

Crehan, K. D. (1997, March). *An investigation into the validity of locally developed performance measures in a school assessment program.* Paper presented at the Annual Meeting of the National Council on Measurement in Education, Chicago.

Cronbach, L. J. (1960). *Essentials of psychological testing* (2nd ed.). New York: Harper & Row.

Crow, L. D. & Crow, A. (1954). *Educational psychology.* New York: American Book Company.

Craik, F. I., & Lockhart, R. S. (1972). Levels of processing: A framework for memory research. *Journal of Verbal Learning and Verbal Behavior, 11,* 671-684.

Crehan, K. D. (1997, March). *An investigation of the validity of locally developed performance measures in a school assessment program.* Paper presented at the Annual Meeting of the National Council on Measurement in Education, Chicago.

Curry, L. (1987). *Integrating concepts of cognitive or learning style: A review with attention to psychometric standards.* Ottawa, ON: Canadian College of Health Service Executives.

Curry, L. (1990). A critique of the research on learning styles. *Educational Leadership, 48,* 50-56.

d'Apollonia, S. & Abrami, P. C. (1997). Navigating student ratings of instruction. *American Psychologist, 52,* 1198-1208.

Darling-Hammond, L., Ances, J. & Falk, B. (1995). *Authentic assessment in action: Studies of schools and students at work.* New York: Teachers College Press.

Dasenrau, P. (1979). The development of a learning strategies curriculum. In H. F. O'Neil, Jr. (Ed.). *Learning Strategies,* pp 1-29. New York: Academic Press.

Davis, G. A. (1983). *Educational psychology: Theory and practice.* New York: Random House.

Davies, M., Stankov, L. & Roberts, R. D. (1998). Emotional intelligence: In search of an elusive construct. *Journal of Personality and Social Psychology, 75,* 989-1015.

Derry, S. & Lesgold, A. (1998). Toward a situated social practice model for instructional design. In D. C. Berliner & R. C. Calfee (Eds.), *Handbook of educational psychology.* New York: McMillan Library Reference USA.

Dewey, J. (1916), *Democracy and education: An introdction to the philosophy of education.* New York: MacMillan.

Dochy, F. J. R. C. (1988). The "prior knowledge state" of students and its facilitating effect on learning: theories and research. ERIC_NO: ED387486. Open University, Secretariaat OTIC/COP, Postbus 2960, 6401 DL Heerlen, The Netherlands.

Dobson, J. (1970). *Dare to discipline.* Wheaton, Il: Tyndale House Publishers.

Dreikurs, R. (1998). *Maintaining sanity in the classroom: Classroom management techniques* (2nd ed.). Bristol, Pennsylvania Hemisphere.

Dreikurs, R., & Cassel, P. (1972). *Discipline without tears: What to do with children who misbehave.* New York: Hawthorn Books.

Dunn, R., & Dunn, K. (1978). *Teaching students through their individual learning styles: A practical approach.* Reston, VA: Reston Publishing.

Dunn, R., Dunn, K., & Price, G. (1982). *Manual: Productivity environmental preference survey.* Lawrence, KS: Price Systems.

Dunn, R., Dunn, K., & Price, G. (1985). *Manual: Learning style inventory.* Lawrence, KS: Price Systems.

Dunn, R., Griggs, S. A., Olson, J. Beasley, M. and Gorman, B. S. (1995). A meta-analytic validation of the Dunn and Dunn model of learning style preferences. *Journal of Educational Research, 88,* 353-362.

Dweck, C. S. (1986). Motivational processes affecting learning. *American Psychologist, 41,* (1040-1048).

Dweck, C. S. & Elliott, E. S. (1983). Achivement motivation. In E. M. Hetherington (Ed.), *Handbook of child psychology: Vol 4. Socialization, personality, and social development*(4th ed.) New York: Wiley.

Dweck, C. S. & Leggett, E. L. (1988). A social-cognitive approach to motivation and personality. *Psychological Review, 95,* 256-273.

Dweck, C. S. & Licht, B. G. (1980). Learned helplessness and intelllectual achievement. In J. Garber & M.E. P. Seligman (Eds.) *Human helplessness: Theory and applications*. New York: Academic Press.

Dwyer, C. A. & Stufflebeam, D. (1996). Teacher evaluation. In D. C. Berliner and R. C. Calfee (Eds.), *Handbook of educational psychology*, pp. 765-786. New York: Simon & Schuster Macmillan.

Earthman, G. I. & Lemasters, L. (1998). *Where children learn: a discussion of how a facility affects learning*. ERIC_document number: ED419368.

Educational Research Service (1980). Class size research: A critique of recent meta-analyses. ERS special report. Arlington, VA: Educational Research Service.

Edward, W. & Newman, J. R. (1982). *Multiattribute evaluation*. (Sage University papers Series in Quantitative Application in the Social Sciences, series no. 07-026). Beverly Hills, CA: Sage.

Engleman, S. (1969). *Preventing failure in the primary grades*. New York: Simon and Shuster.

Environmental Protection Agency Office of Radiation and Indoor Air (1990). *Indoor air quality basics for schools*. Washington DC: Environmental Protection Agency.

Epstein, J. L. (1983). *Friends in school: Patterns of selection and influence in secondary schools*. New York: Academic Press.

Ericsson, K. A. & Charnes, N. (1994). Expert performance. *American Psychologist, 49,* 725-747.

Ericsson, K. A. & Charnes, N. (1995). Abilities: Evidence for talent or characteristics acquired through engagement in relevant activities? *American Psychologist, 50,* 803-804.

Ericsson, K.A., Krampe, R.T., & Tesch-Romer, C. (1993). The role of deliberate practice in the acquisition of expert performance. *Psychological Review, 100,* 3 363,406.

Farr, R. & Tone, B. (1994). *Portfolio and performance assessment*. San Antonio: Harcourt Brace.

Felder, R. M. & Solomon, B. A. (1999). *Learning styles and strategies*. Document retrieved in June, 1999 from Wide World Web : http://www.crc4mse.org/ILS/ILS_explained.html.

Ferguson, D. (1993). Maternal smoking before and after pregnancy: effects on behavioral outcomes in middle childhood. *Pediatrics, 92,* 815-822.

Field, R. (1996). Rise in asthma death baffles docs. *New York Post,* February 13.

Fox, D. J. (1969). *The research process in education.* New York: Holr, Rinehar & Boyd.

Fox, N. A. (1996). The development of emotion regulation, *Monographs of the Society for Research in Child Development, 29,* pp. 25-52.

Freire, P. (1970). *Pedagogy of the oppressed.* New York: Seabury Press.

Fresko, B. (1997). Predicting teacher commitment. *Teaching and Teacher Education, 13,* 429-438.

Furst, E. J. (1981). Bloom's taxonomy of educational objectives for the cognitive domain: philosophical and educational issues. *Review of Educational Research; 51,* 441-53.

Gabriel, R. M., Anderson, B. L., Benson, G., Gordon, S., Hill, R. Pfannenstiel, J. & Stonehill, R. M. (1985). *Studying the sustained achievement of Chapter 1 students.* Washington, DC: US Department of Education.

Gage, N. L. & Berliner, D. C. (1984). *Educational psychology (3rd ed.).* Boston: Houghton Mifflin Company.

Gagné, N. L. (1964). The implications of instructional objectives for learning. In C. M. Lindvall (Ed.), *Defining educational objectives.* Pittsburg: University of Pittsburg Press.

Gagné, N. L. (1985). *The conditions of learning (4rd ed.).* New York: Holt.

Galton, F. (1889). *Natural inheritance.* London: McMillan.

Gamoran, A., Nystrand, M, Berends, M. & LePore, P. C. (1995). An organizational analysis of the effects of ability grouping. *American Educational Research Journal, 32,* 687-715.

Gardner, H. (1989). Assessment in context: The alternative to standardized testing. In B. Gifford (Ed.), *Report to the Commission on Testing and Public Policy.* Boston: Kluwer Academic Press.

Gardner, H. (1993). *Frame of mind: The theory of multiple intelligences.* New York: Basic Books.

Gardner, H. (1995). Why would anyone become an expert? *American Psychologist, 50,* 802-803.

Glasser, W. (1969). *Schools without failure.* New York: Peter H. Wyden Pub.

Goleman, D. (1995). *Emotional intelligence.* New York: Bantam Books.

Gordon, T. (1974). *Teacher effectiveness training.* New York: Peter H. Wyden Pub.

Gredler, G. R.(1984). A viable alternative for the at-risk child? *Psychology in the Schools, 21,* 463-470.

Gronlund, N. E. (1978). *Stating objectives for classroom instruction* (2nd ed.). New York: Macmillan.

Gross, J. (1997, May). *Emotion regulation and its consequences*. A paper presented at the ninth annual convention of the American Psychological Society, Washington, DC.

Grubb, D. (1996). Healthy buildings? ERIC_Document number ED399665.

Guttman, L. (1953). Image threory for the structure of quantitative variates. *Psychometrika, 18,* 277-296.

Hall, S. J. (2000). *The perception of facial, prosodic and lexical emotion across the adult life span.* Unpublished doctoral dissertation, Graduate School and University Center, City University of New York.

Hallahan, D. P. & Kauffman, J. M. (1978). *Exceptional children.* Englewood Cliffs, NJ: Prentice-Hall.

Hambleton, R. K. (1996). Advances in assessment models, methods, and practices. In D. C. Berliner & R. C. Calfee (Eds.), *Handbook of educational psychology*, pp. 899-925. New York: Simon and Schuster Macmillan.

Hambleton, R. K. & Murphy, E. (1991). A psychometric perspective on authentic measurement. *Applied Measurement in Education, 5,* 1-16.

Hanushek, E. (2000). Address on the relationship between student performance and classroom size. *Frontiers in Educational Policy Research: What the Data Show.* Symposium held at The Graduate School and University Center of the City University of New York, May.

Harris, J. R. (1999). *The nature assumption: Why children turn out the way they do..* New York: Simon & Schuster.

Harris, T. A. (1969). *I'm ok—you're ok: A practical guide to transactional analysis.* New York: Harper & Row.

Hedges, L. (2000). Address on the relationship between student performance and classroom size. *Frontiers in Educational Policy Research: What the Data Show.* Symposium held at The Graduate School and University Center of the City University of New York, May.

Herman, J. L., Gearhart, M. & Baker, E. L. (1993). Assessing writing portfolios: Issues in the validity and meaning of scores. *Educational Assessment, 1,* 201-224.

Herrnstein, R. & Murray, C. (1994). *The bell curve.* New York: Free Press.

Hill, C. & Larsen, E. (1992). *Testing and assessment in secondary education: A critical review of emerging practices (Order No. MDS-237)*. Macomb, IL: Materials Distribution Service, Western Illinois University.

Holmes, C. T. & Mathews, K. M. (1984). The effects of non-promotion on elementary and junior high school pupils: A meta-analysis. *Review of Educational Research, 54*, 51-61.

Homme, L. (1970). *How to use contingency contracting in the classroom*. Champaign, Il: Research Press.

House, E. R. (1996). A framework for appraising educational reforms. *Educational Researcher, 25*, 6-14.

Houston, J. P. (1981). *Fundamentals of learning and memory*. New York: Academic Press.

Howell, K. (1993). Bias in authentic assessment. *Diagnostique, 19*, 387-400.

Huff, B. (1999). *Fact sheet on childhood disorders*. Alexandria, Virginia: The National Office of the Federation of Families for Children's Mental Health.

Hurlock, E. B. (1975). *Developmental psychology*. New York: McGrall-Hill.

Illich, I. (1971). *Deschooling society*. New York: Harper and Row.

Ingels, S. & Baldridge, J. (1992). *National education longitudinal study of 1988: conducting trend analyses of NSL-72, HS&B, and NELS:88 seniors. Working paper series*. Chicago: National Opinion Research Center.

Jampole, E. S. (1990). *Effects of imagery training on the creative writing of academically gifted elementary students*. Paper presented at the 40th Annual Meeting of the National Reading Conference.

Jensen, A. R. (1969). *Understanding readiness: an occasional paper*. ERIC document number ED032117.

Jensen, A. (1985). *Bias in mental testing*. New York: The Free Press.

Jensen, A. R. (1993). Why g? *Current Directions in Psychological Science, 2*, 53-56.

Jo, M. L. (1993, January). Hints and learner control for metacognitive strategies in problem solving. Paper presented at the 15th Convention of the Association for Educational Communications and Technology, New Orleans.

Johnson, D. W., Maruyama, G., Johnson, R., Nelson, D. & Skon, L. (`1981). Effects of cooperative, competitive, and individualistic goal structures on achievement: A meta-analysis. *Psychological Bulletin, 89,* 47-62.

Judd, C. H. (1916). *Psychology of high-school subjects.* Boston: Guinnes.

Judd, C. H. (1936). *Education as the cultivation of the higher order mental processes.* New York: Macmillan.

Kauffman, J. M. & Wong, K. L. (1991). Effective teachers of students with behavioral disorders: Are generic teaching skills enough? *Behavioral Disorders, 16,* 225-237.

Kavale, K. A., Hirshoren, A., Forness, S. R. (1998). Meta-analytic validation of the Dunn and Dunn model of learning style preferences: A critique of what was Dunn. *Learning Dissabilities Research and Practice, 13,* 75-80.

Keefe, J. W. (1979). *Learning style: An overview. In NASSP's student learning styles: Diagnosing and prescribing programs (pp. 1-17).* Reston, VA: National Association of Secondary School Principals.

Keefe, J. W. (1989). *Learning style profile handbook: Accommodating perceptual, study and instructional preferences (Vol. II).* Reston, VA: National Association of Secondary School Principals.

Kelleher, K. J., McInerny, T. K. Gardner, W. P., Childs,. G. E. & Wasserman, R. C. (2000). Increasing identification of psychosocial problems, 1979-1997. *Pedriatics, 105,* 1313-1321.

Kibler, R. J., Barker, L. L. & Miles, D. T. (1970). *Behavioral objectives and instruction.* Boston: Allyn and Bacon.

Kimball, S. L. (1994, March). The influence of lead exposure an dtoxicity to children's neurological development and school performance. Paper presented at the Annual National Conference of the American Council on rural Special Education, Austin, Texas.

Kinderman, T.A. (1993). Natural peer groups as contexts for individual development: The case of children's motivation school. *Development Psychology, 29,* 970-977.

King, S. L. (1999). *The delphi procedure and its uses in needs assessment for instructional developers.* Extracted from the World Wide Web on June 11, 1999.

Kline, R. B. (1998). *Principles and practice of structural equation modeling.* New York: The Guilford Press.

Knudson, R. E. (1998). College students' writing: An assessment of competence. *Journal of Experimental Education, 92,* 13-20.

Kolb, D. A. (1984). *Experiential learning: Experience as the source of learning and development.* Englewood Cliffs, NJ: Prentice-Hall.

Kovac, D., Potasova, A., Arochova, O. Biro, V. Halmiova, O. & Kovac, D. (1997). Promptness indicator of the effect of environmental nerotoxins. *Studia Psycholgica, 39,* 275-278.

Kovaks, M. & Bastiaens, L. (1994). The psychotherapeutic management of major depressive and dysthymic disorders in childhood and adolescence: Issues and prospects. In M. Goodyer (ed.), *Mood disorders in childhood and adolescence.* New York: Cambridge University Press.

Krathwohl, D., Bloom, B. S. & Masia, B. (1964). *Taxonomy of educational objectives. Handbook II: Affective domain.* New York: McKay.

Krause, L. B. (1996). *An investigation of learning styles in general chemistry students.* Unpublished doctoral dissertation. Clemson University.

Kropp, R. P. & Stoker, H. W. (1966). *The construction and validation of tests of the cognitive processes as described in the taxonomy of educational objectives.* Florida State University, Institute of Human Learning and Department of Educational Research and Testing. (ERIC ED 010044)

Kulik, C. L, Kulik, J. A., & Bangert-Drowns, R. (1990). Effectiveness of mastery learning programs: A meta-analysis. *Review of Educational Research, 60,* 265-299.

Lang, T. (1998). *An overview of four futures methodologies.* Retrieved by Shirley King on January 29, 1999 from the World Wide Web: http://www.soc.hamaii.edu/~future/j7/LANG.html.

Laosa, L. M. (1982). School, occupation, culture, and family: The impact of parental schooling on the parent-child relationship. *Journal of Educational Psychology, 74,* 791-827.

Lapan, S. D. & Hays, P. A. (1992). Developing special programs for minority gifted youth: Northern Arizona University's teacher training program. *Potential, 18,* 1-3.

LeDoux, J. (1992) Emotion and the limbic system concept. *Concepts in Neuroscience, 2.*

Leiden, L. I. (1990). Learning style inventories and how well they predict academic performance. *Academic Medicine, 65,* 395-401.

Lenneberg, E. H. (1967). *Biological foundations of language.* New York: John Wiley and Sons.

Light, P, E. & Butterworth, G. (1992). *Context and cognition: ways of learning and knowing.* Hillsdale, NJ: Erlbaum Associates, Inc., Publishers

Lindner, R. W. & Harris, B. (1993). Self-regulated learning: Its assessment and instructional implications. *Educational Research Quarterly; 16*, 29-37.

Linn, R. L., Baker, E. L. & Dunbar, S. B. (1991). Complex, performance-based assessment: Expectations and validation criteria. *Educational Researcher, 20*, 15-21.

Loveless, T. (1998). *The tracking and ability group debate. Volume 2, Number 8.* Washington, DC: Thomas B. Fordham Foundation.

Lucangeli, D. (1995). Specific and general transfer effects following metamemory training. *Learning Disabilities Research and Practice, 10*, 11-21.

McCroskey, J. C. & McVetta, R. W. (1978). Classroom sitting arrangements: Instuctional communicaton theory versus student preferences. *Communication Education, 27*, 99-111

Mack, F. (1995, November). *Preschool teacher attitude and knowledge regarding fetal alcohol syndrome and fetal alcohol effects.* Paper presented at the Annual Conference of the National Association of Early Childhood Teacher Educators, Washington, DC.

Madaus, G. F., Woods, E. M. & Nutall, R. L. (1973). A causal model analysis of Bloom's taxonomy. *American Educational Research Journal, 10*, 253-262.

Mager, R. F. (1962). *Preparing instructional objectives*, Palo Alto, California: Fearon Publishers.

Manke, B., McGuire, S., Reiss, D., Hetherington, E. M. & Plomin, R. (1995). Genetic contributions to children's extrafamilial social interactions: Teachers, best friends, and peers. *Social Development, 4*, 238-256.

Marjoribanks, K. (1979). *Families and their learning environments.* London: Routledge & Kegan Paul.

Marjoribanks, K. (1984). Occupational status, family environments, and adolescents' aspirations: The laosa model. *Journal of Educational Psychology, 76*, 690-700.

Marlowe, M. (1986). Metal pollutant exposure and behavior disroders: Implications for school practices. *Journal of Special Education, 20*, 251-264.

Martinez-Pons, M. (1990). *Test of a three-factor model of teacher commitment.* Paper presented at the 1990 Annual Conference of the New England Educational Research Organization, Brockport, Maine.

Martinez-Pons, M. (1991). *A test of Marjoribanks' social-environmental theory of academic achievement.* Paper presented at the 1991 Annual Conference of the New England Educational Research Organization, Portsmouth, New Hampshire.

Martinez-Pons, M. (1996). Test of a model of parental inducement of academic self-regulation. *The Journal of Experimental Education, 64,* 213-227.

Martinez-Pons, M. (1997). *Research in the social sciences and education: Principles and process.* Lanham, MD: University Press of America.

Martinez-Pons, M. (1997-1998). The relation of emotional intelligence with selected areas of personal functioning. *Imagination, Cognition and Personality, 17,* 3-14.

Martinez-Pons, M. (1998). Grounded theory development of a teacher-oriented model of mental ability. *The Journal of Secondary Gifted Education, 9,* 195-206.

Martinez-Pons, M. (1998-1999). Parental inducement of emotional intelligence. *Imagination, Cognition and Personality, 18,* 3-23.

Martinez-Pons, M. (1999a, April). *Cultural differences in parent and teacher inductive behavior of academic self-regulation.* A paper presented at the annual meeting of the American Educational Research Association, Montreal.

Martinez-Pons, M. (1999b). *Statistics in modern research: Applications in the social sciences and education.* Lanham, MD: University Press of America.

Martinez-Pons, M. (2000a, in press). Emotional intelligence as a self-regulatory process: A social cognitive view. *Imagination, Cognition and Personality. 19,* 3-17.

Martinez-Pons, M. (2000b, June). *Transfer as a self-regulatory process: Implications for self-instruction in adult education.* The Second Royaumont Symposium on Self-Learning, Paris.

Martinez-Pons, M. (2000c, June). *Using large data bases to study school-related processes and teacher commitment to teaching.* Paper presented at the ED-MEDIA 2000 Conference, Montreal.

Martinez-Pons, M. & Zimmerman, B. (1989). *Family learning processes among Hispanic groups in the U.S.* Paper presented at the 1989 annual conference of the American Education Research Association, San Francisco.

Mayer, J. D. & Salovey, P. (1993). The intelligence in emotional intelligence. *Intelligence, 17,* 433-442.

Mayer, J. D. & Salovey, P. (1997). What is emotional intelligence? In P. Salovey & D. Sluyter (Eds.), *Emotional development and emotional intelligence: Implications for educators.* New York: Basic Books.

Meyer, J. K. & Levine, D. U. (1977, April). *Concentrated poverty and reading achievement in five big cities.* Paper presented at the Annual Meeting of the Educational Research Association, New York.

Melton, R. F. (1978). Resolution of conflicting claims concerning the effects of behavioral objectives on student learning. *Review of Educational Research, 48,* 291-302.

Meltzer, L. J. (1987). *The surveys of problem solving and educational skills (SPES).* Cambridge, MA: Educator's Publishing Service.

Meltzer, L. J., Solomon, B. A., Fenton, T. & Levine, M. D. (1989). A developmental study of problem-solving strategies in children with and without learning difficulties. *Journal of Applied Developmental Psychology, 10,* 171-193.

Miller, D. W. (1999). The black hole of education research. *The Chronicle of Higher Education, XLV,* 17-18.

Miller, W. G., Snowman, J. & O'Hara, T. (1979). Application of alternative statistical techniques to examine the hierarchical ordering in Bloom's taxonomy. *American Educational Research Journal, 16,* 241-248.

Morris, R. C. (1996). Contrasting disciplinary models in education. *Thresholds in Education, 22* 7-13.

Morrison, T. L. (1979). Classroom structure, work involvement, and social climate in elementary school classrooms. *Journal of Educational Psychology, 71* 471-77

Morrow, J. R., Jr. (1977). Some statistics regarding the reliability and validity of student ratings of teachers. *Research Quarterly; 48,* 372-5.

Mosteller, F. (1995). The Tennessee study of class size in the early school grades. *Future of Children, 5* 113-127.

Myers, I. (1978). *Myers-Briggs Type Indicator.* Palo Alto, CA: Consulting Psychologists Press.

National Center for Educational Statistics (1980). *High school and beyond student file (base year 1980).* Washington, DC: U.S. Department of Education (ED), Office of Educational Research and Improvement (OERI), Information Technology Branch.

National Center for Educational Statistics (1986). *National Education Longitudinal Study: 1988-94 Data Files and Electronic Codebook System.* Washington, DC: U.S. Department of Education

(ED), Office of Educational Research and Improvement (OERI), Information Technology Branch.

Neisser, U. (1976). General, academic and artificial intelligence. In L. B. Ersnick (Ed.), *The nature of intelligence*. Hillsdale, NJ: Lawrence Erlbaum Associates.

Newel, A. & Simon, H. A. (1972). *Human problem solving*. Englewood Cliffs, NJ: Prentcie-Hall.

Newfield, J. (1996). School has breathtaking phew. *New York Post*, February 13.

Oakes, J. (1985). *Keeping track: How schools structure inequality*. New Haven, CT: Yale University Press.

Oakes, J. (1990). *Multiplying inequalities: The effects of race, social class, and tracking on opportunities to learn mathematics and science*. Santa Monica: RAND.

Olds, D. (1994). Intellectual impairment in children of women who smoke cigarettes during pregnancy. *Pediatrics, 93*, 221-227

Orange, C. (1999). Using peer modeling to teach self-regulation. *The Journal of Experimental Education, 68*, 21-38.

Orme, M. E. J. & Purnell, R. F. (1968, February). Behavior modification and transfer in an out-of-control classroom. Paper presented at the American Educational Research Association meeting, Chicago.

Ormrod, J. E. (1999). *Human learning* (3rd ed.). Upper Saddle River, New Jersey: Prentice-Hall.

Ormrod, J. E. (2000). *Educational psychology* (3rd ed.). Upper Saddle River, New Jersey: Prentice-Hall.

Owen, S. A. (1976, April). *The validity of student ratings: a critique*. Paper presented at the Annual Meeting of the National Council on Measurement in Education (San Francisco, California)

Owston, R. D. (1997). The world wide web: A technology to enhance teaching and learning. *Educational Researcher, 26*, 27-33.

Pate-Bain, H, Boyd-Zaharias, J., Cain, V. A., Word, E., Binkley, M. (1997). *STAR Follow-up studies, 1996-1997: the student/teacher achievement ratio (STAR) project*. Lebanon, TN: HEROS, Inc.

Pavlov, I. P. (1927). *Conditioned reflexes*. London: Oxford University Press.

Perrin, J. (1981). *Primary version: Learning style inventory*. Jamaica, NY: Learning Style Network, St. John's University.

Percival, F., Ellington, H. I. & Race, P. (1993). *Handbook of educational technology* (3rd ed.). London: Kogan Page.

Peterson, C., Maier, S. F. & Seligman, M. E. P. (1993). *Learned helplessness: A theory for the age of personal control* New York: Oxford University Press.

Piaget, J. (1951). *Play, dreams and imitation in childhood.* London: Heinemann.

Plomin, R. (1999). Two views about the nurture assumption: Parents and personality. *Contemporary Psychology: APA Review of Books, 44,* 269-271

Popham, W. J. & Baker, E. L. (1970). *Systematic instruction.* Englewood Cliffs, New Jersey: Prentice-Hall.

Popham, W. J. & Baker, E. L. (1973). *Classroom instructional tctics.* Englewood Cliffs, New Jersey: Prentice-Hall.

Pressley, M. & McCormick (1995). *Advanced educational psychology for educators, researchers, and policymakers.* New York: HarperCollins College Publishers.

Raloff, J. (1987). No threshold to lead's learning effect. *Science News, 131,* 374.

Rapp, D. (1990). Allergies: The hidden hazard. *Principal, 70,* 27-28.

Raths, L. E., Harmin, M., Simon, S. B. (1966). *Values and teaching: Working with values in the classroom.* Columbus: Charles E. Merrill Publishing.

Reber, A. S. (1995). *The Penguin dictionary of psychology.* New York: Penguin Books.

Reichmann, S. W., & Grasha, A. F. (1974). A rational approach to developing and assessing the construct validity of a student learning style scale instrument. *Journal of Psychology, 87,* 213-223.

Reigeluth, C. M. (1980). Meaningfulness and instruction: relating what is being learned to what a student knows. Syracuse Univ., NY. School of Education. ERIC_NO: ED195263.

Resnick, L. B. & Resnik, D. P. (1991). Assessing the thinking curriculum: New tools for educational reform. In B. Gifford (Ed.), *Changing Assessments: Alternative Views of Aptitude, Achievement, and Instruction.* Boston: Kluwer Academic Press.

Reynolds, M. (1997). Learning styles: A critique. *Management-Learning, 28,* 115-133.

Rich, Y., Lev, S. & Fischer, S. (1996). Extending the concept and assessment of teacher efficacy. *Educational and Psychological Measurement, 56,* 1015-1025.

Risenberg, R. & Zimmerman, B. (1992). Self-regulated learning in gifted students. *Roeper Review, 15,* 98-101.

Roedl, T. D., Schraw, G. & Plake, B. S. (1994). Validation of a measure of learning and performance goal orientations. *Educational and Psychologivcal Measurement, 54,* 1013-1021.

Rosenthal, T. L. & Zimmerman, B. J. (1978). *Social learning and cognition.* New York: Academic Press.

Rothwell, W. J., & Kazanas, H. C. (1997). *Mastering the instructional design process: A systematic approach.* San Francisco: Jossey-Bass.

Ruble, T. L. & Stout, D. E. (1998). *A critical assessment of kolb's learning style inventory.* ERIK Document Number ED377221

Salovey, P. & Meyer, J. D. (1989). Emotional intelligence. *Imagination, Cognition and Personality, 9,* 185-211.

Salovey, P., Mayer, J. D., Goldman, S. L., Turvey, C. & Palfai, T. (1995). Emotional attention, clarity and repair: Exploring emotional intelligence using the trait meta-mood scale. In J.W. Pennebaker (Ed.): *Emotion, disclosure, & health.* Washington, D.C.: American Psychological Association.

Sanders, J. R. (1990). *Standards for Teacher Competence in Educational Assessment of Students.* Washington, DC: National Council on Measurement in Education.

Scandura, J. M. (1965). Problem solving and prior learning. State Univ. of New York Research Foundation, Albany. ERIC_NO: ED002960.

Schaller, S. (1991). *A man without words.* New York: Summit Books.

Schippmann, J. S., Prien, E. P. & Katz, J. A. (1990). Reliability and validity of in-basket performance measures. *Personnel Psychology, 43,* 837-659.

Schmeck, R. R. (1983). Learning styles of college students. In R. Dillon & R. R. Schmeck (Eds.), *Individual differences in cognition* (pp. 233-279). New York: Academic Press.

Schooler, J. (1998), A multiplicity of memory. *Exploring, 22,* 4-6.

Schultz, F. (1998). *Sources (2nd ed.).* Guilford, Connecticutt: Dushkin/McGraw-Hill Companies.

Schunk, D. L. (1991). *Learning theories: An educational perspective.* New Yoirk: Macmillan Publishing Company.

Schunk, D. L. (1995, April). *Social origins of self-regulatory competence: The role of observational learning through peer modeling.* Paper presented at the 61st Biennial Meeting of the Society for Research in Child Development, Indianapolis, Indiana.

Schunk, D. L. & Hanson, A. R. (1985). Peer models: Influences on children's self-efficacy and achievement. *Journal of Educational Psychology, 77,* 313-322.

Schutte, N. S. & Malouff, J. M. (2000). *Measures of emotional intelligence and related constructs.* Lewiston, NY: Mellin Press.

Seddon, G. M. (1978). The properties of Bloom's taxonomy of educational objectives for the cognitive domain. *Review of Educational Research, 48,* 303-323.

Shanley, D., Martinez-Pons, M., & Rubal-Lopez, A. (1999, October). *Self-regulation of multiple social roles, study skills, and performance on the New York State teacher certification examination.* A paper presented at the 1999 meeting of the New England Psychological Association, Stanford, Connecticut.

Shulman, L. S. & Quinlan, K. M. (1998). The comparative psychology of school subjects. In D. C. Berliner & R. C. Calfee (Eds.), *Handbook of educational psychology.* New York: Macmillan Library Reference USA.

Siegler, R. & Klahr, D. (1982). When do children learn? The relationship between existing knowledge and the acquisition of new knowledge. In R. Glaser (Ed.), *Advances in instructional psychology (Vol. 2).* Hillsdale, NJ: Lawrence Erlbaum Associates, Publishers.

Silberman, C. E. (1973). *The open classroom reader.* New York: Vinatege Books.

Simpson, E. J. (1972). *The classification of educational objectives: Psychomotor domain.* Urbana, Ill: University of Illinois Press.

Skinner, B. F. (1968). *The technology of teaching.* New York: appleton-Century-Crofts.

Slavin, R. E. (1985). Team-assisited individualization: Combining cooperative learning and individualized instruction in mathematics. In R. Slavin, S. Shara, S. Kagan, R. H. Lazarowitz, C. Webb, & R. Schmuck (Eds.). *Learning to cooperate, cooperating to learn* (pp. 177-209). New York: Plenum.

Slavin, R. E. (1999). Rejoinder: Yes, control groups are essential in program evaluation: A response to Pogrow. *Educational Researcher, 28,* 36-38.

Smith, R. M., Neisworth, J. T. & Greer, J. G. (1978). *Evaluating educational environments.* Columbus, OH: Charles E. Merrill.

Sneider, V. E. (1992). Learning styles and learning to read. A critique. *Remedial and Special Education, 13,* 6-8.

Sommer, R. (1967). Classroom ecology. *Journal of Applied Behavioral Science, 3,* 489-503.

Sprenger, M. (1999). Learning and memory: The brain in action. Alexandria, VA: Association for Supervision and Curriculum Development.

Stevens, J. (1996). *Applied multivariate statistics for the social sciences* (3rd ed.). Mahwah, New Jersey: Lawrence Earlbaum Associates, Publishers.

Stevens, J. J. & Clauser, P. (1996, April). *Longitudinal examination of a writing portfolio and the ITBS.* Paper presented at the Annual Meeting of the American Educational Research Association.

Streissguth, A. P., Barr, H. M., Bookstein, F. L., Sampson, P. D. & Olson, H. C. (1999). The long-term neurocognitive consequences of prenatal alcohol exposure. *Psychological Science, 10,* 186-190.

Swanson, D. B., Norman, G. R. & Linn, R. L. (1995). Performance-based assessment: Lessons from the health professions. *Educational Researcher, 24,* 5-11.

Taba, H. (1962). *Curriculum development: Theory and practice.* New York: Harcourt Bace and Company.

Terwilliger, J. (1997). Semantics, psychometrics, and assessment reform: A close look at "authentic" assessments. *Educational Researcher, 26,* 24-27.

Terwilliger, J. (1998). Rejoinder: Response to Wiggins and Newmann. *Educational Researcher, 27,* 22-23.

Thorndike, E. L. (1903). *Educational psychology.* New York: Science Press.

Thorndike, R. L. (1920). Intelligence and its uses. *Harper's Magazine, 140,* 227-235.

Thorpe, L. P. (1946). *Child psychology and development.* New York: The Ronald Press Company.

Turoff, M., & Hiltz, S. R. (1999). Computer based Delphi processes. Invited book chapterAdler, M., & Ziglio, E. (Eds.) *Gazing into the oracle: The Deplhi method and its application to social policy and public health.* London: Kingsley.

Urdan, T. C. (1997). Examining the relations among early adolescent students' goals and friends' orientation toward effort and achievement in school. *Contemporary Educational Psychology, 22,* 165-191.

Veitch, J. & Newsham, G. R. (1996, August). *Determinants of lighting quality II: Research and recommendations.* Paper presented at the 104th Annual Meeting of the American Psychological Association, Toronto, Ontario, Canada.

Webster, R. E. (1981). *Learning efficiency test (LET) manual.* Novato, California: Academic Therapy Publications.

Weinstein, C. & Palmer, D.R. (1998). *Learning & Study Strategies Inventory.* Clearwater, FL: H&H Publishing.

Westman, A. S., Alliston, G. R. & Theriault, E. A. (1997). Lack of correlations of sense-modality-oriented indices of learning styles with each other and with classroom tasks. *Percpetual and Motor Skills, 84,* 731-737.

White, J. M., Yussen, S. R., & Docherty, E. M. (1976). Performance of Montesori and traditionally schooled children on tasks of seriation, classification, and conservation. *Contemporary Educational Psychology, 1,* 356-368.

White, W. F. (1989, November). *Teacher perceptions of the psychology of pedagogy.* Paper presented at the Annual Meeting of the Mid-south Educational Research Association, Little Rock, Arkansas.

Wiggins, G. (1989a). A true test: Toward more authentic and equitable assessment. *Phi Delta Kappan, 70,* 703-713.

Wiggins, G. (1989b). Teaching to the (authentic) test. *Educational Leadership, 46,* 41-47.

Wiggins, G. (1998). Letter to the editor. *Educational Researcher, 27,* 20-21.

Williams, J. (1991). *Writing quality teacher-made tests: a handbook for teachers.* Wheaton, MD: Wheaton High School, 12601 Dalewood Dr.

Williams, W. M. (1999). Two views about the nurture assumption: Peering into the nature-nurture debate. *Contemporary psychology, APA Review of Books, 44,* 267-271.

Williamson, O. E. (1975). *Markets and hierarachies.* New York: Free Press.

Williamson, O. E. (1985). *The economic institutions of capitalism: Firms, markets, and relational contracting.* New York: Free Press.

Witkin, H. A. (1950). Individual differences in ease of perception of embedded figures. *Journal of Personality, 19,* 1-15.

Witkin, H. A., Oltman, P. K., Raskin, E. &Karp, S. A. (1971). Palo Alto, CA: Consulting Psychologists Press, Inc.

Woitaszewski, S. A., Aalsma, M. C. & Gridley, B. E. (1998). Developing emotional literacy programs in schools: Using and expanding skill streaming. *The School Psychologist, 52,* 77-83.

Wolfgang, C. H. (1977). *Helping aggressive and passive preschoolers through play.* Columbus: Charles E. Merrill Publishing.

Wolfgang, C. H. & Glickman, C. D. (1980). *Solving discipline problems.* Boston: Allyn and Bacon, Inc.

Woolfolk, A. E. & Hoy, W. K. (1990). Prospective teachers' sense of efficacy and beliefs about control. *Journal of Educational Psychology, 82,* 81-91.

Wulf, K. M. (1976). Relationship of assigned classroom seating area to achievement variables. *Educational Research Quarterly, 2,* 56-62.

Wulf, M. (1993). Is your school suffering from sick building syndrome? *PTA Today, 19,* 12-13.

Zimmerman, B. J. Triadic model of self-regulated learning. *Journal of Educational Psychology, 81,* 329 -339.

Zimmerman, B. J. & Kitsantas, A. (1997). Developmental phases in self-regulation: shifting from process goals to outcome goals. *Journal of Educational Psychology, 89,* 29-36.

Zimmerman, B. J. & Martinez-Pons, M. (1986). Development of a structured interview for assessing student use of self-regulated learning strategies. *American Educational Research Journal, 23,* 614-628.

Zimmerman, B. J. & Martinez-Pons, M. (1988). Construct validation of a strategy model of student self-regulated learning. *Journal of Educational Psychology, 80,* 284-290.

Index